THE RAILWAY JOURNEY

The Railway Journey

Trains and Travel in the 19th Century

by

WOLFGANG SCHIVELBUSCH

Translated from the German
by
Anselm Hollo

Design by
Brayton Harris

URIZEN BOOKS • NEW YORK

This translation © 1979 by Urizen Books, New York.

The text of this book was also published under the title
Geschichte der Eisenbahnreise by Carl Hanser Verlag,
Munich, West Germany, 1978

First published in Great Britain, 1980
by Basil Blackwell, Oxford

Library of Congress catalogue number 79-67655
ISBN 0-916354-26-1 (cloth)
ISBN 0-89396-028-4 (soft)

British Library Cataloguing in Publication Data

Schivelbusch, Wolfgang
The Railway Journey.
1. Railroads - History
I. Title
385'.09'034   HE1021
ISBN 0-631 19660-9

Printed in the USA

TABLE OF CONTENTS

FOR S.D.C

Acknowledgements:

For their hospitality and assistance I thank the following American libraries: The Library of Congress, The New York Public Library, The New York Historical Society, The New York Academy of Medicine, The Boston Atheneum, The Kress Rare Books Library, and especially, John McLeod of the American Railroads Association Library.

W. S.

Publisher's Note:

The author completed the manuscript in 1977. Therefore, he was unable to incorporate into this book certain scholarly works subsequently published.

"I thought of railway travelling."
Lewis Carroll

1. The Mechanization of Motive Powers

L'industrie est devenue la vie des peuples.
(Marc Séguin, 1839)
[Industry has become the life of the nations.]

In the economic life of the preindustrial era, wood is the prime material, universally used in construction and as combustible matter. The shipbuilding industry of the European maritime powers, the iron works, and the machines built in the manufacturing and early industrial period are all based on the use of wood. Werner Sombart, the economic historian, regarded the exhaustion of this resource (i.e., the deforestation of Western Europe in the eighteenth century) as an essential factor, or perhaps even *the* main incentive for the development of industrial capitalism. In the preindustrial era, "Wood affected all areas of cultural existence, being the prerequisite for the prosperity of all branches of economic life: so general was its use in the production of material goods that the characteristics of culture before the eighteenth century were decidedly wooden, and thus that culture retained an "organic" quality in its material and sensual aspect."[1]

Next to wood, water and wind power are the main energy sources of preindustrial economic life. The industrial revolution, generally seen as having begun in the last third of the eighteenth century, is a complex process of denaturalization. The abolition of "live" workmanship by the division of labor, a process first described by Adam Smith, corresponds in terms of materials and energies to the "emancipation from the boundaries of nature" (Sombart) which

1

*Mouth of the River Tyne
With Coal Ships, 1655.*

In the seventeenth
century coal had largely
replaced wood as a fuel in
England. This large fleet
of ships, which
transported coal from
Newcastle to London,
illustrates this phase of
development preceding
the industrial revolution.

From John U. Nef,
*The Rise of the British
Coal Industry,*
London 1921

occurs when "live" natural materials and energies are replaced by mineral or synthetic ones. Thus wood loses its universal function. Iron becomes the new industrial building material, coal the new combustible.[2] In the steam engine, the prime mover of industry, these two combine to produce energy in theoretically unlimited amounts. The technological development of the steam engine in the eighteenth century exemplifies the gradual process of industry's emancipation from nature. The initial economic utilization of steam power occurs in the early part of the century when Newcomen's atmospheric steam engine is deployed in the Newcastle mining region to pump water out of mine shafts. The Newcastle region can be regarded as Europe's first industrial landscape in that coal begins to determine the physical aspect of the environment. Thus Daniel Defoe, who had a clear understanding of the economics of his day, traveled through the region and expressed his astonishment at the "prodigious Heaps, I might say Mountains, of Coals, which are dug up at every Pit, and how many of those Pits there are; we are filled . . . with Wonder to consider where the People should live that can consume them."[3] The Newcomen engine was a crude contraption, only capable of a back-and-forth motion, consuming incredible amounts of fuel, and comparatively weak in performance. However, as it was used in the coal-producing region, its excessive fuel (i.e., coal) consumption was no problem. As early as 1767, fifty-seven Newcomen engines were working in the area.[4]

2

1788.

Coal Fields around Newcastle, 1788.
A landscape in transition toward industrialization: the sources of power are still largely natural, horses and windmills. However, in the background to the right, we can already see a mechanized conveyor system operated by steam power.

Science Museum. London

Newcomen Steam Engine, Mid 18th Century.
The first commercially used steam engine. Because of its size (compare the size of the man in the illustration) and its enormous consumption of coal, this engine was used exclusively as a water pump in the coal field.

New York Public Library, Picture Collection.

3

James Watt

The waterwheel remains the main energy source for England's manufacturing industry in the eighteenth century. Yet, following the evolutionary pattern characteristic of the industrial revolution, the waterwheel is now aided by a curious intermediate adaptation that points the way to mechanization: waterpowered factories attempted to end their dependence on seasonally variable water levels by installing the Newcomen engine to pump back the used water (i.e., the water that had already passed through the wheel and would have been lost otherwise).[5] This recycling process is a kind of mechanization of the millrace: it regularizes the previously natural and erratic stream of water and turns it into an aqueous driving belt. Thus waterpower has become a merely incidental element in a uniform and regular mechanized process whose true mover is the steam engine.

That bypass becomes obsolete with the development of a steam engine capable of rotary motion. Watt's low-pressure engine, perfected in the 1780s, was such a technological advance. Thus steam power could leave its original, "natural" habitat, the coalfields, and become an essential part of the manufacturing industry. Watt's engine uses only a fraction of the fuel required by Newcomen's. Its performance is also far better and it produces the rotary motion required by industry. (The immediate incentive for Watt's development of the low-pressure engine was the saturation of the coal mine market with Newcomen pump engines. Its manufacturer, the firm of Watt & Boulton, urged Watt to develop an engine for the new market of the manufacturing industries. The success of this speculation demonstrates that industry had in the meantime indeed developed a need for mechanical power.)[6]

At the turn of the eighteenth and nineteenth centuries, the evolution of the steam engine reaches its culmination in Oliver Evans' high-pressure engine. Once again, there was a tremendous improvement: the engine's performance is no longer based solely on condensation, but on the immediate effect of steam pressure. This makes it possible to further reduce the size of the engines, which

4

had been quite unwieldy, while increasing performance and reducing fuel consumption. On the other hand, it becomes necessary, in order to meet the requirements of increased temperature and pressure, to improve the quality of machine technology and its materials.

The intensification achieved by the high-pressure engine — maximal work performance with minimal machinery — permits the mobile use of the steam engine, that is, its use as locomotive. This first takes place at the beginning of the nineteenth century in the coalfields around Newcastle, where the Newcomen engine had found its first application a century before. In the wake of the now fullblown industrial revolution and its increased demand for coal, the region, already transformed by coal production in Defoe's time, has undergone further changes. The land between the mines and the river Tyne is covered by a dense network of railways up to ten miles long — descendants of the rails used in mountain mine shafts since the late Middle Ages. These railways are appendages of the mines and are used exclusively to move coal. The wagons are first pulled by horses, but after the end of the Napoleonic Wars these are progressively replaced by steam-powered locomotives. The changeover to mechanized motive power is possible because in the mining region, fuel (coal) is cheaper than provender — the latter has to be shipped from other regions. From 1815 on, coal became cheaper to use than provender in all of England and that year, Parliament, dominated by agricultural interests, passes a Corn Law which, by imposing steep taxes on imported grain, forces grain prices to rise.[7] Obviously, the artificially high level of grain prices helped replace horsepower by mechanical power in much the same way as the shortage of wood in eighteenth-century Europe had accelerated the development of coal production. Confirmation for this is provided by a contemporary, Thomas Grahame,

The First Railroad System. Railroad Tracks in the Coalfields around Newcastle, 1812.
The tracks are used only for transporting coal to the waterway, the Tyne River. Nevertheless, the distance covered by these tracks *could be up to* 10 miles.

From C.F.D. Marshall, *A History of Railway Locomotion*

Coal Field, 1812.

In contrast to the illustration on page 3, the progress in mechanization can be clearly noticed here. The horse, as a source of power, can still be seen as a small image in the background, but the foreground is dominated by a steam-powered coal train.

Columbia University, Parsons Collection.

Richard Trevithick's Railway Circus, 1809.

This circus-like exhibition — as depicted by Rolandson — represents a curious moment in the history of the Railroad. Although Trevithick had made the steam locomotive technically possible long before George Stephenson, he could not put it to large scale commercial use because the demand for transportation was not great enough at the time. In order to make a profit from his vehicle, he exhibited it for an admission fee.

Science Museum, London.

Title Page of Thomas Gray's "Observations On A General Iron Rail-Way."

(2nd edition, from a total of five editions published from 1820-25).

OBSERVATIONS

ON

A GENERAL,

IRON RAIL-WAY:

SHOWING

ITS GREAT SUPERIORITY OVER ALL THE PRESENT METHODS OF CONVEYANCE,

AND

CLAIMING THE PARTICULAR ATTENTION OF MERCHANTS, MANUFACTURERS, FARMERS,

AND, INDEED,

EVERY CLASS OF SOCIETY.

SECOND EDITION.

LONDON:

PUBLISHED BY BALDWIN, CRADOCK, AND JOY, PATERNOSTER-ROW.

1821.

who in 1834, with steam locomotion an accomplished fact, describes the choice the English industrial capitalists had to make: "The landed capitalists of Britain . . . have by the taxes on corn and provisions more than doubled the price of animal labour, whether of man or horses. To avoid the effects of these taxes the monied capitalists of Britain have been for years devoting their capital to the promotion of those inventions by which taxed animal power may be dispensed with; and their endeavours have been crowned with eminent success."[8]

From the beginning of the nineteenth century, there are plans to develop the railroads into a general and national mode of transportation. The 1820s see the origins of a full-fledged "railroad movement," whose main promoters are agreed that the railroad, which in the meantime carries not only coal but other goods and passengers, must be powered by steam. The high cost of grain is a recurrent and standard argument. According to Adam Smith, the upkeep of a horse costs as much as the feeding of eight laborers. Thus, it is argued, when the one million horses kept for purposes of transportation in England are made redundant by mechanization, they will provide additional foodstuffs for eight million laborers.

Thomas Gray, the most important railroad promoter of the time, whose *Observations on a General Iron Rail-Way* appeared in five editions between 1820 and 1825, considerably expanded each time, argues for his proposed steam-driven railroad as follows: "The exorbitant demands now made on the public, for conveyance of goods and persons by waggons and coaches, are caused principally, if not altogether, by the enormous expense of a stock of horses, the continual renewal of the stock, and the intolerable expense of their keep."[9]

It is possible to see how advanced mechanization was in Britain at this time, in both theory and practice, when one consults a roughly contemporary French statement on the question of animal versus mechanical power. Pierre-Simon Girard, an engineer and member of the Académie des Sciences, who in 1819 had been given the task of planning and realizing a street-lighting system for the city of Paris, ostensibly summarizes the state of the English debate on horsepower versus steam power in an article published in 1827; in fact, his account, tinged with eighteenth-century physiocratic theory, projects French conditions onto England:

> The use of steam engines as locomotives on the railways is still a great open question in today's England. While one is willing to agree with the partisans of this solution that locomotives would be more economical than the use of horses, it is necessary to point out that the fuel on whose consumption these engines depend for the production of their motive power has to be extracted daily from natural deposits whose vast expanses nevertheless are not inexhaustible. . . . The use of horses is not subject to similar hazards; the motive power horses are able to produce is fed by products of the soil that nature renews every year and will continue to reproduce in ever greater abundance as agriculture grows more advanced.[10]

The apprehension that coal resources would be exhausted one day, combined with the notion that organic horsepower can go on reproducing itself

"The Horse Motor,"
1844.
One of the fanciful designs for mechanizing horse power which were never constructed. The anonymous inventor describes the operation of his invention as follows: "The principle consists in relieving the animal's muscular or elastic power of a great part of his weight, by suspending or supporting the horse at the intervals which naturally occur between 'the succession of impulses or strokes of the shoulders against the collar', in his quick paces, and leaving his force free at the recurring periods of action. Thus time will be afforded to renew the elastic power of his muscles, whilst his gravity remains in combination with the momentum of the carriage."

From *Horse-Power Applied to Railways,* London 1844

forever, reflects not only the physiocratic tradition that guides Girard's thinking, but also the economic realities of France during this period: specifically, the state of French coal production. During the first third of the nineteenth century, coal, in France, is *un produit révolutionnaire.*[11] While in England, coal production is sixteen million tons in 1816, thirty million tons in 1836, forty-four million tons in 1846, and fifty-seven million tons in 1851, French production figures are much lower: one million tons in 1820, two million tons in 1837, and five million tons in 1846.[12]

In addition, French production is not centered in one region, but is scattered throughout the country. Unlike the English, whose coal industry is centralized in a way that alters both landscape and consciousness, the French are unable to perceive coal as *the* endlessly available fuel. It is precisely because of the physical reality of the concentration of English coal production, and their awareness of it, that the English are able to mechanize motive power with such ease.

The mechanization of overland traffic subjects it to the same degree of regularization that has already been firmly established in bourgeois self-discipline and in industrial production. Unlike traffic on the waterways,[13] land traffic had until then been the weakest link in the chain of capitalist emancipation from the limits of organic nature, because animal power — on which land traffic was based — cannot be intensified above a certain fairly low level. Yet one should not underestimate the efforts made in the decades before the advent of the railroads to increase the efficiency of land traffic within the framework of these narrow natural limits. These efforts did, in fact, introduce a trend that eventually made mechanization appear as the final logical step. According to Bagwell — who, interpreting the material available to him, sees the English "transport revolution" as beginning as early as 1770 — traveling time between the most important cities was reduced by four-fifths between 1750 and 1830, and cut in half between 1770 and 1830. (Philip S. Bagwell, *The Transport Revolution From 1770,* London, 1974, p. 41.) The trip from London to Edinburgh, which in the

10

1750s still required ten days in the summer, took only forty-five and a half hours in 1836. (Ibid., p. 42; see also p. 43.) With the increase in traveling speed came increases in the number of traveled routes, in traffic intensity, and in the number of transportation enterprises. In the ten most important English cities, there were eight times as many regular departures in 1830 as there had been in 1790; Bagwell thinks that the number of passengers was multiplied by a factor of fifteen, as some of them were now carried "outside" (i.e., on top of the coach) on regular runs. (Ibid., p. 43.) Due to these improvements, the stagecoach surpassed the riding horse as the fastest mode of land transportation. (Bagwell, p. 49.) Karl Philipp Moritz gives us a vivid impression of that highly developed mode of passenger traffic in his *Reisen eines Deutschen in England* (Travels of a German in England). At this time, in the 1780s, the German traveler mostly proceeded on foot. Moritz, who attempts to wander about England in this manner, finds himself regarded as a curiosity. He notes with surprise that in England even the lower orders travel by stagecoach.

Finally, the high degree of development that the coach system achieved can be seen in its economic concentration: of the 342 scheduled daily departures from London listed in John Bates' *Directory of Stage Coach Services* for 1836, 275 are run by the three largest enterprises. The largest of these, owned by William James Chaplin, also has considerable interests in the catering business and employs a total of more than two thousand people and eighteen hundred horses. (Bagwell, p. 50.)

One of the main arguments for replacing the horse teams with steam locomotives is presented by Nicholas Wood, author of the most authoritative technical work of his time on railroads: "The greatest exertions have been used to accelerate the speed of the mails (which have hitherto been the quickest species of conveyance), without being able to exceed ten miles an hour; and that only with the exercise of such *destruction of animal power,* as no one can contemplate with feelings except of the most painful nature; while, upon the Liverpool Rail-way, an average rate of fifteen miles is kept up with the greatest ease.[14] (Italics added.)

*Brandeth's "Cyclopede,"
1829.*

Another unrealized plan for increasing and stabilizing horse power: the horse was to run on a treadmill connected to the wheels by means of a transmission. In this manner, a horse running at 4 mph would propell the vehicle at a speed of 12 mph.

From C.F.D. Marshall, *A Centenary History of the Liverpool and Manchester Railway,* London, 1930

How long overdue the mechanically produced means of locomotion must have seemed to the progressive contemporary consciousness — and how hopelessly anachronistic the animal power still in use — can be seen in a text from 1825 that juxtaposes both forms of locomotion:

> The animal advances not with a continued progressive motion, but with a sort of irregular hobbling, which raises and sinks its body at every alternate motion of the limbs. This is distinctly felt on horseback, and it is the same when an animal draws a load. Even in walking and running one does not move regularly forward. The body is raised and depressed at every step of our progress; it is this incessant lifting of the mass which constitutes that drag on our motions which checks their speed, and confines it within such moderate limits. . . . With machinery this inconvenience is not felt; the locomotive engine rolls regularly and progressively along the smooth tracks of the way, wholly unimpeded by the speed of its own motions; and this, independent of its economy, is one of the great advantages it possesses over animal power.[15]

The mechanical motion generated by steam power is characterized by regularity, uniformity, unlimited duration and acceleration. "No animal strength," says Gray, "will be able to give that uniform and regular acceleration to our commercial intercourse which may be accomplished by railway."[16]

As the motion of transportation is freed from its organic fetters by steam power, its relationship to the space it covers changes quite radically. Preindustrial traffic is mimetic of natural phenomena. Ships drift with water and wind currents, overland motion follows the natural irregularities of the landscape and is determined by the physical powers of the draft animals. Charles Babbage observes concerning the eotechnical utilization of wind and water power: "We merely make use of bodies in a state of motion; we change the directions of their movement, in order to render them subservient to our purposes, but we neither add to nor diminish the quantity of motion in existence."[17]

The earliest perceptions of how steam power dissolves that mimetic relationship can be found in descriptions of the first steam-powered ships. An eyewitness to John Fitch's steamboat experiment in 1790 finds it particularly remarkable that the boat proceeds in a *straight* line, instead of tacking, as one would expect, in the traditional eotechnically "natural" manner of marine vessels.[18] Putting it differently, another account says of steam power that "it *forces* the ships to traverse the ocean against wind and waves."[19] (Italics added.)

Thus steam power appears independent of outward nature and capable of prevailing against it — as artificial energy in opposition to natural forces. While this is first perceived in steamship traffic, it becomes even clearer only a little later, when animal power is abandoned in favor of mechanical power. As long as the conquest of space was tied to animal power, it had to proceed within the limits of the animals' physical capabilities. One way of gaining an immediate perception of the distance traveled was to observe the exhaustion of the draft animals. When they were overtaxed, it was seen as "destruction of animal power." Steam power, inexhaustible and capable of infinite acceleration, reverses the relationship between recalcitrant nature (i.e., spatial distance) and locomotive engine. Nature (i.e., spatial distance), which had caused the animal

Steam-Powered Coaches, 1820's.
While the early development of railroads was taking place in England, attempts were also being made to mechanize carriage traffic. The result was the creation of steam-powered monsters which actually populated the highways for several years — to be resurrected a half century later as automobiles in the modern sense.

From: New York Public Library, Picture Collection.

"locomotive engines" to strain themselves to exhaustion, now succumbs to the new mechanical locomotive engine of the railroad that, in a frequently used metaphor, "shoots right through like a bullet." "Annihilation of time and space" is the *topos* which the early nineteenth century uses to describe the new situation into which the railroad places natural space after depriving it of its hitherto absolute powers. Motion is no longer dependent on the conditions of natural space, but on a mechanical power that creates its own new spatiality.

> We have seen the power of steam suddenly dry up the great Altantic ocean to less than half its breadth. . . . Our communication with India has received the same blessing. The Indian Ocean is not only infinitely smaller than it used to be, but the Indian mail, under the guidance of steam, has been granted almost a miraculous passage through the waters of the Red Sea. The Mediterranean, which is now only a week from us, has before our eyes shrunk into a lake; our British and Irish channels are scarcely broader than the old Firth of Forth; the Rhine, the Danube, the Thames, the Medway, the Ganges, etc., have contracted their streams to infinitely less than half their lengths and breadths, and the great lakes of the world are rapidly drying into ponds![20]

The shrinking of the natural world by means of mechanical transportation is perceived and evaluated in different ways, dependent on the evaluator's economic and ideological position: there is shrinkage as economic gain versus shrinkage as loss of experience. The representatives of industry and free enterprise see transportation's release from nature's fetters as a gain: nature, in the form of distances that were hard to bridge, and exhaustible and unpredictable energy sources, had been an obstacle to the development of world trade.

13

Mechanical energy rendered all transportation calculable. The promoters of the railroad regard steam power's ability to do away with animal unreliability and unpredictability as its main asset. Here is Thomas Gray:

Thomas DeQuincey

> The dangers to which the present coach system is obnoxious (such as the untractableness of horses, the imprudence of drivers, cruelty to animals, the ruggedness of roads, etc.), would not be encountered on the rail-way, whose solid basis and construction render it impossible for any vehicle to be upset or driven out of its course; and as the rail-way must also be perfectly level and smooth, no danger could be apprehended from the increased speed, for mechanic power is uniform and regular, whilst horse-power, as we all very well know, is quite the reverse.[21]

This rational and progressive evaluation is opposed by a contrary position, in which the loss of organic natural power is not seen as an elimination of interfering factors that have hitherto hindered the smooth conduct of business and transportation, but as the loss of a communicative relationship between man and nature. Thus, for instance, Thomas De Quincey describes the lost experience of coach travel:

14

American Stagecoach, Second Half of 19th Century.

New York Public Library, Picture Collection

Seated in the old mail-coach, we needed no evidence out of ourselves to indicate the velocity. . . . The vital experience of the glad animal sensibilities made doubts impossible on the question of our speed; we heard our speed, we saw it, we felt it as a thrilling; and this speed was not the product of blind insensate agencies, that had no sympathy to give, but was incarnated in the fiery eyeballs of the noblest among brutes, in his dilated nostril, spasmodic muscles, and thunder-beating hoofs.[22]

We should not read that account of a past mode of travel as just a reactionary-romantic tirade against the new technology. De Quincey describes the disorientation experienced by the traveler when the traditional, "natural" mode of travel, the one based on traditional technology, is superseded by a new travel technology. Contemporaries perceived the transition from coach to railroad technology as a decisively reduced expenditure of work or power: in the form of animal exhaustion, that expenditure had been immediately perceptible to the senses, and spatial distance had been experienced by means of sensory recognition of that physical exhaustion. As the sensory perception of exhaustion is lost, so is the perception of spatial distance. De Quincey's description of

15

this process is echoed in numerous variations in contemporary literature and journalism, as in this anonymous polemic from the year 1839:

> When we are travelling by stage-coach at the rate of eight or ten miles an hour, we can understand the nature of the force which sets the vehicle in motion: we understand in a general way the nature of animal power: we see how soon it is exhausted; every successive hour do we watch the panting and reeking animals in their stalls, and, in the course of a day's journey, we can appreciate the enormous succession of efforts required to transport a loaded vehicle from London to a distant town.
>
> But, when proceeding on a journey by the rail-road, we are seldom allowed to get a sight of the wondrous power which draws us so rapidly along. The scene is altogether changed, there are no animals yoked to the car, to excite our pity by their apparently short, but really severe labour; we hear the steam gushing from the safety valve, while the machine is for a short time stationary; then we hear a number of rapid beatings: we feel that we are moving; the motion soon increases rapidly, and the journey which by the stage-coach is so tedious, is here, long before we are aware of it, at an end. The traveller then wonders not only at the rapidity of his journey, but often wishes to inspect and comprehend the means by which it was effected.[23]

As the new technology terminates the original relationship between the preindustrial traveler and his vehicle and its journey, the old technology is seen, nostalgically, as having more "soul." In addition to this sentimental line of thought there appears another kind of criticism of steam power that also has a high regard for the old technology, but, while using the same arguments we find in de Quincey and others, invests them with a modern content. This is accomplished by transferring the economically obsolete old technologies to a new realm, that of leisure and sports. What de Quincey deplores as a loss of sensory perception, others now attempt to reinstitutionalize. Thus, for instance,

"The Pleasures of the Journey" (Grandville).

W. B. Adams' *Pleasure Carriages,* published in 1837, is the precursor of a literature of leisure and sports whose ever-increasing growth the century is to witness.[24] In this book, the use of horsepower is no longer treated nostalgically, but
from a point of view that regards the use of steam as merely unsportsmanlike:

*Caricature of Bad Roads,
1850.*

From: *Fliegende Blätter,*

> Steam is a mere labourer — a drudge who performs his work without
> speech or sign, with dogged perseverance but without emotion. . . . He may
> be personified when speaking *of* him; but no one pats his neck or speaks *to*
> him in a voice of encouragement. It is not so with a horse or horses. They
> are beautiful and intelligent animals, powerful yet docile; creatures that
> respond to kindness, and shrink from cruelty and injustice. The driver
> and owner can love them or feel proud of them; they step with grace, and
> can vary their form and movements in a thousand ways. They are crea-
> tures of individual impulses. . . . The man who rides a horse, feels a plea-
> sure when the creature responds willingly to his purposes; and when he
> responds unwillingly, he feels a pride in the exercise of his power to
> compel him to obedience. Even when a horse is vicious, there is a pleasur-
> able excitement in riding him. The rider's nerves are strung, his senses are
> quickened; eye, hand, and ear are alike on the alert; the blood rushes
> through the veins, and every faculty is aroused.[25]

The final fate of carriage-riding, the traditional mode of travel, is to become the amateur sport of the privileged classes. In every day existence, the
new technology takes over. Only during a transitional period do the travelers
who transfer from the stagecoach to the railway carriage experience a sense of

loss due to the mechanization of travel; it does not take long for the industrialization of the means of transport to alter the consciousness of the passengers: they develop a new set of perceptions. Soon the uniform speed of the motion generated by the steam engine no longer seems unnatural when compared to the motion generated by animal power; rather, the reverse becomes the case. Mechanical uniformity becomes the "natural" state of affairs, compared to which the "nature" of draft animals appears as dangerous and chaotic. An anonymous text from the year 1825 gives us an idea of the adaptation to this industrialization of travel. It discusses the "sensitive or nervous man" who will find the new mechanical mode of transport more agreeable than the horse-drawn vehicle:

> It is reasonable to conclude, that the nervous man will ere long, take his place in a carraige, drawn or impelled by a Locomotive Engine, with more unconcern and with far better assurance of safety, than he now disposes of himself in one drawn by four horses of unequal powers and speed, endued with passions, that acknowledge no control but superior force, and each separately momentarily liable to all the calamities that flesh is heir to. Surely an inanimate power, that can be started, stopped, and guided at pleasure by the finger or foot of man, must promise greater personal security to the traveller than a power derivable from animal life, whose infirmities and passions require the constant exercise of other passions, united with muscular exertion to remedy and control them.[26]

The sensitive and nervous man, in whom those horses in front of the coach tended to cause unhealthy excitement, can now relax in the railway carriage, sitting in it without moving a muscle, without "exertion" or any "other passions."

Despite the apparent smoothness of transition to industrialized travel, certain residues of anxiety remain. We get an inkling of this from the report written by the Liberal politician Thomas Creevy about a trip on Stephenson's locomotive in 1829: "It is really flying, and it is impossible to divest yourself of the notion of instant death to all upon the least accident happening."[27]

2. The Machine Ensemble

*Le chemin de fer et les chariots qu'il porte
forme un sorte de machine complexe dont les
parties ne sauraient être envisagées isolément.*

The railroad, and the carriages on it, make
up a complex machine whose parts cannot
be considered separately.

— Anonymous, 1821

Like any other means of transportation, the railroad provides a medium for
moving things from one place to another. Yet the way in which it accomplishes
this distinguishes it from the other means of transportation.

Transportation on roads and canals, as developed in eighteenth-century
England by private enterprise, makes both a technical and an economic distinction between the *route* and the *means*. The capital-investment companies that
provide canals and turnpikes to be used upon payment of tolls do nothing
further: they have nothing to do with the vehicles that are used on their routes.
Anyone using one of these artificially created land routes or waterways does so
with his own vehicle or hires an entrepreneur to transport the goods, and that
entrepreneur, in turn, operates quite independently from the canal or turnpike
company. Route and means of transportation exist independently from one
another, because individual movement of vehicles — their mutual flexibility in
granting right-of-way, etc. — is technically possible.

The railways put an end to that liberal state of affairs. Route and vehicle
become technically conjoined on the railroad: there is no leeway between the
rails and the vehicle running on them, nor is it possible for one train to "pull
over" when confronted by another one. This is realized early on: all initial
definitions of the railroad unanimously describe it as a machine consisting of

the rails *and* of the vehicles running on them. "It is necessary . . . to insist that the railroad and its carriages be considered as one machine, or, as an indivisible entity,"[1] a French author states in 1821. In 1839, Guillaume Tell Poussin goes into somewhat greater detail:

> A railway is far from being the simple construct that a canal or a turnpike is: these have to fulfill quite limited objectives. A railway, on the contrary, is a construct that has to adjust to the eventual exigencies of a new engine, in which each day of experience may cause important new modifications. Consequently, in order for there to be harmony between the two quite distinct parts that a railway consists of, i.e., its rails and its engine, there has to be reciprocal interaction, so that the ameliorations of the one determine the improvements of the other. Thus it is evident that one cannot separate the increasing knowledge of steam engines from the construction of the railways.[2]

In an early phase of the railroad's technological evolution, the concept of "one machine" appears with particular clarity: the locomotive is not seen, as yet, as a self-contained, autonomous motive apparatus, but simply as a steam engine mounted on an undercarriage. Thus, a report in the *Bulletin de la societé pour l'encouragement de l'industrie nationale* (1815) on the railways in the English coal-mining district says: "New application of steam engines. For some time now, a steam engine has been mounted on wheels in Leeds, making it move on rails, by means of a large cogwheel."[3]

Blenkinsop's Cog-Wheel Locomotive, 1815.

One of the many abortive developments in early railroad technology, based on the idea that the iron wheels would not provide enough traction unless they had teeth.

From: C.F.D. Marshall, *A History of Railway Locomotion.*

20

Locomotive by John Stevens, 1825.

In this early form, the composition of the locomotive from the two components of the chassis and the steam engine can be clearly distinguished: the locomotive is indeed a steam engine mounted on a chassis.

From: James Dredge, *Transportation Exhibits at the Columbian Exposition.* New York, 1894.

That steam engine mounted on an undercarriage does not connect with its rails merely by rolling on them, but does so by means of interlocking cogs: it moves by propelling cogwheels along proportionately serrated rails. The latter appear as horizontal cogwheels, providing counterparts to the engine's wheels. In their experimental phase, railways were constructed according to this technical principle; it is hard to imagine a more vivid demonstration of the railways *machine* character. In retrospect, in 1849, Dionysius Lardner describes one of these creations, built by the mining engineer Blenkinsop: "He obtained a patent, in 1811, for the application of a rack-rail. The railroad thus, instead of being composed of smooth bars of iron, presented a line of projecting teeth, like those of a cog-wheel, which stretched along the entire distance to be travelled. The wheels on which the engine rolled were furnished with corresponding teeth, which worked in the teeth of the railroad; and, in this way, produced a progressive motion in the carriage."[4]

This curious, technically redundant form of construction also existed in a variant in which the driving wheel was a cog that connected with a cograil laid between the running rails. The engineers who designed mine railways adhered to this model for a surprisingly long time. Even the illustration that Thomas Gray provides in the fifth edition of his *Observations* in 1825 still shows such a cogwheeled locomotive. The "imaginary difficulty" (Lardner) in the minds of the early railway engineers was the notion that smooth wheels could not provide traction on smooth rails. Until simple experience proved otherwise, smooth steel on smooth steel did not seem capable of sufficient adhesiveness. That such a notion seemed plausible even to engineers, and for a relatively long time, is instructive in a number of ways: it sheds light on the history of cultural and psychological perceptions of iron and steel, and points to a fundamental change in the history of the wheel. For the first time, the wheel is no longer set in motion by a power extraneous to itself — the draft animal — but is, to all appearances, propelling itself along.

The cogwheel episode now looks merely like a symbolically exaggerated demonstration of the concept of rail and carriage as *one* machine: it shows the esthetic exuberance of technology. The final standardized form of the railroad — smooth wheels on smooth rails — retains that concept of unity of parts,

Elevation.

which becomes ever more important as the railroad is technologically perfected. Franz Reuleaux, who in his *Theoretische Kinematik* (1875) sums up the development of machinery in the nineteenth century, agrees with the early chroniclers of the railroad that the joining of rail and wheel was the decisive step *"that joined carriage and road into one machine."*[5] (Italics in original; we will return to Reuleaux's theory of the machine later on in greater detail.)[6] He then describes the development of the machine in the direction of increased performance, intensification, etc., in terms of an ever more precise interaction between its individual parts: "During the last century we have gradually become used to understanding the wheel and its cogs as a unit, a whole, and thus to seeing those cog profiles in context. It is my conviction that, in only a few decades, all cogwheels will operate *without play*."[7] (Italics added.) While Reuleaux is speaking about the cogwheel, he uses it as a paradigm for *the* machine part in general. The disappearance of "play" concerns all parts of the machine.

This tendency in machine development appears early on in the railroad's continuous evolution toward ever greater speed, regularity, and uniformity. In *An Exposition of the Danger and Deficiencies of the Present Mode of Railway Construction,* published in 1846, we find a description that anticipates the prophecy made by Reuleaux thirty years later — or, to put it another way, the descriptions of the railroad in the text of 1846 parallel the theoretical formulations on the development of machines in general made by Reuleaux in 1875:

The wheels, rails, and carriages are only parts of one great machine, on the proper adjustment of which, one to the other, entirely depends the perfect action of the whole. And as the velocity given to the moving parts increases, so does the necessity for perfect adjustment increase also, because the imperfect action, which, at moderate speed, would only cause a *jolt,* will, when moving at high velocity, gain sufficient force to cause an overthrow. Therefore, from this cause it becomes necessary, in order to secure safety when moving at great speed, to have the parts in contact adjusted to each other in such manner as at all times, and under varying circumstances, to preserve a true relationship one to the other, at the same time having a tendency to resist and counteract the impulses which would otherwise destroy their equilibrium, and endanger the safety of the moving body.[8]

The machine character of the railroad is dual: first, the steam engine (locomotive) generates uniform mechanical motion; second, that motion is transformed into movement through space by the combined machinery of wheel and rail.

We observed how the process of the mechanization of formerly organic motive powers by the steam engine was experienced as denaturalization and desensualization. Let us now see how the development of the railway completes the detachment from nature initiated by the discovery of steam power.

As it is the function of the rail to overcome natural resistances, or obstacles, it can be defined as a technical means to implement Newton's First Law of Dynamics, which states: "Every body continues in its state of rest, or of uniform motion in a straight line, unless it is compelled to change that state by forces impressed upon it."[9]

The natural obstacles that are to be overcome by means of the rail are of two different kinds: first, the friction between wheel surface and road surface; second, the irregularity of the terrain. Friction could be called the microphysical resistance; the varying elevation of the land, the macrophysical. How does the rail deal with the microphysical resistance? Lardner provides a definition for the ideal (i.e., frictionless) road, acknowledging that it is directly derived from Newton: *"A perfect road should be smooth, level, hard, and straight.* Were it possible to construct a road between two places, absolutely smooth, absolutely level, absolutely hard, and absolutely straight, then a carriage put in motion from one end of this road would move to the other end without any tractive force at all, except so far as the resistance of the atmosphere would require it."[10] (Italics in original.)

According to Lardner, the railway line is the optimal approximation of that ideal road. Significantly, he bases his argument on a brief delineation of traditional road-building technology. Only when the draft animals are replaced by mechanical motive power does it become possible to construct a road that possesses all four qualities — smoothness, hardness, levelness, and straightness: as long as road traffic relies on animal power, there will be internal contradictions. The smoothness and hardness of the road that the wheel requires are directly opposed to the animals' technical demands, as their hooves cannot get traction on a smooth and hard road; conversely, a road with a soft and uneven surface, ideal for hooves, does not meet the technical demands of the wheel. This contradiction cannot be resolved as long as wheeled vehicles are pulled by draft animals. "A road, then," Lardner concludes, "cannot be perfect, or even nearly perfect, for both purposes." A "compromise between the two principles" is inevitable: a road that is as smooth and hard as possible, while being as soft and rough as is necessary for the horses' hooves.[11]

As the latter are replaced by the locomotive, the contradiction ceases to exist. From now on, the four essentials of the mechanically perfect road can be realized without compromise. The railroad does this first and foremost by means of the rail, which is harder, smoother, more level, and straighter than any road before it. While this revolution in transportation technology occurs in a location separate from the traditional road grid, it influences the latter nevertheless. Serving the need for short-distance transportation not provided by the railroads, the old type of highway survives until the end of the nineteenth century; it becomes obsolete as the automobile begins to mechanize road traffic, and as road-building technology makes an effort to approximate the technical principles of the railroads. When road vehicles are no longer pulled by horses but propelled by the internal combustion engine, the roads they run on tend to become as smooth, hard, level, and straight as the rails. In the twentieth century, their surfaces are covered with asphalt and concrete, whereby they achieve the technical standards set by the railroads in the nineteenth century.

The rail's primary function, which is to minimize the resistance caused by friction, is complemented by its further function of leveling the irregularities of the terrain. To keep friction at a minimum, the rail has to be smooth and hard; to achieve optimal performance with the least expenditure of energy, the rail has to run a level and straight course. Before laying the track, considerable earth moving must be done to lay a level and straight roadbed through uneven terrain. Nicholas Wood provides an illustration and description of this in the third edition of his standard technical work of 1838:

Let A,B,C, Fig. 1, represent a section or the outline of the country over which the railway is to pass, and a, b, c, d, e, the level at which the railway is to be formed. All those parts of the section which are above the line a, b, c, d, e, to the extent of the width required for the railway, will, therefore, require to be cut through, excavated, or levelled down; and those portions which are below that line, will require to be embanked or levelled up. The portions A and C, will, therefore, have to be cut down, and the portion B, raised up or embanked. The portions of railway, a b, and c d, of the section, are, consequently, called *excavations,* or *cuttings;* and the portions b c, d e, *embankments,* or *embanking.* [12] (Italics in original.)

Cuttings and embankments are the staple procedures of railroad construction. Greater irregularities of the terrain, such as valleys and mountains, are overcome by means of tunnels and viaducts.

Rail and Road, 1832.
This is a popular picture motif in the 1830's in England, which illustrates technological progress. The stretch of track cuts across the landscape like a trajectory, while the road winds leisurely through the countryside.

Science Museum, London

The railroad, thus built across the terrain by means of cuttings, embankments, tunnels, and viaducts, made its mark on the European landscape from the 1850s on; it also made its mark on travelers' perceptions. The alienation from immediate, living nature that was initiated by the mechanization of motive power is increased as the railroad is constructed straight across the terrain, as if drawn with a ruler. The railroad is to the traditional highway as the steam engine is to the draft animal: in both cases, mechanical regularity triumphs over natural irregularity. The abandonment of animal power in favor of steam is experienced as the loss of sensorially perceptible animal power/exhaustion, i.e., as the loss of the sense of space and motion that was based on it. As the natural irregularities of the terrain that were perceptible on the old roads are replaced by the sharp linearity of the railroad, the traveler feels that he has lost contact with the landscape, experiencing this most directly when going through a tunnel.

Caricature of a Railroad Survey, 1845.
The construction of railroad lines in Europe — especially in still unindustrialized Germany and Central Europe — cuts a breach not only into the physical landscape but also into popular consciousness. A whole new genre of caricature, the railway caricature, testifies to this phenomenon. Here, the imminent threat of railroad tracks being laid right through a middle-class bedroom.

From: *Fliegende Blätter*, 1845

Railway Journey through a Cutting

"As far as the eye can range, one immense chasm through the earth appears before the observer, and at intervals are bridges carrying roads across the railway at a frightful height . . . . The echoes in this place are very distinct, and whilst traversing its extent you seem shut out from all communication with the world." (Travel log 1839)

Science Museum, London

Early descriptions of journeys on the railroad note that the railroad and the landscape through which it runs are in two separate worlds. Thus, a report on a trip from Manchester to Liverpool in 1833: ". . . we enter the Olive Mount excavation. Here a passage for the railway has been effected through the solid rock by a cutting seventy feet deep and about fifteen wide. . . . Several bridges are thrown over to connect the opposite precipices, and appear to the eye, as we move along the depth below, like communications belonging to beings of another sphere."[13]

Quite similarly, a description of a journey from London to Birmingham, 1839: "As far as the eye can range, one immense chasm through the earth appears before the observer, and at intervals are bridges carrying roads across the railway at a frightful height. . . . The echoes in this place are very distinct, and whilst traversing its extent you seem shut out from all communication with the world."[14]

The empirical reality that makes the landscape seen from the train window appear to be "another world" is the railroad itself, with its excavations, tunnels, etc. Yet the railroad is merely an expression of the rail's technological requirements, and the rail itself is a constituent part of the machine ensemble that the system is. It is, in other words, that machine ensemble that interjects itself between the traveler and the landscape. The traveler perceives the landscape as it is filtered through the machine ensemble.

Cutting as part of the 19th Century Landscape.

Science Museum, London

Cutting in the City, 1837

Science Museum, London

That is the nature of the new perception of landscape and motion. If the material bases for the old perception of landscape and motion were the physical power of the draft animals, the road that followed the contours of the terrain, and the "leeway" given to the vehicle on the road[15], and if the old perception occurred via all these natural and only loosely connected elements of transportation technology, then the character of the new machine ensemble is one of tremendous technical discipline. To follow Reuleaux's argument, the appearance of the machine ensemble signals the end of free play between the individual elements of machines in general. Compared to the old technology, the new appears more deprived, more unnatural, even more restrictive: this is documented in contemporary literature and journalism. Yet it is not only the critical mind of the era that finds it hard to accommodate itself to the new transportation technology. The railroad is such an entirely novel apparatus that even those who advocate its use as a means of public transportation misunderstand it at first. They regard it as a means like any other: they are aware of the peculiarity of rails, but unable to recognize the consequences. It is obvious that an iron wheel running on an iron rail has less friction to contend with than a wheel on a highway, yet at first no one considers the possibility of constructing railroads independent from existing traditional roads. Thus, for instance, Richard Lovell Edgeworth — who in 1802, twenty years before Gray, publishes the first proposal to construct railways for public transport — sees the rail entirely in the context of the road, and thus proposes that the existing roads, more specifically, the ones with the heaviest volume of traffic, be furnished with rails. Here, the railroad is not yet seen as an autonomous traffic system, but

Embankment

From: John Blackmore,
*Views of the Newcastle and
Carlisle Railway.* Newcastle and
London, 1838.

Tunnel

Columbia University,
Parsons Collection.

Viaducts.
The isolation of the railroad tracks from the landscape through which it leads is most clearly portrayed in illustrations of the viaduct. An idyllic, preindustrial scene is usually found in the foreground, but the entire picture is dominated by the railroad running along the line described by the viaduct in the background.

From: John Blackmore, *Views . . .*

British Museum, London

merely as a highway provided with rails while essentially retaining its traditional traffic pattern. The only change perceived is that friction is being reduced. The vehicles remain, as they always were, individual road vehicles, but for the duration of their travel on the rails they have to be lifted onto an undercarriage that is fitted to the rails:

Excursion Coach on the Railroad, 1830's.

Archiv Talbot

Now to accommodate coaches and chaises, etc., to these rail-ways, I would have them carried, wheels and all, in cradles or platforms, *which should have wheels adapted to the rail-ways.* By these means no alteration would be necessary in any of the carriages commonly used; but the horses of any coach or chaise might, as soon as they had got out of town, walk up an inclined plane into the cradle or platform, and draw their respective carriages after them: the horses should then walk out at the farthest end of the platform, upon the road belonging to the rail-ways. They would then draw the chaise not upon its own wheels, but upon the wheels of the platform or cradle in which the *chaise* should be detained.[16] (Italics in original.)

And a little later, in the same text, Edgeworth stresses once more the autonomy retained by the private vehicles using the rails: "The chief convenience of this project arises from the mode of receiving and transporting on rail-ways every carriage now in use *without any change in their structure* so that a traveller may quit and resume the common road at pleasure."[17] (Italics in original.)

While Edgeworth still sees his "rail-way," quite naively, as a potential extension of the common road, he is, however, aware of the rail's tendency to restrict

31

the free and individual maneuvering of vehicles. This gives rise to his suggestion that four separate railways be constructed on a road, two in either direction, and in each pair, one for coaches, one for vehicles carrying goods. That first premonition of a reorganization of traffic according to the technology of the rail was further developed twenty years later in Gray's proposal for a *national* system of railways. Gray still thinks in terms of the categories of individual traffic, but his railways would constitute a traffic system independent from the existing highways.[18] Gray quite clearly demonstrates the ever more acute perception of the inherent contradiction between the rail and individual traffic, a contradiction that remains unresolved until the late 1830s. While the technical concept of the rail does not tolerate individual traffic, the economic thinking of the time can conceive of nothing but such individual traffic. As long as the contradiction remains unresolved, the only way in which both conditions can be satisfied is to multiply the number of parallel railways. Between Edgeworth's time and Gray's, their number has already grown: "In order to establish a general iron rail-way, it will be necessary to lay down two or three rail-ways for the ascending, and an equal number for the descending vehicles. In the immediate neighbourhood of London the traffic might demand six rail-ways."[19]

Stagecoach on Rails, 1826.

On the first railroad line built for public transportation, the Stockton-Darlington Line, the stagecoach "The Union" fulfilled its function the same way as it had formerly done on the turnpikes. Only the wheels had been adapted to the rails; nothing else had been changed. This is one of the few illustrations of individual vehicles on rails, which were soon to be replaced by trains of connected railway cars.

From: C.F.D. Marshall, *A History of British Railways Down to the Year 1830.* London, 1938.

RAPID, SAFE, AND CHEAP TRAVELLING
By the Elegant NEW RAILWAY COACH,

THE UNION,

Which will COMMENCE RUNNING on the STOCKTON and DARLINGTON RAILWAY, on MONDAY the 16th day of October, 1826,

And will call at Yarm, and pass within a mile of Middleton Spa, on its way from Stockton to Darlington, and *vice versa.*
FARES. Inside 1½d.—Outside, 1d. per Mile. Parcels in proportion.
No gratuities expected by the Guard or Coachman.

N. B. The Proprietors will not be accountable for any Parcel of more than £5. value, unless entered and paid for accordingly.
The UNION will run from the Black Lion Hotel and New Inn, Stockton, to the New Inn, Yarm, and to the Black Swan Inn, near the Croft Branch, Darlington; at each of which Inns passengers and parcels are booked, and the times of starting may be ascertained, as also at the Union Inn, Yarm, and Talbot Inn, Darlington.
On the 19th and 20th of October, the Fair Days at Yarm, the Union will leave Darlington at six in the morning for Yarm, and will leave Yarm for Darlington again at six in the evening; in the intermediate time, each day, it will ply constantly between Stockton and Yarm, leaving each place every half hour

PLAN OF A GENERAL IRON-RAIL-WAY FOR GREAT BRITAIN.

Edinburgh
Glasgow
Newcastle
Carlisle
Durham
Scarborough
Leeds
Hull
Liverpool
Manchester
Holyhead
Nottingham
Leicester
Norwich
Birmingham
Harwich
Bristol
LONDON
Dover
Portsmouth
Plymouth
Falmouth

English Miles.

10 20 30 40 50   100

Thomas Gray's Plan of a General Iron Rail-Way for Great Britain, 1821.

The first blue-print of a railroad network with London as the Center and Great Britain's most important industrial cities as connecting stations. This plan was designed four years before the first steps were taken on the construction of the Liverpool-Manchester Line.

From: Thomas Gray, *Observations. . .* 2nd edition, London 1821.

Individual Transport of Rails.

A proposition from 1836 shows how difficult it was even for railroad planners to understand that individual travel was not feasible on rails. *I* proposes reconstruction of a traditional road: "...upon either of the sides is a single track or iron road — the waggons drawn by horses and confined to the proper side of the road, whether travelling to or fro. In the center is seen a mail coach and horses travelling without interruption upon the present turnpike road, and in the act of being passed by another with equal facility as at present time." *II* shows a doubling of the tracks on two levels — because, under the concept of individual transport, an increase in traffic requires an increase in track. *III* shows the absurd situation which would result from this sort of thinking: two two-level tracks in each direction. According to the proud inventor of this monster: "Here is gradually completed a series of lines which afford every degree of speed, the transit of no one track being impeded by that of another. The stream of trade is flowing continuously upon one track from, and upon the opposite one to, any given place. A double number of lines upon the ground is afforded, since the bulk of the traffic upon any road must consist of the carriage of goods; and those also travelling at the slower rate will occupy more time, and thence the road being more continuously filled, a greater space for that species of traffic is seen to be required."

From: Henry Fairbairn, *A Treatise on the Political Economy of Railroads.* London, 1836.

PLATE I.

PLATE II.

PLATE III.

In the writings of Edgeworth and Gray, the conflict between the rail and individual traffic still appears merely in the form of proposals and projections for ways of organizing railways for public transportation; however, the actual practice of such transportation, as it becomes a reality in the 1820s, becomes more and more seriously impeded by that conflict.

In 1855, Lardner retrospectively describes the economic views of the early period, when the railroad was regarded simply as a means of transportation similar to canal and turnpike, to be used by individual vehicle owners upon the payment of tolls:

It was expected that the public should be admitted to exercise the business of carriers upon them [the rails], subject to certain specified regulations and by-laws. It soon became apparent, however, that this new means of transport was attended with qualities which must exclude every indiscriminate exercise of the carrying business. A railway, *like a vast machine,* the wheels of which are all connected with each other, and whose movement requires a certain harmony, can not be worked by a number of independent agents. Such a system would speedily be attended with self-destruction. The organization of a railway requires unity of direction and harmony of movement, which can only be attained by the combination of the entire carrying business with the general administration of the road.[20] (Italics in original.)

It took a while before the technological necessity of the railroad companies' *monopoly* on transportation (i.e., the management of both rails and carriages under *one* supervisory agency) prevailed against the liberal view that was based on principles applicable to canals and turnpikes. As late as 1838, there were private vehicles on the Liverpool-Manchester line.[21] W. T. Jackman enumerates the following reasons for the termination of such individualism in transportation, which was occurring despite the fact that "laissez-faire doctrines were so predominant in every other aspect of the national life":

1) Dangers caused by non-coordination of trains of vehicles traveling on the line.
2) The absence of technically necessary facilities along the line (coal and water depots).
3) Negligible profits for the private transport entrepreneurs.
4) The disregard evinced by those entrepreneurs and private users of the line towards the railroad's technical regulations.[22]

Jackman describes the end of individual rail traffic:

Soon it became evident to the railway companies that, with due regard to the efficiency of their line and to the public convenience and safety, they could not allow rival parties to run engines and carriages on the same line; and it was eventually acknowledged that these lines of communication must be placed under undivided control and authority. Accordingly, a Parliamentary Committee of 1839 urged the necessity of prohibiting, as far as locomotive power was concerned, the rivalry of competing parties on the same line of railway; and the Committee of 1840 decided that railway companies using locomotive power possessed a practical monopoly for the conveyance of passengers, from the nature of their business.[23]

Thus, finally, after many vain efforts to accommodate the new transport technology to juridical concepts appropriate to the old, the inherent character of that new technology prevailed even in the juridical realm. The railroad as a machine ensemble receives its legal and politicoeconomic sanction in the form of the transport monopoly.

English Railways, 1840 and 1850.

By comparing the two maps, we can clearly see how the few unconnected lines of 1840 had grown into such a dense railway network a mere ten years later.

From: Wilfred Smith, *An Economic Geography of Great Britain*. New York.

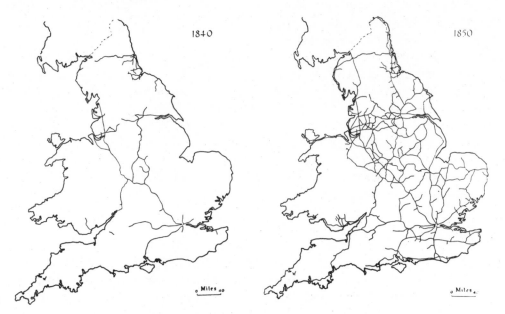

The process by which the institutions accommodate themselves to the railroad as a machine ensemble does not end with the acceptance of the transport monopoly. The chaos caused by individual traffic on the rail lines, now terminated by the monopoly, repeats itself on a higher level. In England (but not in Belgium and France) the railroad system grows without central planning, on a purely private-enterprise basis. The railway network grows denser through the construction of more and more lines, which never becomes a unified entity: it remains merely the sum of numerous local and regional lines that operate independently from each other. Technologically, it is a national transportation grid, providing fast and comfortable access to all its parts; but as an organization, based on private enterprise, it is a multitude of individual lines, isolated, working without coordination, or even working against each other. While objectively the expansion of the system should facilitate travel, in fact it increases the difficulties involved in changing trains and in transferring goods from one line to another, by creating impediments such as uncoordinated schedules and stations located at long distances from one another.

The unification of the railway network proceeds just as slowly and reluctantly as did the development of the transport monopoly. Finally, in 1842 the English railway companies create a cooperative and coordinative authority to deal with the traffic moving along more than one line — i.e., the *through* traffic, as distinct from the merely local and regional traffic.[24] This through traffic is becoming more and more important to the national economy.

Thus the railroad as a machine ensemble finally becomes institutionalized even in this respect, despite the resistance offered by the economic thought of the period, which was based on the principle of competition. The machine ensemble, consisting of wheel and rail, railroad and carriage, expands into a unified railway system, which appears as one great machine covering the land.[25]

In order to guarantee the proper functioning of this machine, juridical and politicoeconomic regulations have to be revised, but technological improvements prove equally necessary. The most important technological addition to the railways is the electrically operated telegraph system.

While this telegraph system already had been technically perfected at the beginning of the nineteenth century, before the advent of the railroad, it did not, at first, find any practical application, as there was no particular need for it. That changed with the coming of the railways, on which signals play a vital part from the very beginning. The machine ensemble, whose parts have to be minutely adjusted to each other, must not be prey to catastrophes. Contemporary illustrations demonstrate the tense watchfulness that characterized early journeys on the railroad. On *each* carriage of the train we can see one, two, and sometimes three persons, whose sole task it is to scan the line ahead for obstacles, approaching trains, etc. The first optical and acoustical signals that were devised to assist in this activity soon proved insufficient in dark, foggy, or noisy conditions, and of course when going through tunnels.

Train Crew.
This illustration from Thomas Gray's "Observations" (5th ed., 1825) is interesting for two reasons. First, the number of guards on each railway car is obviously an expression of an immense mistrust of machinery, which, in this manner, could be continually observed. Second, the design of the passenger car (see Chapter 5): here we can still clearly see the outlines of the coal lorry, upon which a double coach body has been mounted. When this illustration was published (1825), trains were not yet used for passenger traffic, which means that rail vehicles were not being built for this purpose. Gray's illustration simply documents a *concept* for combining a coal lorry with a passenger car. This is what makes the illustration so notable and peculiar.

From: Thomas Gray, *Observations. . .*, London, 1825.

*Allegory of the Electric
Telegraph, USA 1861.*

New York Public Library,
Picture Collection

Tunnel passages provide the telegraph with its first practical application.[26] The system devised for its use (first in tunnels, later all along the line), the "space interval system," consists of a division of the entire line into separate "blocks," each one of them served by a telegraph transmitter. This transmitter signals to the block ahead when the line is clear; the engine-driver then receives an optical signal that tells him to go ahead. The system relieves the engine-driver from any remaining obligation to exercise his personal powers of perception and judgment on the conditions that prevail around him and his train: all he needs to do now is to follow the signals he is given by a distant telegraph center. Because a train runs on a predetermined line, an engine-driver can never aspire to the social role of a "captain on dry land": the electric telegraph confirms his true status, that of an industrial worker, an operator of a machine. The telegraph becomes an integral element of the machine ensemble; Max Maria Von Weber, a philosophical-minded railroad expert and son of the well-known composer, observes that without the telegraph, the railway would be like an organism without a nervous system: ". . . as the muscle of a human body without the nerve flashing through it would be a mere lifeless hunk of flesh, so would the flying muscles that Watt's and Stephenson's inventions have lent to humanity be only half as capable of winging their way, if they were not animated by the guiding thought imperiously flashing through the nerves of the telegraph wires."[27]

However, the electric telegraph does not gain tremendous significance solely for its effect on the actual running of the machine ensemble. Its very appearance, too, becomes a major emblem of railway travel: the outer world beyond the compartment window is mediated to the traveler by the telegraph poles and wires flashing by — no longer does he see only the landscape through

BOOK

OF THE

TELEGRAPH.

BOSTON:
PUBLISHED BY DANIEL DAVIS,
428 WASHINGTON STREET.
1851.

Telegraph and Railroad
Originally developed to regulate railroad traffic, the telegraph differentiated itself as an independent means of communication toward the middle of the 19th century. However, the railroad line and the telegraph usually continued to exist side by side, one keeping the other company, the telegraph wires 'dancing' before the traveller's eyes.

From: *Book of the Telegraph.*
Boston, 1851

which he is traveling, but also, continuously, these poles and wires that belong to the railroad as intimately as the rails themselves do. The landscape appears *behind* the telegraph poles and wires; it is seen *through* them. As we noted earlier, the rail traveler's perceptions are changed by the intervention of the machine ensemble between him and the landscape; now we see a material demonstration of that intervention, in those poles and wires which are a part of the machine ensemble. They interpose themselves, both physically and metaphorically, between the traveler and the landscape.[28] To use Dolf Sternberger's term, the resulting perception can be called "panoramic." Verlaine, in the seventh poem of his cycle *La Bonne Chanson,* describes it with technical precision. The hurtling railroad train appears here as the very motion of writing, and the telegraph poles and wires are the calligraphic instruments with which the new perception inscribes the panoramic landscape upon the real one:

> Le paysage dans le cadre des portières
> Court furieusement, et des plaines entières
> Avec de l'eau, des blés, des arbres et du ciel
> Vont s'engouffrant parmi le tourbillon cruel
> Où tombent les poteaux minces du télégraphe
> Dont les fils ont l'allure étrange d'un paraphe.

> The scene behind the carriage window-panes
> Goes flitting past in furious flight; whole plains
> With streams and harvest-fields and trees and blue
> Are swallowed by the whirlpool, whereinto
> The telegraph's slim pillars topple o'er,
> Whose wires look strangely like a music-score.[29]

3. Railroad Space and Railroad Time

Economically, the railways' operation
. . . causes distances to diminish . . . Lille suddenly finds itself transported to Louvres;
Calais to Pontoise; le Havre to Poissy; Rouen
to Sèvres or to Asnières; Reims to Pantin;
Strasbourg to Meaux; Lyon to a place half-
way between Melun and Corbeil; Marseilles
to Nemours; Perpignan to Pithiviers; Bordeaux to Chartres or to Étampes; Nantes to
Arpajon, etc.
— Constantin Pecqueur, 1839

"Annihilation of space and time" is the early nineteenth-century characterization of the effect of railroad travel. The concept is based on the speed that the
new means of transport is able to achieve. A given spatial distance, traditionally
covered in a fixed amount of travel time, can suddenly be dealt with in a
fraction of that time; to put it another way, the same amount of time now
permits one to cover the old spatial distance many times over. In terms of
transport economics, this means a shrinking of space: "Distances practically
diminish in the exact ratio of the speed of personal locomotion," Lardner says
in his *Railway Economy*.[1]

The average traveling speed of the early railways in England is twenty to
thirty miles an hour, which is roughly three times the speed previously achieved
by the stagecoaches.[2] Thus, any given distance is covered in one-third of the
customary time: *temporally* that distance shrinks to one-third of its former
length. In early nineteenth-century writings the temporal diminution is expressed mostly in terms of a shrinking of space. An article published in the
Quarterly Review in 1839 speaks of "the gradual annihilation, approaching almost to the final extinction, of that space and of those distances which have
hitherto been supposed unalterably to separate the various nations of the
globe," and continues:

For instance, supposing that railroads, even at our present simmering
rate of travelling, were to be suddenly established all over England, the
whole population of the country would, speaking metaphorically, at once
advance *en masse*, and place their chairs nearer to the fireside of their
metropolis by two-thirds of the time which now separates them from it;
they would also sit nearer to one another by two-thirds of the time which

now respectively alienates them. If the rate were to be sufficiently accelerated, this process would be repeated; our harbours, our dock-yards, our towns, the whole of our rural population, would again not only draw nearer to each other by two-thirds, but all would proportionally approach the national hearth. As distances were thus annihilated, the surface of our country would, as it were, shrivel in size until it became not much bigger than one immense city.[3]

The image of a temporal shrinkage seen as a spatial one appears in an even more extravagant guise in the work of Constantin Pecqueur, the economist and Saint-Simonian, whose *Economie sociale* received a prize from the Institut de France in 1838. Here, the temporally shrunk transport space appears as a new geography of France, a geography based on the new conditions of speed, a condensed geography, as it were. The cities of France approach each other while simultaneously advancing on Paris. These changes in location, enumerated in the epigraph to this chapter, are summarized in Pecqueur's statement

The Age of Coach Travel in England around 1750.

From: Philip S. Bagwell, *Transportation Revolution.* London 1974.

that it is now possible to see "the new France as fitting into the space of the *old* Île-de-France, or its equivalent."

The diminution of transport distances seems to create a new, reduced, geography, yet it does not actually alter the size of the spaces between the points connected by the new mode of transport. "Yet by a sort of miracle," says the *Quarterly Review* article, after describing the shrinking process, "every man's field would be found not only *where* it always was, but *as large* as ever it was." Pecqueur expresses the same notion in literary hyperbole: the diminished transport geography of France contains the true geography of France within it in a condensed form: "Each bit of terrain, each field on this surface would still remain intact; so would every house in a village, the village itself, or the town; every territory with its village in the center would remain a province; on the map of the imagination, all of these would finally be reproduced and reduced down to the infinitely small! As for Louvres, or Pontoise, or Chartres, or Arpajon, etc., it is obvious that they will just get lost in some street of Paris or its suburbs."[4]

The notion that a French town will fit into a Paris street demonstrates that the alteration of spatial relationships by the speed of the railroad is not simply a process that diminishes space, but that it is a dual one: it both diminishes and expands space. The dialectic of this process states that this diminution of space (i.e., the shrinking of transport time) causes an expansion of transport space by incorporating new areas into the transport network. The nation's contraction into a metropolis, as described in the *Quarterly Review*, conversely appears as an expansion of the metropolis: by establishing transport lines to ever more outlying areas, the metropolis tends to incorporate the entire nation. The epoch of the suburbs, of the amoebic proliferation of the formerly contained cities into the surrounding countryside, begins with the railroads. This is Lardner in 1851:

> It is not now unusual for persons whose place of business is in the centre of the capital, to reside with their families at a distance of from fifteen to twenty miles from that centre. Nevertheless, they are able to arrive at their respective shops, counting-houses, or offices, at an early hour of the morning, and to return without inconvenience to their residence at the usual time in the evening. Hence in all directions round the metropolis in which railways are extended, habitations are multiplied, and a considerable part of the former population of London has been diffused in these quarters.[5]

The notion that the railroad annihilates space and time is not related to that expansion of space that results from the incorporation of new spaces into the transport network. What is experienced as being annihilated is the traditional space-time continuum which characterized the old transpsort technology. Organically embedded in nature as it was, that technology, in its mimetic relationship to the space traversed, permitted the traveler to perceive that space as a living entity. What Bergson called the *durée* (duration, the time spent getting from one place to another on a road is not an objective mathematical unit, but a subjective perception of space-time. The dependence of this perception on transport technology illustrates Durkheim's notion that a society's space-time perceptions are a function of its social rhythm and its territory.[6] "What is decisive," says Erwin Straus, discussing the psychology of distances, "is not the objectively measured distance, but the relation of such distance to potentiality."[7] Transport technology is the material base of potentiality, and equally the material base of the traveler's space-time perception. If an essential element of a given sociocultural space-time continuum undergoes change, this will affect the entire structure; our perception of space-time will also lose its accustomed orientation. Sorokin, who following Durkheim, distinguishes between sociocultural and physicomathematical notions of space-time, describes the hypothetical effects of a sudden replacement of customary sociocultural time measures with purely mathematical ones: "If we try to replace sociocultural time by a purely quantitative time, time becomes devitalized. *It loses its reality, and we find ourselves in an exceeding difficult position in our efforts to orient ourselves in the time process, to find out 'where we are' and where are the other social phenomena on 'the bridge of time'.*" (Italics in original.)[8]

Thus, the idea that the railroad annihilates space and time has to be seen as the reaction of perceptive powers that were formed by a certain transport technology who suddenly find that technology replaced by an entirely new one. Compared to the eotechnical space-time relationship, the one created by the railroad appears abstract and disorienting, because the railroad — in realizing Newton's mechanics — negates all that characterized eotechnical traffic; the railroad does not appear embedded in the space of the landscape the way coach and highway are, but seems to strike its way through it.

Heinrich Heine captures the disorientation experienced by the traditional space-time consciousness when confronted by the new technology; apropos the opening of railway lines from Paris to Rouen and Orléans in 1843, he speaks of the "tremendous foreboding such as we always feel when there comes an enormous, an unheard-of event whose consequences are imponderable and incalculable," and calls the railroad a "providential event," comparable to the inventions of gunpowder and printing, "which swings mankind in a new direction, and changes the color and shape of life." Heine continues in this vein:

> What changes must now occur, in our way of looking at things, in our notions! Even the elementary concepts of time and space have begun to vacillate. Space is killed by the railways, and we are left with time alone. . . . Now you can travel to Orléans in four and a half hours, and it takes no longer to get to Rouen. Just imagine what will happen when the lines to Belgium and Germany are completed and connected up with their railways! I feel as if the mountains and forests of all countries were advancing on Paris. Even now, I can smell the German linden trees; the North Sea's breakers are rolling against my door.[9]

We have now clearly stated the two contradictory sides of the same process: on one hand, the railroad opens up new spaces that were not as easily accessible before; on the other, it does so by destroying space, namely, the space between points. That in-between space, or travel space, which it was possible to "savor" while using the slow, work-intensive eotechnical form of transport, disappears on the railroads. The railroad knows only points of departure and destination. "They [the railways] only serve the points of departure, the way stations, and the terminals, which are mostly at great distances from each other," says a French author in 1840; "they are of no use whatsoever for the intervening spaces, which they traverse with disdain and provide only with a useless spectacle."[10]

As the space between the points — the traditional traveling space — is destroyed, those points move into each other's immediate vicinity: one might say that they collide. They lose their old sense of local identity, which used to be determined by the spaces between them. The isolation of localities, which was created by spatial distance, was the very essence of their identity, their self-assured and complacent individuality. Heine's vision of the North Sea breaking on his doorstep in Paris is tinged with "tremendous foreboding" because both localities — Paris and the North Sea — are still presented in their mutually isolated state, "worlds apart": thus their collision appears unfathomable. Thirty years later, as an interlocking network of railroad lines connects all of Europe, that kind of consciousness is no longer realistic. The regions appear, regardless of their geographical remoteness, as close and as easily accessible as the railroads have made them. One generation after Heine, the more privileged inhabitants of Paris have the option of letting themselves be transported, in a matter of hours, to a region that is as distant from their city as Heine's North Sea. The Mediterranean does not extend its shores right up to Parisian thresholds, but it can be reached so much more quickly than before, that the journey there is no longer experienced as such. The Parisians who migrate south in the winter see nothing but blue skies and the sea. As Mallarmé writes in the winter of 1874/5, in *La Dernière Mode,* the journal he edits, they are "calm, self-absorbed people, paying no attention to the invisible landscapes of the journey. To leave Paris and to get to where the sky is clear, that is their desire."[11] These are no longer travelers — rather, as Ruskin puts it, these are human parcels who dispatch themselves to their destination by means of the railroad, arriving as they left, untouched by the space traversed.

Even though the railroad cannot bring the remote regions physically to Paris, the speedy and comfortable accessibility of those regions creates a consciousness of distance that approximates Heine's vision of space, but without the sense of foreboding. The region that can be reached by train from Paris *realizes itself* for the Parisians by means of the train. It then appears as the product or appendage of the railroad, as in a phrase of Mallarmé's: "Normandy, which, like Brittany, is part of the Western Railway."[12]

But if Normandy and Brittany are part of the Western Railway, being its destinations, then the point of departure of that same railway, the station in Paris, becomes the entrance to those regions. This is a common enough notion in the nineteenth-century: it can be found in every one of Baedeker's travel guides that recommends a certain railroad station as the point of departure for each excursion.

The identification of the railrad station with the traveler's destination, and the relative insignificance of the journey itself, are expressed by Mallarmé, who prints in *La Dernière Mode,* under the heading *Gazette et Programme de la Quinzaine,* the following subheadings representing equally important institutions for entertainment: *Les Librairies, Les Théâtres, Les Gares* (the last sometimes replaced by *Les Voyages*). Thus a railroad journey appears not different from a visit to the theater or the library — the purchase of a train ticket is equivalent to that of a theater ticket.

A generation after Mallarmé, Marcel Proust, in *Remembrance of Things Past*, discusses the difference between a journey by train and one in a motorcar:

> The journey was one that would now be made, probably, in a motor-car, which would be supposed to render it more interesting. We shall see too that, accomplished in such a way, it would even be in a sense more genuine, since one would be following more clearly, in a closer intimacy, the various contours by which the surface of the earth is wrinkled. But after all, the special attraction of the journey lies not in our being able to alight at places on the way and to stop altogether as soon as we grow tired, but in its making the difference between departure and arrival not as imperceptible but as intense as possible, so that we are conscious of it in its totality, intact, as it existed in our mind when imagination bore us from the place in which we were living right to the very heart of a place we longed to see, in a single sweep which seemed miraculous to us not so much because it covered a certain distance as because it united two distinct individualities of the world, took us from one name to another name; and this difference is accentuated (more than in a form of locomotion in which, since one can stop and alight where one chooses, there can scarcely be said to be any point of arrival) by the mysterious operation that is performed in those peculiar places, railway stations, which do not constitute, so to speak, a part of the surrounding town but contain the essence of its personality just as upon their sign-boards they bear its painted name.[12a]

The fate wrought upon the outlying regions by the railroads affects *goods* even sooner: as long as production and consumption are strictly regional — which they were until the beginning of modern transportation — the goods remain part of the local identity of their place of production. Their route of circulation can be perceived at a glance. Only when modern transportation creates a definite spatial distance between place of production and place of consumption do the goods become uprooted commodities. In *Grundrisse*, Marx makes an observation about the relation between spatial distance and the nature of commodities; it tells us a good deal about how modern transportation has affected our perception of goods: "This locational movement — the bringing of the product to the market, which is a necessary condition of its circulation, except when the point of production is itself a market — could more precisely be regarded as the transformation of the product *into a commodity*."[13] (Italics in original.)

With the spatial distance that the product covers on its way from its place of production to the market, it also loses its local identity, its spatial presence. Its concretely sensual properties, which are experienced at the place of production as a result of the labor process (or, in the case of the fruits of the land, as a result of natural growth), appear quite different in the distant marketplace. There the product, now a commodity, realizes its economic value, and simultaneously gains new qualities as an object of consumption. No longer is it seen in the context of the original locality of its place of production but in the new locality of the marketplace: cherries offered for sale in the Paris market seem to be products of that market, just as Normandy seems to be a product of the railroad that takes you there. Pecqueur touches on the notion of the unity of the realization of economic value and the biological process, using the example of the ripening of fruit: "For instance, economically speaking, and for the sake of freshness and price, the cherries of Montmorency really ripen on the uncultivated summits of the Quartier Lafayette; the roses of Fontenay burst into bloom and fragrance in the flower beds of the Jardin du Luxembourg; the peaches of Montreuil in the Parc de Monceaux, and the grapes of Fontainebleau, too, ripen on some hill closer to Paris than the one where the Surênes is still greening."[14]

The regions, joined to each other and to the metropolis by the railways, and the goods that are torn out of their local relation by modern transportation, share the fate of losing their inherited place, their traditional spatial-temporal presence or, as Walter Benjamin sums it up in one word, their aura.

The detaching of the remote region from its original isolation, its opening-up by the railroad, can well be defined as the loss of its aura, as Benjamin characterizes the aura and its loss in his essay "The Work of Art in the Age of Mechanical Reproduction." The notions of spatial-temporal presence and distance are integral parts of Benjamin's concept of the aura. He defines the "aura of natural objects" as "the unique phenomenon of a distance, however close it may be."[14a] The aura of a work of art is "its unique existence at the place where it happens to be."[14b] This spatial-temporal singularity, this "happening-but-once-ness," this *genuineness* of the object, is, according to Benjamin, destroyed by reproduction. "The situations into which the product of mechanical reproduction can be brought may not touch the actual work of art, yet the quality of its presence is always depreciated."[14c] It is tempting to apply this statement to the outlying regions that have been made accessible by the railroad: while being opened up to tourism, they remain, initially at least, untouched in their physical actuality, but their easy, comfortable, and inexpensive accessibility robs them of their previous value as remote and out-of-the-way places. "The staple of the district is, in fact, its beauty and its character of seclusion and retirement," Wordsworth writes in 1844, defending the Lake District against the intrusion of the railways.[15] The *devaluation* of outlying regions by their exploitation for mass tourism, by means of the railroad in the nineteenth century and air traffic in the twentieth, is a familiar occurrence. As soon as the railroad reaches the seaside towns of southern England that had been strongholds of the aristocracy far into the nineteenth century, the middle classes take them over. Then the aristocracy retires to remote localities such as Scotland, Ireland, and the Lake District.[15a] Contemporary airplane tourism is engaged in further devaluation of formerly exclusive, very remote regions.

The destruction of aura by means of reproduction of which Benjamin speaks is an expression of the same trend that brought the masses "closer" to the outlying regions in the nineteenth century: "The desire of contemporary masses to bring things 'closer' spatially and humanly . . . is just as ardent as their bent toward overcoming the uniqueness of every reality by accepting its reproduction."[15b] The remote regions are made available to the masses by means of tourism: this is merely a prelude, a preparation for making *any* unique thing available by means of reproduction. When spatial distance is no longer experienced, the differences between original and reproduction diminish. In the filmic perception — i.e., the perception of *montage*, the juxtaposition of the most disparate images into one unit — the new reality of annihilated in-between spaces finds its clearest expression: the film brings things closer to the viewer as well as closer together.

The regions lose their temporal identity in an entirely concrete sense: the railroads deprive them of their local time. As long as they remained isolated from each other, they had their individual times: London time ran four minutes ahead of time in Reading, seven minutes and thirty seconds ahead of Cirencester time, fourteen minutes ahead of Bridgewater time.[15c] This patchwork of varying local times was no problem as long as traffic between the places was so slow that the slight temporal differences really did not matter; but the temporal foreshortening of the distances that was effected by the trains forces the differing local times to confront each other. Under traditional circumstances, a supraregional schedule would be impossible: times of departure and arrival are valid only for the place whose local time is being used. For the next station, with its own time, that previous time is no longer valid. Regular traffic needs standardized time; this is quite analogous to the way in which the machine ensemble constituted by rail and carriage undermined individual traffic and brought about the transportation monopoly.

In the 1840s, the individual English railway companies proceed to standardize time, while not coordinating their efforts with each other. Each company institutes a new time on its own line. The process is so novel that it is repeated daily, in the most cumbersome manner, as Bagwell describes, apropos of the Grand Junction Company's procedure: "Each morning an Admiralty messenger carried a watch bearing the correct time to the guard on the down Irish Mail leaving Euston for Holyhead. On arrival at Holyhead the time was

Timetable of the London & Birmingham Railway, 1840.

From: *Bradshaw's Railway Companion,* London 1840.

Distance from London.	London to Birmingham STATIONS.	Mixed. 6 a.m.	3rd class train, 7 a.m.	*Mixed Class 8 a.m.	First calling at M. Stns. 9 a.m	Mixed. 9½ a.m.	*Mail. 9¾ a.m.	Mixed Class. 11 a.m.	Mixed Class 12 Noon	*Mixed calling at 1st.cl.Stns.1 p.m	Mixed Class. 2 p.m.	Mixed Class 3 p.m.	*Mixed calling at 1st.cl.stns.5 p.m	Mixed Class. 6 p.m.	*Mail, Mixed. 8½ p.m.	Mixed, calling at mail sts. 9 p.m.	FARES. ¼ in. car. by day, or l class 6in. by night s. D.	1st class carriage, 6 in-side, by day s. D.	2nacuus carriage, closed, by night s. D.	2d class open, by day s. D.
Mls.	LONDON ..	6 0	7 0	8 0	9 0	9 30	9 45	11 0	12 0	1 0	2 0	3 0	5 0	6 0	8 30	9 0				
11¼	Harrow ..	..	7 40	8 30	..	..	..	..	12 30	..	2 30	3 30	5 30	6 30	..	..	3 6	3 0	2 6	2 0
17¾	Watford ..	6 45	8 0	8 50	..	..	..	11 45	12 45	1 45	2 50	3 50	5 45	6 54	..	..	5 0	4 6	4 0	3 0
24¼	Boxmoor..	..	8 30	9 10	..	..	..	..	1 5	..	3 10	4 10	..	7 10	..	..	7 0	6 6	5 6	4 6
28½	B.Hampstd	..	8 45	9 20	..	..	..	..	1 20	..	3 20	4 20	..	7 20	..	..	8 0	7 6	6 6	5 0
31	Tring	7 25	9 0	9 35	10 22	10 52	11 0	12 25	1 35	2 25	3 35	4 35	6 25	7 35	9 56	10 26	9 6	8 6	7 0	5 6
	Aylesbury	..		10 15	..	..	..	..	2 15	..		5 15		8 15	..	..		8 6		5 6
41	Leighton ..	7 50	10 0	10 0	..	..	..	12 50	..	2 50	4 0	..	6 50	8 0	..	..	12 0	11 0	9 0	7 6
	Bletchley ..	..	10 25	10 15	..	..	..	..	..	..	4 15	..	..	8 15	..	..	13 6	12 6	10 6	8 6
52½	Wolverton ..	8 15	10 45	10 30	11 7	11 37	12 0	1 15	..	3 15	4 30	..	7 15	8 30	10 54	11 24	15 6	14 0	11 6	9 6
60	Roade	..	12 30	10 55	..	..	..	..	..	..	4 55	..	7 40	..	..	..	17 6	16 0	13 6	10 6
63¼	Blisworth ..	8 50	12 45	11 5	..	12 0	12 23	1 50	..	3 50	5 5	..	7 50	..	11 15	11 45	18 6	17 0	14 0	11 6
69½	Weedon ..	9 5	1 15	11 25	11 50	12 20	12 40	2 5	..	4 5	5 25	..	8 5	..	11 50	12 20	20 6	18 6	15 6	12 6
75¼	Crick	..	1 35	11 45	..	..	..	..	..	..	5 45	..	..	..	..	..	22 0	20 0	17 0	13 6
83¼	Rugby	9 40	2 0	12 5	..	12 55	1 15	2 40	..	4 40	6 5	..	8 40	..	12 30	1 0	24 6	22 0	18 6	15 0
89¼	Brandon ..	..	2 20	12 20	..	..	..	..	..	..	6 20	..	..	..	..	..	26 0	24 0	20 0	16 0
94	Coventry	10 10	2 40	12 35	12 55	..	1 45	3 10	..	5 10	6 35	..	9 10	..	1 0	..	27 6	25 0	21 0	16 6
100¼	Hampton	10 35	3 10	1 0	1 28	..	..	..	..	5 35	7 0	..	..	..	..	..	30 0	27 6	23 0	18 6
112¼	Birminghm	11 30	3 45	2 0	2 15	..	2 30	4 30	..	6 30	8 0	..	10 30	..	2 0	..	32 6	30 0	25 0	20 0

The 3rd Class train takes passengers, private carriages, and horses, at the following charges:—From London to Birmingham, Passengers 14s, private carriages £3, horse boxes £4, and in proportion for intermediate stations.

ROUTES FROM NEW YORK.

To Albany, by Steam Boat.		
Fort Gansewort,		2
Hamilton's monument,	2	4
Manhattanville,	3	7
Fort Lee,	3	10
Spuyten Duyvel Cr.	2	12
Phillipsburg,	4	16
Dobb's Ferry,	6	22
Tappan Landing,	3	25
Tarrytown,	1	26
Nyack, on Tappan sea,	3	29
Sparta, & State Prison,	3	32
Tellers Point,	2	34
Haverstraw & Croton,	1	35
Stony Point,	3	38
Verplank's Point,	1	39
Peckskill,	2	41
St Anthony's nose,	2	43
Fort Clinton,	1	44
West Point,	7	51
Highlands. { Crows Nest Mt.	4	55
Butter Hill,	1	56
Caldwell,	1	57
Canterbury,	1	58
New Windsor,	1	59
Newburg, West side, } Fiskill landing, E. S. }	2	61
Hamburg,	6	67
Hampton,	1	68
Barnegat,	2	70
Poughkeepsie,	5	75
Hyde Park,	5	80
Pelham,	3	83
Walkill Cr.	6	89

Rhinebeck,	1	90
Redhook, L. L.	6	96
Glasgow,	3	99
Redhook, U. L.	1	100
Saugerties,	1	101
Bristol,	1	102
Catskill,	9	111

(Thence to Pine Orchard, 14 miles.)

Hudson and Athens,	5	116
Columbiaville,	5	121
Coxackie,	3	124
Kinderhook Landing,	1	125
New Baltimore,	5	130
Coeymans,	2	132
Schodack,	2	134
Castleton,	1	135
Albany,	10	145

For routes from Albany, see article " Albany."

The stage route from N. York to Albany, does not differ materially from the above.

To Boston, by Steam Boat.		
Newtown Creek,		4
Hell Gate,	5	9
Flushing Bay,	4	13
Frogs Point,	3	16
Cow Neck,	2	18
New Rochelle L.,	6	24
West Greenwich,	11	35
Stamford,	8	43
Oldwell,	8	51

Timetable of an American Steamship, 1834.

This timetable does not yet contain arrival and departure times, but only the distances between the individual ports. The figures in the left column indicate the distances between consecutive ports. The right column summarizes the distances of the entire voyage.

From: Henry Tanner, *The American Traveller, for the year 1834.*

passed on to officials on the Kingston boat who carried it over to Dublin. On the return mail to Euston the watch was carried back to the Admiralty messenger at Euston once more."[16]

When, after the establishment of the Railway Clearing House, the companies decide to cooperate and form a national railroad network, Greenwich Time is introduced as the standard time valid on all the lines.[17] Yet railroad time is not accepted as anything but schedule time until late in the century. As the rail network grows denser, incorporating more and more regions, the retention of local times becomes untenable: in 1880, railroad time becomes general standard time in England. In Germany, official recognition comes in 1893; as early as 1884, an international conference on time standards, held in Washington, D.C., divided the world into time zones.

In the United States, the process is more complicated, as there is no cooperation whatsoever between the private railroad companies. Each company has its own time, in most cases, the local time of the company's headquarters. In stations used by several different lines there are clocks showing different times: three of these in Buffalo, six in Pittsburgh.[18] In 1889, the United States is divided into four time zones, essentially unchanged to this day; officially, at first, the times within the zones are regarded only as railroad time; in practice, these become regional standard times, although they are given legal recognition only in 1918.

Excursion:
The Space of Glass Architecture

The railroad reorganizes space. In architecture, a similar reorganization occurs with the introduction of glass and steel as new building materials. The railroad machine ensemble multiplies speed and capacity of traffic; steel and glass multiply the capacity of roofed structures. Both the railroad and the glass buildings are direct expressions of the multiplied productivity brought about by the industrial revolution. The railroad brings new quantities of goods into circulation; the edifices of glass architecture — railroad stations, market halls, exhibition palaces, arcades — serve as places of transit and storage. The spatial capacity of glass architecture stands in a similar relation to the capacity of traditional architecture as the railroad's capacity stands to that of preindustrial transportation. This is due to the greater strength and resistance to stress characteristic of steel, the necessary complement to glass, compared to the previously utilized building materials. According to Alfred Gotthold Meyer, steel, in terms of stress resistance, is forty times as strong as stone, ten times as strong as wood.[1] The combination of steel as the carrier and glass as the filler leads to a reappraisal of all previously recognized architectural principles; Meyer expresses it as follows:

1) *The reappraisal of strength and mass.* By means of mathematical calculation, it is possible to determine the statistically possible minimum of material required for a given structure, using a material that has hitherto unheard-of powers of resistance. The opposing forces are rationally divided into vectors of push and pull and then dealt with by appropriately formed cross sections. The result is strength without mass.

2) *The reappraisal of spatial boundaries.* The wall masses shrink to thin boundary surfaces. The contained space no longer functions in terms of walls and vaults: it stands on its own, and does so inside as well as outside, without intermediaries.

3) *The reappraisal of light and shadow.* New purposes demand maximal interior light: thus we get the glass roof, and with it, a diffuse light without contrast, lacking plastic definition of form, but also lacking painterly indefiniteness.

4) To greater extent than with other building materials, the effective form of glass and steel architecture is based primarily on the structure itself, with its ubiquitous logical pattern of girders: The essential thing is now *the line,* not the self-contained mass.[2] (Italics in original.)

To sum up: it is the very nature of glass architecture that puts an end to traditional architecture and its inevitable contrasts of light and shadow. As Meyer says, glass architecture creates a "light-space." "The striving for lightness," he writes, "is one of the main motivating forces in the developmental history of interior space. In the walls erected by stone or wood architecture, it could express itself only by breaking through the surfaces, in order to provide light for the interior; there was a conflict between light and shadow, between light and dark. It is, primarily, that contrast that gives us our sense of interior space and that gives a building its character, inside as well as outside."[3]

The Crystal Palace, erected for the World Exhibition in London in 1851, was the first true large-scale realization of glass and steel architecture; it caused perceptual shocks similar to those experienced by the first railway travelers. "The enormous areas of glass introduced into the vaulting," Giedion says, describing contemporary reaction, "almost blinded contemporary spectators, who were unaccustomed to the amount of light that was admitted."[4]

In his report on the 1851 World Exhibition, Lothar Bucher — an emigré after the German Revolution of 1848, and later a collaborator of Bismarck — gives a vivid picture of the dazzling effect of ferrovitreous architecture on the customary patterns of light and shadow perception:

We see a fine network of symmetrical lines that does not, however, provide any clues whereby one could estimate its distance from the eye or the actual size of the mesh. The side walls stand too far apart to be taken in at a

Space in Glass Architecture: The Crystal Palace, 1851.

The shock in perception created by the interior space is analogous to the perception shock of a railroad trip. From a contemporary description of the Crystal Palace: "We see a delicate network of lines without any clue by means of which we might judge their distance from the eye or the real size. The side walls are too far apart to be embraced in a single glance. Instead of moving from the wall at one end to that at the other, the eye seeps along an unending perspective which fades into the horizon..." (L. Bucher). New York Public Library, Picture Collection

glance, and instead of meeting a facing wall, the eye moves upward over an endless perspective, or one whose end appears diffuse and blue. We do not know whether that mesh hovers a hundred or a thousand feet above us, or whether the ceiling is flat or formed by a number of small parallel ceilings; this is due to the total absence of shadows, which normally aid the psyche in comprehending the impression received by the optical nerve. If we let our gaze slowly move downward again, it encounters the filigreed girders, painted blue, far apart from each other at first, then moving ever closer, then superimposed on each other, then interrupted by a shining band of light, and finally dissolving in a remote background in which everything corporeal, even the lines themselves, disappears and only the color remains. Looking at the side walls, we orient ourselves, by seeking out, from among the profusion of carpets, tapestries, animal skins, mirrors, and a thousand other draperies, a single uncovered pillar — so slender that it does not seem to be able to hold up any weight, but is there only to satisfy the eye's need to recognize a support; we can estimate its height by comparing it to some person passing by, and by observing a second and a third one above it.[5]

The impression of glass architecture can be summed up in one word: evanescence. The uniform quality of the light and the absence of light-shadow contrasts disorient perceptual faculties used to those contrasts, just as the rail-road's increased speed disorients the traditional perception of space. The motion of the railway, proceeding uniformly and in a straight line, is experienced as abstract, *pure* motion, dissociated from the space in which it occurs. Analo-gously, the space of ferrovitreous architecture appears as pure abstract light-space, dissociated from all customary architectural form, a space without qual-ities and contrasts. Richard Lucae describes the space of the Crystal Palace as an "artificially created environment" that "no longer is a space," and continues with an elegant simile: "As in a crystal, there no longer is any true interior or exterior. We have been separated from nature, but we hardly feel it. The barrier erected between us and the landscape is almost ethereal. If we imagine that air can be poured like a liquid, then it has, here, achieved a solid form, after the removal of the mold into which it was poured. We find ourselves within a cut-out segment of atmosphere. . . . It is, in my opinion, extraordinar-ily difficult to arrive at a clear perception of the effect of form and scale in this incorporeal space."[6]

World Exhibition Pavilions — Hot-Houses of 19th Century Industry.
Here the Crystal Palace is manifestly reminiscent of a hot-house: a fully-grown tree found on the construction site has been incorporated into the enclosed space. In addition, an abundance of decorative plants, mostly palm trees, are interspersed with the actual exhibits. The total impression is one of a space which harmoniously combines palm trees, industrial products, machinery, etc.: Industry as a gigantic hot-house.

New York Public Library, Picture Collection

53

Glass Architecture and Exotic Plants: Jardin des Plantes, Paris, 1840's.

19th Century glass architecture originated from garden architecture. Joseph Paxton, the architect of the Crystal Palace in London, had been a garden architect; the Crystal Palace itself is a gigantic version of the hot house which Paxton built for the "Victoria Regis" waterlilly.

New York Public Library, Picture Collection

In dissociating light and atmosphere from the context of the natural overall atmosphere by means of "an almost ethereal" barrier, ferrovitreous architecture creates a novel condition. Light and atmosphere are now perceived as independent qualities, no longer subject to the rules of the natural world in which they had hitherto manifested themselves. This process is comparable to the experience of *pure* speed on the railroad, that is, speed perceived as an independent quality because it is divorced from the organic base of horsepower. (In the beginning of the twentieth century, the human voice is subjected to that same process of dissociation from its natural habitat, its natural condition, by the microphone and the radio.)*

*I owe this realization to Hans-Thies Lehmann who applies the thought successfully in his analysis of Bertolt Brecht's early poetry.

Considering the newly gained independence of light from nature and the dissolution of corporeality that characterize Bucher's and Lucae's perceptions of the Crystal Palace, one might call their descriptions "Impressionist." Max Raphael's definition of the Impressionists' method of painting corresponds, in detail, to their perceptions of the inner space of the Crystal Palace: "a dissolution of the object, in its closed form as well as in its inherent significance within the atmosphere; a cancellation of the material concepts, e.g., the local color, the line of three-dimensional form, in favor of a relationship with light; an emphasis on appearance that simultaneously removes it into distance; the removal of space from the realm of visual representation."[7] Siegfried Giedion[8] understands the effect of the Crystal Palace on its contemporaries as objectively Impressionist in intention, and makes a connection between Turner's painterly objectives and those of the architect of the Crystal Palace; that seems far-fetched, but it does seem justifiable to view Impressionism as a codification of a certain nineteenth-century perception of an evanescence whose most powerful material manifestations are the railroad and ferrovitreous architecture.[9]

This digression on the novel spatiality of that architecture would not be complete without a reference to the developments that led to its demise. The Crystal Palace is the culmination and termination of ferrovitreous architectural functionalism: it is followed, in the latter half of the century, by restorative developments. Ferrovitreous methods of construction are relegated to tasks of roofing and dome-building. Builders revert to the erection of massive and pompous stone fronts: these cover up the ferrovitreous constructions which cannot yet be abandoned entirely, due to the lighting requirements of large interior spaces.

By the turn of the century, as it becomes possible to generate inexpensive artificial electric light by industrial means, ferrovitreous architecture becomes redundant. The need for large structures for the display, storage, and merchandising of commodities remains, but the dependence on natural light disappears. The ferrous mode of construction, which remains necessary for the stability of large rooms and buildings, detaches itself from the vitreous aspect and takes the form of steel skeletons for edifices that are once again constructed in the traditional massive materials.

Artificial electric light as a mass phenomenon originates and achieves its most extended potential in the United States of Edison's day. It is another giant step in the direction of independence from nature. Although ferrovitreous architecture was an initial development in that same direction, it was still dependent upon and oriented toward nature, in that it attempted to maximize the use of natural light. The new, artificially lighted type of enclosed space requires the very opposite — the minimization of glass windows. No longer is daylight an exploitable raw material: now it is an uncertain factor that should be eliminated, as Matthew Luckiesh points out in his work *The Lighting Art,* published in 1917: "Natural light does not possess the potentiality that artificial light does because it is generally less readily controlled and adapted to the problems."[10] Windows are not only sources of irregular, unreliable, and difficult-to-control natural light, they also present problems of expenditure. Luckiesh: "The cost of natural light for indoor illumination is considerable because of the floor and wall area that has to be sacrificed for window space; in addition there are various minor factors which increase the cost of natural light indoors."[11]

The solution that determines the future development of commercial building spaces is *artificial light,* i.e., the production of the same amount of light that filled the inner space of vitreous architecture *by technical means.* "In considering future applications of artificial daylight it is well to note that even when natural daylight is available *it cannot be brought into interiors without cost.* The construction of the daylight entrance is more expensive than ordinary roofing and blank walls."[12]

In less than a century, the problem of lighting undergoes two revolutionary transformations. In the first half of the nineteenth century, ferrovitreous architecture dissolves the elements of traditional architecture in order to gain natural light. This is followed, as a result of the development of artificial light, by a movement in the opposite direction, by a closing off of interior spaces *against* uncontrollable daylight, a tendency leading to the elimination of windows and glass buildings.[13]

This second turn did not have anything like the effect on contemporary consciousness and perception that the "light-space" of glass architecture had. It is not difficult to see why this was so: glass architecture dissolved the traditional forms because it had to fulfill a dual function — it was architecture as well as lighting technology. It was a technical and architectural surrogate for the artificial light that was not yet available. It prepared the way for artificial lighting by making the natural light appear artificial. (This process is comparable to the previously mentioned development of the water wheel which initially receives its regular water supply by means of a steam-powered water pump before it is replaced by the steam engine.)

4. Panoramic Travel

Dreamlike travelling on the railroad. The towns which I pass between Philadelphia and New York make no distinct impression. They are like pictures on a wall. The more, that you can read all the way in a car a French novel.

— Emerson, *Journals,* February 7, 1843

In Goethe's journal on his trip to Switzerland in 1797, we find the following entry:

Left Frankfurt shortly after 7:00 A.M. On the Sachsenhausen mountain, many well-kept vineyards; foggy, cloudy, pleasant weather. The highway pavement has been improved with limestone. Woods in back of the watchtower. A man climbing up the great tall beech trees with a rope and iron cleats on his shoes. What a village! A deadfall by the road, from the hills by Langen. *Sprendlingen.* Basalt in the pavement and on the highway up to Langen; the surface must break very often on this plateau, as near Frankfurt. Sandy, fertile, flat land; a lot of agriculture, but meager . . .[1]

As Goethe tells Eckermann, this journal was "merely jotted down as given by the moment." Thus it is no poetic text, but a description of a journey by coach in the late eighteenth century, a record of impressions received on that journey. Goethe's trip from Frankfurt to Heidelberg consists of a continuous sequence of impressions that demonstrates how intense the experience of the traversed space has been. Not only the villages and towns on the way are noted, not only the formations of the terrain, but even details of the material consistency of the pavement of the highway are incorporated into his perceptions.

57

The railway puts an end to this intensity of travel, which reached its peak in the eighteenth century and found its cultural expression in the genre of the "novel of travels." The speed and mathematical directness with which the railroad proceeds through the terrain destroy the close relationship between the traveler and the traveled space. The space of *landscape* becomes, to apply Erwin Straus' concept, *geographical* space. "In a landscape," says Straus, "we always get to one place from another place; each location is determined only by its relation to the neighboring place within the circle of visibility. But geographical space is closed, and is therefore in its entire structure transparent. Every place in such a space is determined by its position with respect to the whole and ultimately by its relation to the null point of the coordinate system by which this space obtains its order. Geographical space is systematized."[2] Straus sees the railroad as the essential agent of the transformation of landscape into geographical space:

> The modern forms of traveling in which intervening spaces are, as it were, skipped over or even slept through, strikingly illustrate the systematically closed and constructed character of the geographical space in which we live as human beings. Before the advent of the railroad, geographical connections evolved, for the traveler, from the change in landscape. True, today the traveler also goes from place to place. But now we can get on a French train in the morning, and then, after twelve hours on the train (which is really being nowhere), we can get out in Rome. The old form of traveling provided for a more and better balanced relationship between landscape and geography.[3]

The nineteenth century found a fitting metaphor for this loss of continuity: repeatedly, the train is described as a projectile. First, the projectile metaphor is used to emphasize the train's speed, as in Lardner: a train moving at seventy-five miles an hour "would have a velocity only four times less than a cannon ball."[4] Then, as Greenhow points out, there is the cumulative power and impact that turns a speeding train into a missile: "when a body is moving at very high velocity, it then, to all intents and purposes, becomes a projectile, and is subject to the laws attending projectiles."[5] In 1889, after the complete cultural assimilation of the railroad, the projectile metaphor is still quite attractive. "Seventy-five miles an hour," says a technical text published in that year, "is one hundred and ten feet a second, and the energy of four hundred tons moving at that rate is nearly twice as great as that of a 2,000-pound shot fired from a 100-ton Armstrong gun."[6]

The train is experienced as a projectile, and traveling on it, as being shot through the landscape — thus losing control of one's senses. "In travelling on most of the railways . . .," says an anonymous author of the year 1844, "the face of nature, the beautiful prospects of hill and dale, are lost or distorted to our view. The alternation of high and low ground, the healthful breeze, and all those exhilarating associations connected with 'the Road,' are lost or changed to doleful cuttings, dismal tunnels, and the noxious effluvia of the screaming engine."[7] Thus the rails, cuttings, and tunnels appear as the barrel through which the projectile of the train passes. The traveler who sits inside that projectile ceases to be a traveler and becomes, as noted in a popular metaphor of the century, a mere parcel.[8] "It matters not whether you have eyes or are asleep or blind, intelligent or dull," says Ruskin, "all that you can know, at best, of the country you pass is its geological structure and general clothing."[9]

This loss of landscape affects all the senses. Realizing Newton's mechanics in the realm of transportation, the railroad creates conditions that will also "mechanize" the travelers's perceptions. According to Newton, "size, shape, quantity, and motion" are the only qualities that can be objectively perceived in the physical world. Indeed, those become the only qualities that the railroad traveler is now able to observe in the landscape he travels through. Smells, sounds, not to mention the synesthetic perceptions that were part of travel in Goethe's time, simply disappear.

The change effected in the traveler's relationship to the landscape becomes most evident in regard to his sense of sight: visual perception is diminished by velocity. George Stephenson testifies to this in a statement given at a parliamentary hearing on safety problems on the railways in 1841: when asked for his estimation of the engine-driver's ability to see obstacles, he replies, "If his attention is drawn to any object before he arrives at the place, he may have a pretty correct view of it; but if he only turns himself round as he is passing, he will see it very imperfectly."[10]

Unlike the driver, the travelers have only a very limited chance to look *ahead:* thus all they can see is an evanescent landscape. All early descriptions of railroad travel testify to the difficulty of recognizing any but the broadest outlines of the traversed landscape. Victor Hugo describes the view from a train window in a letter dated August 22, 1837: "The flowers by the side of the road are no longer flowers but flecks, or rather streaks, of red or white; there are no longer any points, everything becomes a streak; the grainfields are great shocks of yellow hair; fields of alfalfa, long green tresses; the towns, the steeples, and the trees perform a crazy mingling dance on the horizon; from time to time, a shadow, a shape, a spectre appears and disappears with lightning speed behind the window: it's a railway guard." (Quoted in Baroli, *Le Train dans la Littérature Française,* Paris, 1964, p. 58). And Jacob Burckhardt writes in 1840: "It is no longer possible to really distinguish the objects closest to one — trees, shacks, and such: as soon as one turns to take a look at them, they already are long gone."[11] In a text from 1838 we find the statement that it is impossible to "recognize a person standing by the road while driving past him" at the "greatest speed,"[12] which prompts the following advice: "He who has good eyesight . . . does well to acquire the habit of observing from a certain distance everything that attracts his attention while traveling: given some power of observation, he will not miss anything at all, not even during the stage of utmost velocity."[13]

The recommendation to look at things "from a certain distance" does not seem entirely realistic, in view of the traveler's situation in train compartment: enclosed in it, the traveler has no way of distancing himself from the objects — all he can do is to ignore the objects and portions of the landscape that are closer to him, and to direct his gaze to the more distant objects that seem to pass by more slowly. If he does not modify his old way of observing things while traveling — if he still tries to perceive proximity and distance in

59

equal measure — the result, as noted in 1862 by the *Lancet*, a medical journal, is fatigue:

> The rapidity and variety of the impressions necessarily fatigue both the eye and the brain. The constantly varying distance at which the objects are placed involves an incessant shifting of the adaptive apparatus by which they are focused upon the retina; and the mental effort by which the brain takes cognizance of them is scarcely less productive of cerebral wear because it is unconscious; for no fact in physiology is more clearly established than that excessive functional activity always implies destruction of material and organic change of substance.[14]

Increased velocity calls forth a greater number of visual impressions for the sense of sight to deal with. This multiplication of visual impressions is an aspect of the process peculiar to modern times that Georg Simmel has called the development of urban perception. He characterizes it as an *"intensification of nervous stimulation* which results from the swift and uninterrupted change of outer and inner stimuli."[15] (Italics in original.) "Lasting impressions," Simmel says, "impressions which take a regular and habitual course and show regular and habitual contrasts — all these use up, so to speak, less consciousness than does the rapid crowding of changing images, the sharp discontinuity in the grasp of a single glance and the unexpectedness of onrushing impressions."

The difference between the quality of stimuli in the metropolis and those of railroad travel need not concern us here: what is decisive, is the quantitative increase of impressions that the perceptual apparatus has to receive and to process. Contemporary texts that compare the new travel experience with the traditional one demonstrate how that stimulus increase produced by increased velocity is experienced as *stressful*. The speed causes objects to escape from one's gaze, but one nevertheless keeps on trying to grasp them. This is implied in Eichendorff: "These travels by steam keep on shaking the world — in which there really is nothing left but railway stations — like a kaleidoscope, incessantly, the landscapes speeding by in ever-changing grimaces even before one has been able to perceive any genuine traits of physiognomy; the flying salon presents one with ever new coteries, even before one has been able to really deal with the old ones."[16]

John Ruskin

John Ruskin, whose dislike of the railways created the most sensitive descriptions of the peculiar traits of preindustrial travel, proposes an almost mathematical negative correlation between the number of objects that are perceived in a given period of time and the *quality* of that perception: "I say, first, to be content with as little change as possible. If the attention is awake, and the feelings in proper train, a turn of a country road, with a cottage beside it, which we have not seen before, is as much as we need for refreshment; if we hurry past it, and take two cottages at a time, it is already too much: hence to any person who has all his senses about him, a quiet walk along not more than ten or twelve miles of road a day, is the most amusing of all travelling; and all travelling becomes dull in exact proportion to its rapidity."[17]

That final statement — "travelling becomes dull in exact proportion to its rapidity" — represents the evaluation of railroad travel made by all those nineteenth-century travelers who were still accustomed to preindustrial travel

Monotony of the Railroad Journey
Sleeping Travellers (Daumier)

Archive Roger Viollet, Paris

and thus not able to develop modes of perception appropriate to the new form of transportation. Dullness and boredom result from attempts to carry the perceptual apparatus of traditional travel, with its intense appreciation of landscape, over to the railway. The inability to acquire a mode of perception adequate to technological travel crosses all political, ideological, and esthetic lines, appearing among the most disparate personalities of the nineteenth century. Flaubert writes to a friend in 1864: "I get so bored on the train that I am about to howl with tedium after five minutes of it. One might think that it's a dog someone has forgotten in the compartment; not at all, it is M. Flaubert, groaning."[18] Before a railway journey, Flaubert stays up all night in order to be able to sleep through the journey and not experience it at all: he can do nothing with the vista offered to him by the compartment window.[19] The most diverse sources provide any number of similar complaints. To indicate the width of the spectrum, and its independence from attitudes based on *weltanschauung,* let us

61

attend to one more piece of evidence: the report given on a railroad journey in the United States by the politically liberal German-American Francis J. Lieber in 1834:

> From Albany to Schenectady, you travel by rail-road; and the least exciting of all travelling, it seems to me, is decidedly locomotion by steam on a rail-road. The traveller, whose train of ideas is always influenced by the manner in which he proceeds, thinks in a steam car of nothing else but the place of his destination, for the very reason that he is moving so quickly. Pent up in a narrow space, rolling along on an even plain which seldom offers any objects of curiosity, and which, when it does, you pass by with such rapidity, that your attention is never fixed; together with a number of people who have all the same object in view, and think like you of nothing else, but when they shall arrive at the journey's end — thus situated, *you find nothing to entertain or divert you,* except now and then a spark flying into the window of the car. . . . There is no common conversation, no rondo-laugh, nothing but a dead calm, interrupted from time to time, only by some passenger pulling out his watch and uttering a sound of impatience. . . .[20] (Italics in original.)

While the consciousness molded by traditional travel finds itself in a mounting crisis, another kind of perception starts developing which does not try to fight the effects of the new technology of travel but, on the contrary, assimilates them entirely. For such a pair of eyes staring out of the compartment window, all the things that the old consciousness experiences as losses become sources of enrichment. The velocity and linearity with which the train traverses the landscape no longer destroys it — not at all; only now is it possible to fully appreciate that landscape. Thus, a description of a trip from Manchester to Liverpool in the year 1830:

> The passenger by this new line of route having to traverse the deepest recesses where the natural surface of the ground is the *highest,* and being mounted on the loftiest ridges and highest embankments, riding above the tops of the trees, and overlooking the surrounding country, where the natural surface of the ground is the *lowest* — this peculiarity and this variety being occasioned by that essential requisite in a well-constructed Railway — a level line — imposing the necessity of cutting through the high lands and embanking across the low; thus in effect, presenting to the traveller all the variety of mountain and ravine in pleasing succession, whilst in reality he is moving almost on a level plane and while the natural face of the country scarcely exhibits even those slight undulations which are necessary to relieve it from tameness and insipidity.[21]

That is not a picturesque landscape destroyed by the railroad; on the contrary, it is an intrinsically monotonous landscape brought into an esthetically pleasing perspective by the railroad. The railroad creates a new landscape. The velocity that atomizes the objects of Ruskin's perception, and thus deprives them of their contemplative value, becomes a stimulus for the new perception. Now it is the velocity that makes the objects of the visible world attractive. Let us compare the following quote to Ruskin's comments, and we shall see how differently velocity and evanescence can be experienced during the same period of time: "The beauties of England," an American traveler writes in 1853, "being those of a dream, should be as fleeting"; and further:

> They never appear so charming as when dashing on after a locomotive at forty miles an hour. Nothing by the way requires study, or demands meditation, and though objects immediately at hand seem tearing wildly by, yet the distant fields and scattered trees, are not so bent on eluding observation, but dwell long enough in the eye to leave their undying impression. Every thing is so quiet, so fresh, so full of home, and destitute of prominent objects to detain the eye, or distract the attention from the charming whole, that I love to dream through these placid beauties whilst sailing in the air, quick, as if astride a tornado.[22]

To Benjamin Gastineau, whose newspaper essays on travel were collected in 1861 in book form as *La Vie en chemin de fer,* the motion of the train through the landscape appears as the motion of the landscape itself. The railroad choreographs the landscape. The motion of the train shrinks space, and thus displays in immediate succession objects and pieces of scenery that in their original spatiality belonged to separate realms. The traveler, gazing through the compartment window at such successive scenes, has acquired a novel ability that Gastineau calls "la philosophie synthétique du coup d'oeil" (the synthetic philosophy of the glance). It is the ability to perceive the discrete, as it rolls past the window, indiscriminately. The scenery that the railroad presents in rapid motion appears in Gastineau's text as a *panorama,* without being explicitly referred to as such: "Devouring distance at the rate of fifteen leagues an hour, the steam engine, that powerful stage manager, throws the switches, changes the decor, and shifts the point of view every moment; in quick succession it presents the astonished traveler with happy scenes, sad scenes, burlesque interludes, brilliant fireworks, all visions that disappear as soon as they are seen; it sets in motion nature clad in all its light and dark costumes, showing us skeletons and lovers, clouds and rays of light, happy vistas and somber views, nuptials, baptisms, and cemeteries."[23]

In another, roughly contemporary, French text we find all three essential characteristics of the *panorama* described. Jules Clarétie, a Parisian journalist and publicist, characterizes the view from the train window as an evanescent landscape whose rapid motion makes it possible to grasp the whole, to get an *overview;* defining the process, he makes specific use of the concept of panorama: "In a few hours, it [the railway] shows you all of France, and before your eyes it unrolls its infinite panorama, a vast succession of charming tableaux, of novel surprises. Of a landscape it shows you only the great outlines, being an artist versed in the ways of the masters. Don't ask it for details, but for the living whole. Then, after having charmed you thus with its painterly skills, it suddenly stops and quite simply lets you get off where you wanted to go."[24]

What, exactly, does this new perception that we are referring to as "panoramic" consist of? Dolf Sternberger uses this concept of the panorama and the panoramic to describe European modes of perception in the

The Railroad Journey as Panorama.

For the opening of the Paris-Orléans Line in 1843, the landscape along the journey was reproduced on three large sheets, in a sequence of pictures entitled "Vues panoramiques du chemin de fer de Paris à Orléans" (the first of these is reproduced here). In contrast to the usual representations of railroad scenes, the tracks themselves are not depicted in this picture. Obviously, this was an attempt to illustrate the view from a compartment window.

Columbia University, Parsons Collection.

nineteenth century — the tendency to see the discrete indiscriminately. "The views from the windows of Europe," Sternberger says, "have entirely lost their dimension of depth and have become mere particles of one and the same panoramic world that stretches all around and is, at each and every point, merely a painted surface."[25] In Sternberger's view, modern transportation, the railroad first and foremost, is the main cause for such panoramization of the world: "The railroad transformed the world of lands and seas into a panorama that could be experienced. Not only did it join previously distant localities by eliminating all resistance, difference, and adventure from the journey: now that traveling had become so comfortable and common, it turned the travelers' eyes outward and offered them the opulent nourishment of ever changing images that were the only possible thing that could be experienced during the journey."[26]

What the opening of major railroads provides in reality — the easy accessibility of distant places — was attempted in illusion, in the decades immediately preceding that opening, by the "panoramic" and "dioramic" shows and gadgets. These were designed to provide, by showing views of faraway landscapes, cities, and exotic scenes, " a substitute for those still expensive and onerous journeys."[26a] A newspaper of the year 1843 describes the Parisian public "reclining on well-upholstered seats and letting the five continents roll by at its pleasure without having to leave the city and without having to risk bad weather, thirst, hunger, cold, heat, or any danger whatsoever."[26b] That the diorama fad dies out in Paris around 1840[26c], more or less at the same time that the first great railways are opened (lines from Paris to Orléans and Rouen appearing in 1843) would seem corroborative evidence for the presumed connection. The simultaneous rise of photography provides more support for the thesis. According to Buddemeier, the public became fascinated, at first,

> Not by the taking of a picture of any specific object, but by the way in which any random object could be made to appear on the photographic plate. This was something of such unheard-of novelty that the photographer was delighted by each and every shot he took, and it awakened unknown and overwhelming emotions in him, as Gaudin points out. . . . Indeed, the question arises: why did the exact repetition of reality excite people more than the reality itself? Gaudin hints at an answer: he describes how intensely the first photographs were scrutinized, and what people were mostly looking for. For instance: looking at a picture of the building across the street from one's own window, one first started counting the roof shingles and the bricks out of which the chimney was constructed. It was a delight to be able to observe how the mason had applied the mortar between the individual stones. Similar instances occur in other texts dealing with photographs. Tiny, until then unnoticed details are stressed continuously: paving stones, scattered leaves, the shape of a branch, the traces of rain on the wall.[26d]

Thus the intensive experience of the sensuous world, terminated by the industrial revolution, undergoes a resurrection in the new institution of photography. Since immediacy, close-ups, and foreground have been lost in reality, they appear particularly attractive in the new medium.

Sternberger observes that the vistas seen from Europe's windows had lost their dimension of depth; this happened first with the vistas seen from the train compartment window. There the depth perception of preindustrial consciousness is literally lost: velocity blurs all foreground objects, which means that there no longer is a foreground — exactly the range in which most of the experience of preindustrial travel was located. The foreground enabled the traveler to relate to the landscape through which he was moving. He saw himself as part of the foreground, and that perception *joined* him to the landscape, included him in it, regardless of all further distant views that the landscape presented. Now velocity dissolves the foreground, and the traveler loses that aspect. He is removed from that "total space" which combines proximity and distance: he becomes separated from the landscape he sees by what Richard Lucae, speaking of ferrovitreous architecture, has called an "almost immaterial barrier." The glass separates the interior space of the Crystal Palace from the natural space outside without actually changing the atmospheric quality of the latter in any visible manner, just as the train's speed separates the traveler from

65

the space that he had previously been a part of. As the traveler steps out of that space, it becomes a stage setting, or a series of such pictures or scenes created by the continuously changing perspective. Panoramic perception, in contrast to traditional perception, no longer belongs to the same space as the perceived objects: the traveler sees the objects, landscapes, etc. *through* the apparatus which moves him through the world. That machine and the motion it creates become integrated into his visual perception: thus he can only see things in motion. That mobility of vision — for a traditionally oriented sensorium, such as Ruskin's, an agent for the dissolution of reality — becomes a prerequisite for the "normality" of panoramic vision. This vision no longer experiences evanescence: evanescent reality has become the new reality.

While the railroad causes the foreground to disappear, it also replaces looking at the landscape with a new practice that did not exist previously. *Reading* while traveling becomes almost obligatory. The dissolution of reality and its resurrection as panorama thus became agents for the total emancipation from the traversed landscape: the traveler's gaze can now move into an imaginary surrogate landscape, that of his book. By the mid-nineteenth century, reading while traveling has become an established custom. The following observation is found in the minutes of an 1860 congress of French physicians: "Practically everybody passes the time reading while traveling on the train. This is so common that one rarely sees members of a certain social class embark on a journey without first purchasing the means by which they can enjoy this pastime."[27]

The idea of reading while traveling on trains is as old as the railroad itself. An article in the *Quarterly Review* of 1830 notes that the journey is "so easy, that a passenger might read a newspaper with perfect comfort."[28] A German text of 1833 makes a connection between the dissolution of the outer world by means of velocity, and the opportunity to compensate for this by developing an activity within the train compartment that will engage one's attention. Lips speaks of "a speed at which the objects outside rush past the eye without color or contour, and thus cannot be recognized anymore," and continues: "And yet, the motion of such a steam-car is so imperceptible, smooth, and comfortable, that it is not only possible to *read* but even to *write* in it with the greatest ease; thus, a great number of people, such as scholars, officials, merchants, etc., need no longer rest or interrupt their regular routine while traveling, but can pursue it while sitting in the steam-car."[29] (Italics in original.)

In the late 1840s, English booksellers establish stalls in railway stations, as well as a peculiar kind of lending library, to meet the general demand for things to read while traveling. John W. Dodds describes this development:

The development of railways encouraged the sale of books of all kinds. Until 1848 no systematic attempt had been made to supply passengers with either books or papers at the railway stations. In that year W.H. Smith got the exclusive right to sell books and papers on the Birmingham Railway. His first bookstall was at Euston Station. Shortly he had the franchise for the entire London and Northwestern System. By 1849, the station library at Paddington terminus contained one thousand volumes, chiefly works of fiction. Here, for the charge of one penny, a passenger had free access to the use of the library while waiting for trains, and for slightly more could take a volume with him on his journey, turning it in at his destination. To meet this new demand Routledge launched his *Railway Library* — novels by Cooper, James, Hawthorne, James Grant, Dumas, and others. Murray advertised his "Literature for the Rail" — "works of sound information and innocent amusement."[30]

Railroad Station Bookstore of the Hachette Publishing House.

From: Jean Mistler, *La Librairie Hachette, de 1826 a nos jours.* Paris, 1964

In 1852 Louis Hachette emulates the English model in France: in a communication to the French railroad companies he proposes a "large-scale operation of bookselling that apart from its advantages for the companies would also be both useful and pleasing to the public." The monotony and boredom of travel by rail, mentioned in so many contemporary descriptions, reappears here as a commercial argument for the establishment of railroad bookstalls:

The traveler finds himself condemned to idleness as soon as he enters the carriage. The monotony of the trip soon takes effect: boredom arrives, and, what is worse, impatience engulfs the unfortunate traveler, pulled along by the machine like a piece of baggage. . . . L. Hachette and Company have come up with an idea for turning the enforced leisure and the boredom of a long trip to the enjoyment and instruction of all. They have

THE FIRST-CLASS PASSENGER.

Reading During a First Class Trip.

From: *The Railway Cartoon Book,* Ed. by Ken and Kate Baynes, Newton Abbot 1976.

Title Page of a Volume from the "Railway Library."

thought of establishing a railway library that will provide only interesting volumes in a handy format and at a moderate price.[31]

Only two years after the opening of the first railway bookstall in France, of whose income the rail companies receive thirty percent, Hachette operates sixty branches in the whole of France. In 1864, the income exceeds for the first time one million francs, while the sale of books is still greater than that of newspapers. A little later that ratio is reversed: in 1866 the income from the sale of newspapers is 969,000 francs, that from the sale of books, 527,000 francs.[32]

A glance at the offerings of the English and French railway bookstalls shows that the reading public is almost exclusively bourgeois. An English survey of 1851 shows that, in contrast to the supply of trashy mass literature in the regular bookstores, the railway bookstalls and lending libraries in London carry highly respectable nonfiction, fiction, travel guides, etc.[33] Hachette's catalogue has the following categories: travel guides, books about travel, French literature, classics, agriculture and industry, children's books.[34]

Reading while traveling is an exclusively bourgeois occupation. The lower classes who use the railroad do not read not only because they cannot afford to, but also because they have no desire to do so. Their traveling situation is quite different from that of the more privileged strata. The carriages of the third and fourth class are not divided into compartments: they have no formal resemblance to the traditional means of travel, while the compartments of the

3rd Class Passengers
(Daumier).

first and second class do. The lower classes, who really join the ranks of travelers only after the advent of the railroad, are unencumbered by memories of previous forms of travel: thus the new forms are not as strange to them as they are to those classes that have to abandon their private coaches for the train. The primitive, spacious third- and fourth-class carriages into which the proletarian traveling public is crowded characteristically promote continuous communication: in the compartments of the bourgeois first- and second-class carriages, such communication has died out, at least by the end of the nineteenth century. "How often . . . I have . . ., while traveling alone or with people with whom it was impossible to start a conversation, envied the travelers of the third and fourth class, from whose heavily populated carriages merry conversation and laughter rang all the way into the boredom of my isolation cell," says P.D. Fischer, in his *Betrachtungen eines in Deutschland reisendeu Deutschen* (Observations of a German traveling in Germany), published in 1895.[35]

The emergence of reading while traveling is not only a result of the dissolution and panoramization of the outside landscape due to velocity, but also a result of the situation inside the train compartment. The railroad disrupts the travelers' relationships to each other as it disrupts their relationship to the traversed landscape. Constantin Pecqueur explains the phenomenon of dissolution, dispersal, and trivialization of perception and communication, by the greatest *number* of objects and persons with which the travelers' powers of attention (which have remained constant) now have to deal: "In these great halls, and in the cheerful caravans of the trains and steamships, one's affections tend to go out to a greater number of objects and individuals, and consequently become less intense or durable in each case. This encourages inconstancy and creates excitement over variety; life and affections are seen to lose in depth what they gain in range; the social and general sentiments, on the other hand, find this to be a most pleasing state; while the private sentiments, the familial ones, would seem to suffer from it."[35a]

Travelers of the eighteenth century, prior to the railroads, formed small groups that, for the duration of the journey, were characterized by intensive conversation and interaction: the travel novels of the period testify to this quite eloquently. The travelers in the train compartment do not know what to do with each other, and reading becomes a surrogate for the communication that no longer takes place. This connection between reading and the alienation of railroad travelers from one another is made by all authors dealing with the subject of travel reading. It appears in the following contribution to the medical congress of 1866, in which travel reading is cited as the general and sole activity of travelers:

> Nowadays one travels so fast and sees, if the journey is of any duration, such a succession of new faces, that one frequently arrives at the destination without having said a single word. Conversation no longer takes place except among people who know each other, at least not beyond the exchange of mere generalities; any attempt to go beyond these often lapses due to the indifference of some travelers. Thus one might say that the railroads have in this respect, too, completely changed our habits. Whenever, in the past, one knew that one was going to pass several hours, sometimes several days, in the company of others, one tried to establish a rapport with one's companions that often lasted beyond the duration of the journey. Today we no longer think about anything but the impatiently awaited and soon reached destination. The traveler one takes one's leave from may get off at the next station where he will be replaced by another. Thus reading becomes a necessity.[36]

The effects of reading while traveling are generally discussed in medical circles in the 1860s. The debate as to whether it is harmful or beneficial relates the practice to the special stresses put on the optical sense by rail travel, and to visual perception in general. According to one side of the argument, reading while traveling is harmful to the eye because "when the traveller sets himself to read, he imposes yet further labour on the eye in tracing the shifting characters of his book or newspaper, and also on the brain."[37] The traveler who *concentrates* on his reading behaves in just as old-fashioned a manner as the traveler who, accustomed to the pace of the stagecoach, attempts to fix his stare on the objects flitting past the compartment window. In both cases, the result is exhaustion of the senses and of the mind. To adapt to the conditions of rail

71

travel, a process of deconcentration, or dispersal of attention, takes place in reading as well as in the traveler's perception of the landscape outside: Hachette's rising sales of newspapers and falling sales of books attest to that. The afore-mentioned contribution to the medical congress of 1866 states that travel reading may have deleterious effects on eyesight, but adds that it would be impossible to curtail it: "Nevertheless, no matter what one says or does, reading will remain the most natural occupation of railway travelers, in this new form of locomotion that has so profoundly altered the travelers' relations to each other."[38]

5. The Compartment

Cette boite ambulante où j'ai dû me cloîtrer.
Je n'en puis plus sortir, mai nul n'y peut
entrer.

This ambulatory box in which I have had to
  enclose myself:
I can't get out of it, but nothing can come in,
  either.
                    — Eugène Manuel, 1881

To adherents of progressive thought in the first half of the nineteenth century, the railroad appears as the technical guarantor of democracy, harmony between nations, peace, and progress. According to them, the railroad brings people together both spatially and socially. This current of European thought found its most pathetic expression in the followers of Saint-Simon: the intellectual generation that appears on the French political and economic stage around 1825, the year Saint-Simon died, projects all the egalitarian hopes left unfulfilled by revolution and empire, onto industry and its spectacular spearhead, the railroad: to them it is the material force that will realize the equality and fraternity of 1789 more effectively than any merely formal political emancipation.

Pecqueur formulates the belief that the railroad, as a part of industry, works for human emancipation:

"The communal journeys on trains and steamships, and the great gatherings of workers in the factories, inspire, to a great degree, the sentiment and habits of equality and liberty. By causing all classes of society to travel together and thus juxtaposing them into a kind of living mosaic of all the fortunes, positions, characters, manners, customs, and modes of dress that

73

each and every nation has to offer, the railroads quite prodigiously advance the reign of truly fraternal social relations and do more for the sentiments of equality than the most exalted sermons of the tribunes of democracy. To thus foreshorten for everyone the distances that separate localities from each other, is to equally diminish the distances that separate men from one another."[1]

If Pecqueur is convinced that trains and steamers "truly are the chariots of equality, freedom, and civilization," he does, on the other hand, recognize the possibility that old privileges and inequalities may reappear in the creations of industry, even though their essential nature is egalitarian and democratic. The equality and democracy of industry in general and the railroad in particular has to be safeguarded by "a certain degree of preexisting equality between the diverse classes or races that constitute the nation: without this, we might end up creating subdivisions in the railway carriages and thus a separation and distinction between social and economic ranks analogous to *stagecoaches, private vehicles for rent,* and *livery stables.*"[2] (Italics in original.)

Pecqueur regards the division of rail carriages into classes as a baleful possibility. At the time of the writing of his *Economie sociale* that division does not yet exist in France, simply because the railroads have not yet instituted passenger service. Until the early 1840s, apart from one short line, the railroad exists in France only in the form of descriptions of the railways in England and Belgium. In those two countries, however, the railways' division into classes is a fact from the start. Yet the progressives of the early nineteenth century, especially the Saint-Simonian industry enthusiasts, hardly pay any attention to that fact, being dazzled by the overwhelming fascination exerted by steam power. In the face of the unheard-of energy and productivity made possible by the railroad, the traditional social privileges seemed to be so hopelessly outdated that it appeared hardly worthwhile to deal with them. Even though Pecqueur does not entirely discount the possibility of a survival of inequality, he regards the ultimate victory of equality based on technology as certain. The travelers in a train, he argues, are all equal because they find themselves in a situation of technological equality: "It is the *same convoy*, the *same power* that carries the great and the

Origins of the Railway as a Means of Transporting Coal.
The train that opened the Stockton-Darlington Line pays hommage to this evolution. It is a coal and passenger train in one.

Science Museum, London

74

The Freight Car as Passenger Car.
Well into the 1840's, members of the poorer classes were transported in open freight cars which were coupled to the end of a train consisting of covered passenger cars.

Musée Carnavalet,
Cabinet des Estampes

small, the rich and the poor; thus, the railroads most generally provide a continuous lesson in equality and fraternity."[3]

But the continuing history of the railroad, manifesting separation of classes even on French trains, exploded (along with many other Saint-Simonian hopes) the notion that social equality would result from the technically equal situation of the travelers. Yet that history has shown that Pecqueur's idea has a core of truth in it, although it is very different from what Pecqueur believed. The fact that the members of different classes travel on the same train, moved by the same power, does not render them social equals, but it is ever present in their minds. Travel by rail, being pulled by the power of steam, is experienced as participation in an industrial process. For the lower classes this experience is quite immediate: in England they are transported in open boxcars on freight trains, up to the 1840s. They are not regarded as recipients of passenger service but as freight goods. The Gladstone Act of 1844 requires the carriages of the third and fourth class to be covered, yet they still look more like covered boxcars than passenger cars. The traveling situation of the more privileged classes is entirely different: their carriages look like coaches mounted on rails.

Mounting of a Coach Body onto a Chassis, France 1840's.

Archiv Talbot

Not only is this design forgetful of the industrial origin and nature of the railroad, it is literally an attempt to repress awareness of them. The compartment, an almost unaltered version of the coach chamber, is designed to reassure the first-class traveler (and, to a lesser degree, the second-class traveler as well) that he is still moving along just as he was in his coach, only at less expense and greater speed. Its effect is the exact opposite of the one desired. Exactly because the compartment is so closely linked to traditional preindustrial travel — imbued with its spirit as it were — the new industrial mode of transportation is experienced as even more traumatic. Bourgeois first-class travelers complain that they no longer feel like travelers but mere parcels: this makes their subjective experience of travel just as industrial as is the objective experience of the lower classes. Yet the bourgeois experience is only subjective to the extent that it actually occurs in a well-upholstered and outfitted compartment instead of the boxcarlike traveling space of the lower classes: it is equally objective in its realization that the traveler *is* the object of an industrial process — all the upholstery in the world cannot make him forget it.

76

The End of Conversation While Traveling

Transplanted from the coach to the railroad train, the compartment loses some of its functions. What was functional in the time of preindustrial travel now becomes redundant. The essential social function of the coach chamber arises out of its form, namely, the seating arrangement: in the U-shaped coach chamber the travelers face each other, and such an arrangement encourages conversation while traveling. The historical genesis of the coach as a means of travel justifies the classification of that communicative form of seating as a specifically bourgeois idea; a brief digression should make this clear.

In the Middle Ages, people traveled exclusively on foot or on horseback, depending on their class. The custom of traveling in coaches arises at the beginning of the modern age, concurrently with a great number of other practices arising from the processes of defeudalization and urbanization of Western European life. Thus Werner Sombart describes the origin of coach travel:

> In the course of the sixteenth century, presumably due to the improvement of the roads, travel by horse-drawn carriage became more common. True, we encounter the merchants of the sixteenth with increasing frequency in their "coaches": but as late as in the mid-seventeenth century we find resistance against coach travel on the grounds that it is detrimental to the welfare of the nation — it makes the people too soft, it ruins horsebreeding, etc. By the end of the seventeenth century travel by coach had finally established itself as equally acceptable as travel on horseback.[4]

According to Jackman,[5] the coach finds its first mass propagation at the beginning of the seventeenth century in and around London — a region where Europe's urbanization has progressed farthest.

The form and seating arrangement of the coach harks back to another specifically urban vehicle for the transporation of persons, the sedan chair.[6] One might say that the coach consists of two frontally joined sedan chairs. The creation of this curious arrangement during the same period that sees the rise of other bourgeois institutions of communication, such as coffeehouses, clubs, newspapers, and theaters, indicates that the coach has to be seen as part of that larger configuration.

Evolution of the Coach Body from the Sedan Chair.

a) Sedan Chair (Model)

b) Double Sedan Chair, Early 18th Century

c) English Coach, 17th Century

d) French "Chaise de Poste," 18th Century

e) English Stagecoach, late 18th Century.

a) New York Public Library, Picture Collection
b) New York Public Library, Picture Collection
c) From: G.A. Thrupp, *The History of Coaches,* London, 1877
d) From: Thrupp
e) From: Thrupp

a.

b.

c.

d.

e.

Travel in the coach is characterized not only by the travelers' intensive relationship to the world outside, the traversed landscape, but also by their lively communication with each other. Coachtravelers are talkative folk, providing material for numerous novels published in the eighteenth and early nineteenth century. The railroad puts an end to all that. As a Frenchman reminisces in 1857: "In the coach, conversation got off to an easy start after a few moments of preliminary study of one's companions; at the moment of parting, one oftentimes regretted the brevity of the journey, having almost made friends. How different it is on the train. . . .!"[7]

The face-to-face arrangement that had once institutionalized an existing need for communication now becomes unbearable because there no longer is a reason for such communication. The seating in the railroad compartment forces the travelers into a relationship that no longer is based on living need but has become an embarrassment. Georg Simmel's explanation of the way in which modern perception both orients itself and is disoriented by the optical sense refers to modern transportation as one of the agents of that development:

> Generally speaking, what we *see* of a person is interpreted by what we *hear* of him, the reverse being a much rarer case. Therefore one who sees without hearing is far more confused, undecided, upset than one who hears without seeing. This must have an important bearing on the sociology of the big city. Compared to the traffic in the small town, the traffic in the city creates an infinitely greater proportion of cases of seeing rather than hearing others; this is so not only because a great proportion of encounters on a small-town street involve either acquaintances with whom we exchange a few words or those whose appearance allows us to reproduce their entire personality, not only the visible part, but, above all, because of the fact of public transportation in the big city. *Before the development of buses, trains, and streetcars in the nineteenth century, people were quite unable to look at each other for minutes or hours at a time, or to be forced to do so, without talking to each other.* Modern traffic increasingly reduces the majority of sensory relations between human beings to mere sight, and this must create entirely new premises for their general sociological feelings.[8] (Italics in long passage added.)

What Simmel describes as a feeling of being confused, undecided, and upset may be simply described as the embarrassment of people facing each other in silence in the train compartment. As we have seen, the perusal of reading matter is an attempt to replace the conversation that is no longer possible. Fixing one's eyes on a book or a newspaper, one is able to avoid the stare of the person sitting across the aisle. The embarrassing nature of this silent situation remains largely unconscious: any insight into it will therefore appear only in hidden terms, hinted at "between the lines." We find one example of such hidden implication in M.M. von Weber's railroad handbook of 1857, in which the author considers the pros and cons of the European compartment car versus the American car. (The American standard carriage differs, as we shall see in the next chapter, from the European in that the seats have not been arranged in compartments and facing each other, but in a long car and facing one way.) Weber believes that the American type would be

Bâtard Coupé
(Half-Compartment).

From: M.M. von Weber,
Schule des Eisenbahnwesens.
Leipzig 1857.

unsuitable for European conditions. He champions the compartment system and then states that he has a particular fondness for the half compartments (*bâtard-coupés*) "which, placed at both ends of the car, have the advantage that *the passengers have no one facing them*, while being able to look outside through the windows that open out to three sides of the compartment."[9]

One of the few open criticisms of the compartmental seating arrangement can be found in an 1838 issue of the *Railway Times*. A Letter to the Editor, signed with irony An Enemy to Imprisonment for Debt and in Travelling, suggests an alternative:

> With reference to the interior arrangement of Railway Carriages . . ., I beg to suggest . . . to the public, whether their comfort could not be promoted, by having some of them, in each train, fitted up, so that the passengers should sit back to back, and look out upon the country, from a range of windows the whole length of the carriage. By this plan, a man going to and from Southampton or Bristol might, by taking opposite sides of the carriage, on each journey, see all the country within view of both sides of the road; and, surely, *this would be pleasanter than a three or four hours' study of physiognomy at a stretch, for want of any better occupation.*[10] (Italics added.)

Only the privileged classes undergo this experience of no longer speaking to each other and being increasingly embarrassed by their companions. In the carriages of the third and fourth class, which mostly have not been divided into compartments but consist of one large space, there is neither embarrassed silence nor general perusal of reading matter. On the contrary, the sounds emanating from these carriages can even be overheard in the compartments of the privileged: "merry conversation and laughter rang all the way into the boredom of my isolation cell," remarks P.D. Fischer in a previously quoted passage. The French novelist Alphonse Daudet gives his impression of the lively goings-on in the proletarian carriages in the following vivid sketch that is

Third Class Passengers among Themselves.
(Gustav Doré)

Musée Carnavelet,
Cabinet des Estampes

reminiscent of Honoré Daumier's caricatures of train scenes: "I'll never forget my trip to Paris in a third-class carriage . . . in the midst of drunken sailors singing, big fat peasants sleeping with their mouths open like those of dead fish, little old ladies with their baskets, children, fleas, wetnurses, the whole paraphernalia of the carriage of the poor with its odor of pipe smoke, brandy, garlic sausage and wet straw. I think I'm still there."[11]

Isolation

There are occasions when the first-class traveler finds himself untrammelled by the displeasing presence of fellow travelers. Being alone in the compartment is an ambivalent situation. This solitude can be experienced as a state of satisfaction, of safety, of happiness. "Alone in the compartment," says Taine in his *Carnet de voyage,* "I have spent three of the sweetest hours I have experienced in a long time."[12] Another passage in the *Carnet* gives concreteness to this state of serenity: "I was alone in my carriage . . . the wheels rolled on indefatigably, with a uniform noise like that of a prolonged roaring note played on an organ. All mundane and social ideas faded from my mind. No longer did I see anything but the sun and the countryside, in bloom, smiling, all green and with a greenness so various and illuminated by that gentle rain of warm beams that caressed it."[13]

It is tempting to give a psychoanalytic explanation for that pleasurable feeling of self-forgetfulness which is brought on by the isolation of the ego in the compartment and the powerful mechanical motion of the train. Freud and Karl Abraham have indicated the connection between mechanical agitation and sexual arousal and have called the railroad the most powerful agent of that arousal.[14] The joy of riding trains finds its counterpart, as soon as there is repression, in what Freud termed "fear of trains." Karl Abraham interprets the fear experienced by neurotics in the face of accelerating or uncontrollable motion as the fear of their own sexuality going out of control: "Their fear is related to the danger of finding themselves in a kind of unstoppable motion that they can no longer control. The same patients generally exhibit fear of locomotion in any vehicle they cannot bring to a halt themselves at any time."[15]

The travelers themselves experience that fear of the independence of their own sexuality as a fear of derailment. The fear of derailment is ever present on train journeys in the early days. The greater the ease and speed with which the train is *flying* (a typical nineteenth-century term for rail travel)[16] the more acute the fear of catastrophe becomes: we have already quoted Thomas Creevy's statement made in 1829, that the railroad journey is "really flying, and it is impossible to divest yourself of the notion of instant death to all upon the least accident happening." A German text of 1845 speaks of "a certain constriction of the spirit that never quite leaves one no matter how comfortable the rail journeys have become." It is the fear of derailment, of catastrophe, of "not being able to influence the motion of the carriages in any way."[17]

The fear of derailment is in fact a feeling of impotence due to one's being confined in a fast-moving piece of machinery without being able to influence it in the least. The isolation of the compartment that encloses the passenger intensifies this feeling of helpless passivity. While the compartment facilitates the pleasurable experience of mechanical motion, it becomes, in equal measure, a locus of trauma. Its enclosed nature hides whatever happens in it from outside glances: once the traveler has seated himself in it, he remains alone with himself or with fellow travelers for the duration of the journey, or at least for the time it takes to get from one station to the next. There are no channels of communication to the outside world, and there are actual risks involved in that. Peter Lecount, an English engineer, writes in 1839: "In road travelling, a passenger suddenly taken ill, or from any other cause, has nothing to do but to put his head out of the coach window and make his wants known; the coach can be stopped, and he can receive the necessary assistance. But how different is the case in railway travelling! There, unless he has by accident a seat just under the guard, he might exert his voice in vain and could by no possibility receive the least help if he was dying; in fact, the more he wanted it, the less able he would be to endeavour to obtain it."[18]

The compartment's total optical and acoustical isolation from the rest of the train and its inaccessibility during the journey (until the 1860s, even the compartments of express trains could be entered only from outside: there was no communication between them) cause the travelers' interrelationships to change from mere embarrassment at silence to fear of potential mutual threat. The train compartment becomes a scene of crime — a crime that takes place unheard and unseen by the travelers in adjoining compartments. This novel danger captivates the nineteenth-century imagination: "The loudest screams are swallowed up by the roar of the rapidly revolving wheels, and murder, or violence worse than murder, may go on to the accompaniment of a train flying along at sixty miles an hour. When it stops in due course, and not till then, the ticket collector coming up may find a second-class carriage converted into a 'shambles'. We are not romancing."[19]

Drama in the Compartment

In the January 1861 issue of the *Annales d'Hygiène Publique,* we find the headline "Dangers Run by Travelers on Trains" and the following description:

On the sixth of December last year, the train from Mulhouse entered the Paris station at a quarter past three in the morning. The passengers made haste to leave their compartments; as the door of one of them remained closed, a railway employee went to open it. How great was his surprise when he perceived the shape of a man lying between the seats! He then asked the man to get out, but received no answer. He found it difficult to see clearly in the uncertain light of the fixture in the compartment that was further dimmed by the black silk shade designed to make it more agreeable; he reached out, and upon withdrawing his hand, found it covered in blood. He notified the stationmaster and the police commissioner, and it was soon ascertained that the man was nothing but a cadaver bathed in a pool of blood.[20]

The dead man was Chief Justice Poinsot. The ensuing investigation reveals that he shared his compartment with a single fellow passenger, his murderer. No trace of the latter can be found. The case arouses unusual interest. "The painful interest excited in Paris by the dreadful death of M. Poinsot has been extraordinarily great," *Galignani's Messenger*, an English-language newspaper published in Paris, reports on the ninth of December, "and a certain feeling of uneasiness has arisen at the idea of the extreme facility with which the crime appears to have been perpetrated."

"What is so strange, so inexplicable," says an article in the *Journal des Débats*

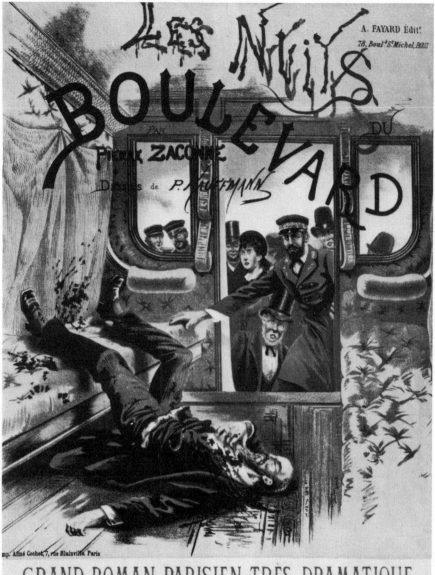

Murder on Rails as a Subject of Popular Imagination.

Title page of an 1880's novel, obviously based on the Poinsot murder.

Musée Carnavelet, Cabinet des Estampes

of the eighth of December that expresses the general public's fearful interest in the case, "is that the travelers who were in the compartment next to M. Poinsot's had not heard a single shot; without being able to affirm this in any certain manner, they thought that they had heard a shout, but only one."

In the days following the discovery of the crime, the columnists of the Parisian press published pieces whose satirical surface is a transparent attempt to conceal the deeper fears that this murder had stirred. In the *Figaro* of the twentieth of December we find this suggestion: "In every well-arranged train we find a carriage reserved for smokers and another one for ladies who desire to travel by themselves. Why not provide a carriage with the legend: *compartment reserved for assassins*? But we know those gentlemen well: they are perhaps too shy to want to attract attention." (Italics in original.)

85

On the twenty-fifth of December *Figaro* publishes a satirical description of the atmosphere of anxiety that pervaded railroad travel: "M. Poinsot's assassination still has the privilege of being a matter of concern to the public. . . . There is a great deal of egotism in that general preoccupation. Everyone feels menaced in his mortal condition as a traveler. For the employees of the railroad, the affair has become a comedy. We now see well-known millionaires boarding third-class carriages. Others have started traveling in the company of their valet, their coachman, and their cook. Those whom fortune has not blessed with such accessories remain prey to terrible perplexities."

This is followed by a satirical demonstration of such perplexities, a fictitious dialogue between two unaccompanied passengers in one compartment:

Not too long ago, the train from Brussels carried to Paris, in a compartment of the first class, two voyagers who were hermetically sealed in their topcoats and scarves. After a very defiant study of their respective physiognomies, one of the two passengers decided to speak to his traveling companion.

"Monsieur," he said, "one really is lucky to find an honest man traveling first-class these days. I congratulate myself on the stroke of luck that has joined us here, seeing as I might have fallen upon a villain. By the way, I am a cautious man. I do not carry any money, nor a watch, nor any jewelry. I'm wearing an old pair of trousers in order not to excite anyone's greed, and as for my topcoat, a ragdealer refused to give me forty sous for it. Besides, anyone who dares to attack me will find himself out of luck. I have here a Catalan dagger, two saddle pistols, and a revolver that has as many barrels as one of M. Alexandre's organs has pipes. In this game bag I carry bullets and gunpowder. I have more than a hundred and ten shots that I can fire before surrendering. . . ."

"Well, that's just like me, Monsieur," replied the other traveler. "I've been pretending to sleep, just pretending. But I'm never more formidable than when I seem to be snoring. You see, I know how to take care of myself. . . . I can take you into my confidence, since you seem to be such an honest man. At the very moment when some scoundrel thinks he can assassinate me, I can riddle his chest with holes. . . ."

"By what means, Monsieur?"

"Look, Monsieur, it's very simple. I told M. Godillot of the travelers' outfitters to make me a breastplate armored with thirty bayonet points. See, it's very ingenious. . . . I only have to embrace my adversary heartily in order to turn him into a sieve."

Reassured by their reciprocal confidences the two travelers fell asleep with one eye open, clutching their pistols.

A look at entirely nonsatirical official reports and technical works that appear a few years later demonstrates how realistic that satirical sketch of the new attitudes of first-class passengers toward one another is. When another compartment murder occurs in England in 1864, it receives both official and satirical comment. A series of *Punch* cartoons deals with the mutual distrust of first-class passengers, and an official report describes the same phenomenon as follows: "There has been, indeed, a panic amongst railway passengers. Ladies,

Caricatures on Travel Companions' suspecting each other as potential Killers.

From: Punch 1864.

SCENE IN A TUNNEL. HOW TO CLEAR A CARRIAGE FOR A CIGAR.

Ferocious Looking Passenger (to Old Gent who objects to Smoking). "THAT'S A PRETTY KNIFE; AIN'T IT? THAT'S THE SORT O' THING WE USE IN CALIFORNIA! JOLLY THING TO STICK INTO A FELLOW, EH?"

[OLD GENT *fears his Companion is not "quite right," and changes his Carriage at the next Station.*

RAILWAY MORALS.

Guard. "NOW, MISS! ARE YOU GOING BY THIS TRAIN?"
Miss Rebecca. "YES! BUT I MUST HAVE A CARRIAGE WHERE THERE ARE NO YOUNG MEN LIKELY TO BE RUDE TO ONE."

unable, of course, to discriminate at the moment between those whom they should avoid and those who should be their protectors, shun all alike; and gentlemen passengers, as well as railway officers of all classes, constantly refuse to travel singly with a stranger of the weaker sex, under the belief that it is only common prudence to avoid in this manner all risk of being accused, for purposes of extortion, of insult, or assault."[21]

The above is from the report prepared by a committee of experts for the House of Commons in 1865: the committee's task was to find out what technical possibilities there were for the creation of means of communication between train compartments, so that further compartment murders could be averted. Similar deliberations take place in France and Germany. The feverish search for ways to end the isolation of the compartment is based on the nightmarish vision of the compartment as such being a provocation to murder.[22] That fantasy recurs even in purely technical dissertations, such as *Le matériel roulant de chemins de fer au point de vue du comfort et de la sécurité des voyageurs* (The rolling stock of the railroads from the point of view of the passengers' comfort and security) by Ernest Dapples: "If one is not alone in the compartment, one has one or several fellow passengers on the journey. If there is only one of them, and this is often impossible to avoid . . ., one may be exposed, by that solitary fellow passenger, to all kinds of disagreeable things, possibly even robbery and murder, as has been shown, unfortunately, by certain well-known events."[23]

As late as 1870 we find this in the *Handbuch für spezielle Eisenbahntechnik* (Handbook for special railway technology): "The passenger is so pleased when he finds a vacant compartment; but he is not so fortunate when he acquires a fellow passenger who robs him in his sleep, or perhaps even murders him, and then ejects his body from the compartment piecemeal, without attracting the train personnel's attention."[24]

The Compartment as a Problem

After the Poinsot murder in France in 1860 and the Briggs murder in England in 1864, two traumatic experiences for Europeans, the search is begun for ways to end the isolation of the compartment. That only two cases of murder, occurring four years apart and in two different countries, were able to trigger a collective psychosis tells us as much about the compartment's significance for the nineteenth-century European psyche as does the fact that it took so long to become conscious of the compartment's dysfunctionality. The surprising aspect of the history of the train compartment is, indeed, that it remained unchanged for so long, and that it has, in fact, survived to the present day in modified form, despite its drawbacks that were so plain from the very beginning. While the railroad itself was recognized to be fundamentally different from the highway from the very beginning,[25] the form of the passenger carriage moving on it was kept strictly imitative of the traditional form of the coach. As far as I know, in Europe there were no attempts to create a passenger car that would be compatible in its form with the modern technology of the railroad — i.e., one that would no longer have anything to do with the coach-derived compartment. The closest thing to such a "utopian" carriage is a proposal published by the Scots journalist MacLaren in 1825. It appears to be entirely free of any formal reminiscences of the stagecoach: MacLaren proposes a shiplike space, "a form analogous to that of the steam-boat and track boat would be the best." Nevertheless, another arrangement slips in covertly and it can be easily recognized as the familiar compartment system: "It might, for instance, consist of a gallery seven feet high, eight wide, and one hundred feet in length, *formed into ten separate chambers* ten feet long each, connected with each other by joints working horizontally, to allow the train to bend where the road turned. A narrow covered footway, suspended on the outside over the wheels on one side, would serve as a common means of communication for the whole."[26] (Italics added.) Thus we get, on the one hand, the idea of a large room on wheels, a ship on land, as it were (not long after, a similar proposal is made in America),[27] but, on the other, the subdivision of that large room into a row of smaller, compartmentlike spaces. Admittedly, these have the advantage of being connected with each other — an innovation predictive of the one realized forty years later.

MacLaren's proposal remained on paper. The carriage consisting of a series of unconnected compartments — as it had been first introduced on the Manchester-Liverpool line — remained, in spite of all obvious shortcomings and dangers, the European standard for half a century thereafter. This persistent survival of an impractical form appears even less explicable considering that Europe became cognizant, around 1840, of a technically functional type of carriage — the American car. This type has all the advantages the European type lacks. Due to its open spatial arrangements, problems such as heating and toilets,[28] insurmountable in the compartment system, are easily solved; nor need the traveler in the American car fear for his life, being at all times in communication with a great number of other passengers.

In the public discussion to which the compartment system becomes subjected in the 1860s, the American car appears as an alternative. With a few marginal exceptions,[29] the European rail companies reject its adoption. The psychology of the European traveling public is an important reason for this: the English and French commissions appointed to study the problems of the compartment all agree that the European rail passenger *wishes* to be left alone while traveling. "The passengers," Dapples says in summing up the French Commission's report, "would complain if they were obliged to spend a long time in public carriages, subjected to all the noises, vulnerable to all eyes and all ears...."[30]

The proposals for ways to improve communication between the compartments that come up in the 1860s, in the wake of the Poinsot and Briggs murder cases, all take the "desire to be left alone" into account. In them, the compartment remains essentially unchanged. There is talk of various alarm systems which would enable passengers to transmit calls of help when they found themselves in acute danger: these include a speaking tube running the entire length of the train, a cord that can be pulled to activate an alarm bell, an arrangement of mirrors that enables the train personnel to see into the compartments; and an electric alarm system. The French commission, appointed in 1861 after the

Poinsot murder, suggests that the simplest and most effective solution would be to open up small peephole windows in the dividing walls between compartments:

> The dormer window placed in the upper part of the compartment wall offers, in its modest way, some of the advantages of communication between the compartments. In certain cases it could be of useful assistance to the passengers, inspire a healthy fear in wrongdoers, and thus be a material and moral deterrent. It has no detrimental effect whatever on the comfort or privacy of the passengers, as these would always be at liberty to cover it up should they think this advisable. It could also be introduced at very small expense. It does not transmit, from one compartment to the next, words spoken by the travelers, nor drafts, nor tobacco smoke.[31]

This peephole was actually introduced on numerous lines, and it soon became a subject of caricature.[32] It assuaged the immediate cause of the compartment controversy, i.e., the fear of murder. It did not, however, solve the problem of actual physical communication; for that, mobility between compartments and carriages would be absolutely necessary. (This mobility was also a prerequisite for toilets, heating installations, dining and sleeping cars, and ticket control during the journey.)

The most primitive form of physical communication between the compartments was a footboard mounted on the outside of the carriage and running its entire length. The French commission recommended this, in addition to the peephole, for general adoption. The peephole facilitated optical communication between adjoining compartments; the footboard was designed to enable the train personnel to gain access to the compartments during the journey. Passengers, obviously, were not supposed to avail themselves of the daredevil contraption which caused numerous deaths every year.

Effective, safe, and comfortable communication between compartments and carriages could be established only by means of a passageway in the interior of the carriage: this meant at least partial adoption of the American system. At the beginning of the 1860s, the Swiss Northeast Line introduced a type of carriage that represents a first step in that direction. The carriage remains divided into compartments, but these are connected by means of doors in the dividing partitions. The arrangement did, however, meet with the same line of criticism that prevented the introduction of the American system. It was said that the compartment's privacy and quiet was disturbed by the traffic through it. Heusinger von Waldegg, the man who finally came up with the definitive solution to the compartment problem, summarizes that criticism:

> As essential as are the advantages gained by these various means of intercommunication, it cannot be denied that the main argument against the American system, that of the continuous disturbance of the travelers due to the passage through the middle, was not resolved even in the compartmental arrangement of the first and second class, and that such disturbance is most annoying to travelers, particularly in the nighttime. The only way to avoid it would be to either provide sliding doors or curtains between the two sides of the compartment and the passageway, or to move the latter . . . to the side of the carriage.[33]

NOVELTY IN GLASS.

BELINDA, ABOUT TO ARRANGE HER BONNET AT WHAT SHE SUPPOSES TO BE THE NEW LOOKING-GLASSES (" AND A VERY GRACEFUL AND CONSIDERATE IDEA, TOO, ON THE PART OF THE RAILWAY ! "), SPEEDILY DISCOVERS HER MISTAKE, AS SHE IS CONFRONTED BY THE FACE OF AN IMPERTINENT YOUNG MAN IN THE NEXT COMPARTMENT.

Caricature of "Muller's Window."
After a murder in 1864, various possibilities of eliminating the isolation of railroad compartments were explored in England. According to popular opinion, this isolation constituted a provocation to crime. In one of many attempts to solve this problem, small windows were built into partitions between compartments. In common parlance, these were called "Muller's Windows" after the perpetrator of an 1864 murder, Franz Müller.

From: Punch, 1865.

Heusinger von Waldegg's solution is to move the corridor to one side and to separate it from the compartments by sliding doors. Now the compartments can no longer be entered from the outside but only indirectly, through the corridor. The carriage has entrances at both ends, similar to the American system. This remains the current arrangement of European passenger carriages. The compartment has been preserved as an intimate, enclosed traveling space. Intercommunication does not take place by movement through but *past* the compartment. The side corridor is not regarded as part of the actual traveling space: it is merely a compromise with technical necessity to establish communication. It is not an offshoot of the compartment but of the footboard: this becomes apparent from the first publication of Waldegg's proposal.[34] For the European public, the essential traveling space is and remains the compartment: in order to preserve its quiet and isolation, experienced as both pleasurable and frightening, the nineteenth century had to come up with Von Waldegg's monstrous spatial design. The entirely different development of the railroad and the railroad carriage in the United States demonstrates to what a great degree the compartment is an expression of European traditions and class relationships, and how far it is from being the "natural" form of railroad travel.

6. The American Railroad

Un train de chemin de fer est dans ce pays-là considéré comme une voiture ordinaire. On est habitué à s'en garder comme nous nous gardons d'un cabriolet qui passe dans la rue.

In that country, a railroad train is just another vehicle. People are accustomed to watch out for it the way we watch out so as not to be knocked over by a buggy in the street.

— French travel account, 1848

The history of the railroad in the United States differs from its history in Europe in that the American railroad was not the industrial successor to a full-fledged preindustrial transportation system: in America, the railroad served to open up, for the first time, vast regions of previously unsettled wilderness. "With the construction of railroads, American culture *began* what European culture completed with them," says Max Maria von Weber; "*before* the humble footpath, before the cattle road, the railroad stretched itself through the wild savannah and primeval forest. In *Europe*, the railroad system *facilitates* traffic; in America, it creates it."[1] (Italics in original.)

That difference has to do with the specific nature of the industrial revolution in America: here, it did not begin with manufacture, but with agriculture and transportation. In England the revolution in transportation was a consequence of the prior development of industrial production, i.e., the textile industry, first and foremost. The prime mover in the construction of the first railroad between Manchester and Liverpool was the increased need for transportation between the main cotton port, Liverpool, and the main center of the textile industry. In England, the increased productivity of the transportation system provided input to the entire economy and gave it a tremendous boost, but this does not alter the initial order of events — first came the industrial revolution in manufacture, then the transport revolution.[2]

93

Weber indicates the reason for the reversal of that order in the United States. The first prerequisite for opening up the wilderness to civilization and economic utilization was the creation of an effective transport system. W.W. Rostow says of the American railroad system between 1850 and 1875 that it was "the instrument for launching the American industrial revolution"[3]; this is true from the very beginning, and applies equally to the railroad's predecessor, the river steamboat, and to the mechanization of agriculture.

In order to understand the American relationship to machinery, mechanization, and industrialization, one has to bear in mind the initial application of machinery in transportation and agriculture. While Europe experiences mechanization and industrialization as largely destructive, as they replace a highly developed artisan culture and an equally highly developed travel culture, the case of America is the exact opposite. At the beginning of the nineteenth century, when steam power is first introduced, there is no developed American culture of artisanship or of travel. The American situation is characterized by enormous and practically worthless (because unutilized) natural resources on the one hand and a chronic shortage of labor power on the other. As it does not cause any unemployment, every form of mechanization is experienced as creative. The mechanization of transportation is not seen, as in Europe, as the destruction of a traditional culture, but as a means to gaining a new civilization from a hitherto worthless (because inaccessible) wilderness. As the transport system does not merely take over preexisting traffic but opens up new territories for traffic, it appears productive to a degree unimaginable to Europeans. This productivity finds its clearest expression in the policy of land grants.[4] The mechanized transportation system becomes, as it were, a producer of territories, in the same way that mechanized agriculture becomes a producer of goods. Since American history really begins with the industrial revolution (all else being colonial prehistory), that revolution is a constituent part of American national and cultural identity to a far greater degree than it is in Europe. Steam power is perceived as a guarantor of national unity,[5] since the latter would be as impossible without it as would be the extraction of wealth from the vast, seemingly endless land by means of mechanized transportation, agriculture, and industry.

In the United States the industrial revolution is seen as a natural development, not only because it appears right at the beginning of American history, but also because it happens first in agriculture and transportation, and is thus directly related to nature. The main instruments of American industry in the early nineteenth century are not machines in factories, as in England, but river steamboats, railroad trains, sawmills, harvesting combines, etc. This immediate relation with (or embedding in) nature provides the material base for the American notion, classically described by Leo Marx, of machinery and industry as forces that do not destroy nature but actually realize its potential by cultivating it. Paraphrasing Emerson, Marx says that the industrial revolution appears as a "railway journey in the direction of nature."[6]

In nineteenth-century American thought, the machine appears closely linked to nature, and simultaneously the American landscape is seen as closely linked to the machine.[7] The material foundation for those perceptions lies in the peculiarity of American economic life in the nineteenth century that

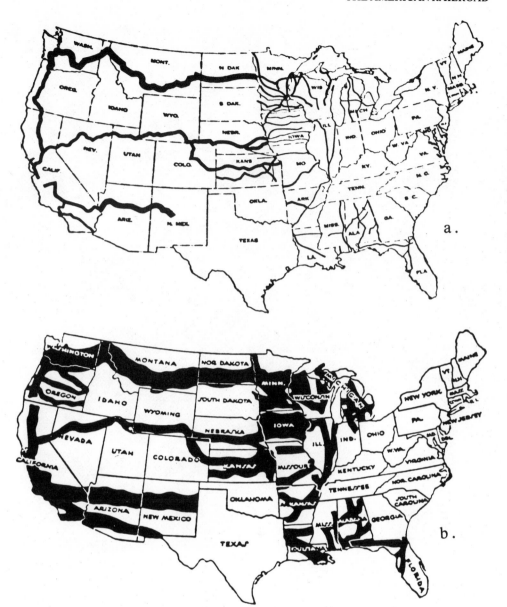

Landgrants to American Railroads.

Map (a) gives an idea of the amount of land given to the railroad companies by the Federal government in the 19th century to finance the construction of railroad lines. Map (b) was often printed in school books and similar publications to illustrate the octopus-like grip of the railroads on America. As generous as these grants of public lands to private companies may have been, it never actually attained such fantastic proportions.

From: Steward H. Holbrook, *The Story of the American Railroads.*

Habakkuk has formulated as the "substitution of natural resources for capital."[8] The shortage of capital and labor in the United States led to new forms of raw-material production, to an uninhibited exploitation of seemingly inexhaustible natural resources; the lack of restraint was merely a form and expression of the low investment of capital and shortage of labor. The application of the same principle to transportation led to entirely different results: here, there was no unrestrained exploitation of nature, but practically mimetic utilization of the existing natural routes, i.e., the waterways. "The inland routes which required the least capital to utilize in a primitive way were the rivers," explain Cleveland and Powell,[9] discussing early transportation in the United States, which was indeed based almost exclusively on the natural waterways. The motivation to utilize the waterways is the same one that leads to extensive and

95

"Across the Continent."
One of the best known illustrations of Currier & Ives, a firm famous for its landscapes with railroads and steamships. Here, at the inauguration of the transcontinental railroad in 1869, the picture symbolically captures the opening and civilizing of the wilderness by the railroad.

New York Public Library, Picture Collection.

heedless exploitation of resources ("substitution of natural resources for capital"). The results differ: the first leaves nature intact, the second leads to its destruction. In both cases, however, nature is experienced at closer range and with greater immediacy than in Europe. The history of American transportation in general and of its railroads in particular can only be understood in terms of that immediate relationship to nature which is not esthetic but economic.

Transportation Before the Railroad

At the beginning of the nineteenth century, the United States does not possess a network of roads and highways comparable to those of Europe. Only in New England and between the cities of Boston, New York, Philadelphia, Baltimore, and Washington is there a genuine highway system traveled by regular stagecoach traffic. In the rest of the country, the roads are "unbelievably poor" (as noted by G.R. Taylor),[10] being of merely local importance, and functioning as service connections to the waterways. The latter constitute the essential transportation system. Settlement proceeds along the natural waterways,[11] and these are, long into the nineteenth century, the main routes of traffic for goods as well as persons. We can still note to what an extent water traffic has shaped the American consciousness of transportation in the common American usage of the verb *to ship* for all forms of transport, whether they take place on dry land or across water.[12] The abundance of waterways, in marked contrast to Europe, made it possible for them to gain paramount importance. Contemporary travel journals testify to this, as for example, G.T. Poussin, in 1836: "One of the most curious circumstances is, no doubt, the abundance of its [America's] vast and navigable rivers, its great bays, straits, and lakes, all of which contribute to a coherent interior navigation system incomparable to that of any other continent."[13] Thus passenger travel uses these waterways in the absence of highways. From the eighteenth century on (at the latest), the dominant form of travel in Europe takes place overland, by stagecoach or on horseback; Kitchener's, *The Traveller's Oracle*, an English handbook of 1827, lists travel on foot, on horseback, and by coach with no mention of travel by water, this being seen strictly as a form of transoceanic travel. The American situation is exactly the reverse. Here one travels by water, wherever possible. Thus, for instance, the Englishman W. Bullock, who travels through the United States from the South to the North using only the waterways, writes in 1827: "On my return from Mexico to England, in the spring of the present year, I was induced, by the representation of an American friend, to pass through the United States by way of New Orleans, up the Mississippi and Ohio, by Lake Erie, the Falls of Niagara, the Erie Canal, and Hudson River, to New York . . .; nearly the whole journey being now performed by commodious steam and tow boats on the rivers, lakes and canals in the interior of the states."[14]

The technical innovation that enabled water traffic to gain such prominence was the river steamboat. Henry Adams calls it "the most efficient instrument yet conceived for developing such a country."[15] The development of the American riverboat could be called the first transport revolution, preceding the railroad. Only by means of steam power did the Mississippi and Ohio rivers become navigable in both directions. Freight rates were reduced to such a degree that the railroad, when it appeared later, did not provide further economy but merely extended freight traffic into regions that were not accessible to waterways.[16] The great numbers of riverboats also indicate their importance: until the mid-nineteenth century, the tonnage of riverboats navigating only on the "Western Waters" (the Mississippi and the Ohio) is equal to that of the entire British steamship fleet traveling the high seas.[17] Louis C. Hunter, the historiographer of the American river steamboat, sums up its importance as follows: "The steamboat was not America's first contribution to the technology of the Industrial Revolution, but in scale and complexity of mechanisms as well as in range of social and economic influence it was in many ways the most notable achievement of our industrial infancy. Before the railroad age it was the chief technological means by which the wilderness was conquered and the frontier advanced, and the principal instrument by which steam power was introduced and spread in the United States."[18]

The Construction of the Railroad

The American railroad continues what the river steamboat began. This applies, as we shall see, even to the design of its carriages, and in equal degree, to the design of the railroad lines themselves. In England such a line is built to be as straight as possible, partly because railroad technology favors this, partly for economic reasons. Labor is cheap, land expensive. Thus it pays to construct tunnels, embankments, and cuttings in order to make the rails proceed in a straight line, at a minimum of land cost. Diametrically opposed American conditions produce opposite results. Labor is expensive, land practically worthless. In accordance with the principle of "substitution of natural resources for capital," the American railroad does not proceed in a straight line through natural obstacles, but runs around them like a river. An article published in 1858 in the *Atlantic Monthly* observes that the English railroad engineer "defies all opposition from river and mountain, maintains his line straight and level, fights Nature at every point, cares neither for height nor depth, rock nor torrent. . . . On the other hand, the American engineer, always respectful (though none the less determined) in the presence of natural obstacles to his progress, bows politely to the opposing mountain-range. . . ."[19] The American engineer proceeds in this manner not so much out of a respect for nature as out of the wish to build the line as cheaply as possible. As Von Gerstner, one of the first European railroad experts to visit America in the 1830s, notes, "a great deal of earthwork is avoided" by building the line around natural obstacles. Indeed, the cost per mile of the American lines is only a fraction of the English, even though the rails have to be imported from England at considerable expense. According to Von Gerstner, the building of a mile of an American railroad costs only a tenth of what it would in England;[20] according to a report presented to the House of Commons in 1857, the cost is roughly a third, and this would seem closer to the truth.[21]

All European observers note how the American railroad lines proceed by curves instead of straight lines: from the very beginning, this is the main characteristic of American railroads. As early as 1827, when the first reports of the English railroad experiments inspire the proposal for the first American railroad (the Baltimore and Ohio), one of its promoters, Minus Ward, states that the English innovation would have to be modified to suit American conditions: among other things, he mentions "the necessity of departing from the transatlantic system of straight rail-roads."[22] In a survey report for the Baltimore and Ohio Company, S.H. Long concludes in 1830 that the English mode of construction would be uneconomical in American circumstances. He exprsses his preference for a line with numerous curves, justifying it by the observation "that . . . the expense of avoiding a hill or valley, by a prolongation of the route, in a manner to maintain a uniformity in its vertical direction, is less than that of *cutting* and *filling*."[23] (Italics in original.) To what extent the curving route appears to be the only economical and sensible one to the American engineers can be realized from their incomprehension of the English mode of construction. Thus an American text of 1844 fails to grasp the reason for the English engineer's method: "To approximate to an air-line and a dead level . . ., recourse has been had to cuts, embankments, and tunnels, involving great expense and an immense annual outlay for repairs, which might have been easily avoided by waving the line, increasing the gradients, and conforming to the surface of the country."[24]

The Twists and Turns of the American Railroad System.

Here is the extreme case of serpentine tracks winding up a slope. In England, they would have built a tunnel instead. These illustrations demonstrate that in 19th century America, railroad tracks were looked upon in basically the same way as ordinary roads and treated accordingly.

From: *The American Railway,* New York, 1889.

In this somewhat condescending evaluation tinged with pity, the American commentator shows his ignorance of the fact that the English straight-line manner of contruction is not based on esthetics but on purely technical considerations. The rigid axles of the English rolling stock require a line that is as straight as possible: an English car would inevitably derail in the attempt to take a sharp curve.

Let us look at the reason why the American railroads with their abundance of curving lines did not have that technical problem.

The New Type of Carriage

In rigid-axle construction, the sharper the curves of a railroad line, the closer together the axles of a carriage would have to be placed, to avoid derailment. Technically, the frequently curving American route would require so short a distance between the axles that an economical-sized carriage would be an utter impossibility. Thus the innovation of the curving route required a complementary technological innovation, that of a carriage capable of dealing with those curves. The mechanical solution of the problem required a synthesis of contradictory requirements: both rigidity and mobility of the individual axle, and simultaneity of a long and a short distance between the axles. In 1834, Ross Winans provides the solution in his patented invention, which becomes the basis for the development of the specifically American type of railroad car. Winans suggests a new design for the undercarriage — the "bogie." It combines the seemingly contradictory requirements. Two rigid axles are combined in an undercarriage, with an extremely short distance between them: this guarantees that wheels and rails will remain parallel even on the sharpest curve. Mobility is added to this rigid component by attaching it to the body of the car by means of a swiveling pivot. One of these double-axled "bogies" is at each end of the car. In his patent application Winans says: "I construct two bearing carriages, each with four wheels, which are to sustain the body of the passenger or other car, by placing one of them at or near each end of it. . . . The two wheels on either side of these carriages are to be placed very near to each other: the spaces between their flanges need to be no greater than is necessary to prevent their contact with each other."[25]

This constitutes a breakthrough against the earlier prevalent principle of technical unity between undercarriage and car body. That unity is dissolved into two mutually independent technical complexes, an achievement that coincides, more or less, with Colt's and Whitney's development of the technology of interchangeable parts.

Technically emancipated from the rails, the car can now be extended in length, virtually ad infinitum. Winans modestly proposes cars that will be only twice as large: "The body of the passenger or other car I make is double the

Bogie.
A dual-axle chassis
devloped in America in
the 1830's, enabling cars
to negotiate even the
sharpest curves.

From: August Mencken, *The
Railroad Passenger Car.*
Baltimore, 1957.

ordinary length of those which run on four wheels, and capable of carrying double their load."

This is an elegant example of the thesis that a technological innovation becomes a historically significant one only when there is an actual economic demand for it: Winan's bearing carriage is the second discovery of the same idea developed twenty years earlier in England. In 1812 William Chapman patented the same technical principle of a four-wheeled bearing carriage in England.[26] No real need for it existed because the straight line appeared as "natural" and economically sensible to the English — due to high real estate costs and low wages, and also to the Newtonian tradition — as the curving track seemed in the United States.[27]

The timing of Winans' patent and its quick adoption by the American lines in the 1830s and early 1840s is revealing. At first, at the beginning of the 1830s, the compartment design of the English railroad had been adopted along with the rest of the technology. As the curving tracks of America demanded an extremely short distance between axles, it was found to be impossible to place three compartments in a series on one bearing carriage: there was room for only one.[28] This cultural lag between the already-Americanized (curving) mode of construction of the road and the still-European type of car lasted for a few

101

years. Only after the "bogie" had *technically* solved the problem of how to build a car suited to the American routes was it possible to develop an entirely new *form* of car.

That form, the long car without compartments, devoid of reminiscences of the stagecoach, becomes the standard in America from the 1840s on. A report on the American railroads, commissioned by and presented to the British House of Commons in 1857, contains the following description:

> The bodies of the passenger cars are from thirty to forty-five, and even sixty, feet in length. . . . On lines of four feet eight and one half inches gauge the cars are about nine feet, and on the New York and Erie, ten feet wide, and from six feet to seven feet six inches high. . . . The interior of the car forms a large room, with a passage, of from one foot nine inches to two feet wide, down the centre, upon each side of which cross seats are arranged. These seats are intended for two passengers each; they are from three feet three inches to three feet six inches long, about one foot six inches wide, and one foot apart. The back is arranged to be turned, so that the passenger may sit with his face in either direction. . . . In winter the cars are warmed by means of an iron stove in the centre; and they are lighted at night by lamps placed at the sides. In a certain proportion of the passenger cars, a portion, about seven feet long, three feet six inches wide, is partitioned off, in which is a small room for the convenience of ladies nursing, and a watercloset.[29]

How different this type of car is from the compartmentalized one becomes apparent merely by a glance at scale specifications. The first-class compartment of the London-Birmingham line in the 1830s is six feet six inches wide, five feet six inches long, six feet high.[30] The different spatial dimensions are an expression as well as a cause of different attitudes toward travel. Travel in the compartment is characterized by immobility, whereas in the American car there is a great deal of mobility during the trip. A situation of embarrassed sedentary confrontation such as the one Simmel describes is unthinkable in the American car, simply because the seats have not been arranged to face each other (their

*Prototype of the
American Railroad Car
since ca. 1834.*

This car was made
possible by the bogies on
either end of the car — a
type of construction
which was entirely dif-
ferent from the European
and early American
railroad car with coach
design. This type of car
could be built in virtually
any length.

From: Mencken, *The
Railroad Passenger Car.*

*Floorplan of Standard
American Passenger Car.*

The interior is not divided
into compartments as in
Europe, but forms one
continuous space. Rows
of seats lined both sides,
in the middle was an aisle
with washing facilities
and, at the end, there was
a toilet. All these ap-
pliances were technically
not possible for decades in
the European com-
partment cars.

From: 1836-1886. *Semi-
Centennial Memoir of the
Harlan and Hollingsworth Co.*
Wilmington 1886.

backrests can be reversed), but also because of the general communication and mobility possible in the American car. Poussin stresses this autonomy of movement during the journey and goes on to say: ". . . in this manner, a traveler is free to go and sit down next to whoever he likes, and also to change places again. An American would not much care for our way of traveling in a fixed seat, in a cramped carriage, under lock and key; he would sense a lack of air, of suffocation."[31] Americans traveling in European trains do indeed mention "confinement in a small, locked-up compartment,"[32] and find it an unpleasant experience to be unable to move freely through the cars and the entire train during the journey,[33] and to have only inaccessible sanitary facilities or none at all — a problem that persists on European trains for so long. The European evaluation of the American car is, as we have already seen, somewhat ambivalent. There are many statements of approval, particularly during the compartment hysteria of the 1860s. "There is no danger of robbery, murder, or other outrage, as in the small, locked, and inaccessible compartments of European roads," writes an English author on America, in 1864.[34]

As the history of the compartment demonstrates, the obvious advantages of the American car do not, however, seem sufficient reason to abandon the quiet and immobility of the European train compartment. Thus Captain Tyler in his report to the House of Commons: ". . . as regards the American arrangement, it is obvious that it is so opposed to the social habits of the English, and would interfere so much with the privacy and comfort which they now enjoy, that these considerations, apart from others, nearly as important, would forbid its adoption in this country."[35] M. Couche, a member of the French commission appointed after Poinsot's murder, is even more explicit: he says that the American car is suited to American conditions but not for those prevailing in Europe, since Europeans are not accustomed to move around during the journey, and there is thus no advantage in mobility: "The traveler is not, in actual fact, free to move around beyond the compartment that he occupies."[36]

The explanation for the American railroad car's particular interior form is not as uncomplicated as the compartment's derivation from the coach chamber. There is, in fact, a whole series of explanations, all of which apply. We have mentioned the invention of the undercarriage ("bogie or truck") that permitted the construction of virtually endless cars. The American car can also be described as the simplest and cheapest type of passenger car: just as the lack of capital in the United States during the early and mid-nineteenth century led to the cheapest mode of railroad construction, it also resulted in the least expensive kind of passenger car. That purely economic state of affairs is, however, closely related to the indigenous American democracy of the nineteenth century as described by Tocqueville and Chevalier. The classless open car is economically, politically, psychologically, and culturally the appropriate travel container for a democratic pioneer society, while the compartment car, on the other hand, expresses the social conditions prevailing in Europe.

These general explanations are not entirely satisfactory. It obviously would have been possible to simply build a cheaper and more primitive kind of compartment car. We get closer to the core of the question why Americans travel in a big room and Europeans in a tiny cell if we consider the remarkable difference between average travel distances in Europe and the United States. The

The American Railroad Car from a European Viewpoint.

Both of these French illustrations from 1848 tell us less about the actual interior of American passenger cars than about the space perception of the illustrator. The interior appears to be much larger than it actually is, and its bleakness reminds one of a prison. The open spaces of the American car appear suspect to the European eye, which is accustomed to the intimacy of the compartment.

From: Illustration, 1848.

first American lines on the East Coast are still relatively short, although they do bridge larger distances than the first European connections between cities. With the westward expansion the American lines grow increasingly longer. Already in the 1830s, when European train journeys are merely a matter of hours and are undertaken only in the daytime, the first sleeping cars appear in the United States.[37]

Couche refers to the development of new forms of travel due to longer distances. While a train journey in Europe takes place in the surrounding environment of stations and their installations — such as buffets, toilets, etc., — America boasts very few of these. Thus, Couche argues, the American traveler has to find those facilities in the train itself. "A train has to be self-sufficient. The travelers have to be able to find all that is necessary on board, as would be the case on a steamship that puts into port only rarely and briefly."[38]

The steamship, mentioned by Couche as a convenient analogy, does indeed upon closer scrutiny yield many clues to the rise of a certain type of car on American railroads.

The Riverboat Cabin as Model for the American Passenger Car.

(a) shows the daytime cabin of a smaller riverboat in the first half of the 19th century; (b) is the interior of a railroad passenger car around the middle of the century. Form and dimensions of the space are strikingly similar from the vaulted ceiling to the arrangement and size of the windows. This similarity in form becomes even clearer when we notice how the rooms are arranged for the night: (c) shows the main cabin of an 1850 riverboat arranged for the night, while (d) shows a sleeping car of the New York Central Railroad in 1859.

All illustrations: New York Public Library, Picture Collection

a.

b.

c.

d.

River Steamboat and Canal Packet as Models for the American Train Car

Noting that the American train car differs from European compartment cars in its spaciousness and ease of communication, some contemporary authors proceed to state that this type of car reminds them more of the interior of a seagoing vessel than of a stagecoach. Von Waldegg is reminded of the "cabin of a ship."[39] Galton, in the report to the House of Commons in 1857: "In designing their rolling stock, the Americans appear to have taken their ideas more from a ship than from an ordinary carriage."[40] The French railroad engineers Lavoinne and Pontzen find the opportunity to move around during the journey "analogous to what is possible on board a ship, instead of the immobility imposed on European travelers."[41]

In the literature (sparse, and more popular than scientific)[42] dealing with the development of design on the railroads, we do not find anyone pursuing this obvious resemblance between American railroad car and ship design. The only mention known to me of their analogous form, in the framework of a serious study, occurs in John Gloag's work *Victorian Comfort*. Gloag speaks of the extreme importance of the river steamboats in American travel before the railroad era and concludes: "The design of these river steamers had a permanent effect on American standards of comfort and travel." Then he conjectures: "The long and spacious saloons may well have been the prototypes for the American railroad cars."[43] In corroboration, he then presents side-by-side illustrations of a riverboat saloon and a Pullman car interior. The similarity of these spaces seems even less accidental when considering what a dominating role the river steamers played in American transportation, and thus in American transportation consciousness, during the early part of the nineteenth century. In other words, the riverboat became for the American railroad train what the stagecoach had been for the European: a means and form of travel that was representative of the period before the introduction of railroads, and thus one upon which the railroad modeled itself.

There is one singularly striking piece of proof for that formal influence which otherwise manifests itself only relatively indirectly and becomes evident only by means of historical reconstruction: it is Morgan's never-realized design for a railroad car, published in the Boston journal *the American Traveler* in 1829, when the United States had not yet built its first actual railroad. As the designer himself notes, what is proposed and illustrated here is not so much a carriage as rather "what may be emphatically termed a *Land Barge,* and to the Traveller will furnish an idea of all the convenience and comfort which belong to the best steam boats." (Italics in original.) The spatial divisions correspond exactly to those of a steamer: "It is constructed with a cabin, berths, etc. below; a promenade deck, awning, seats, etc. above" — with "below" and "above" referring to

MORGAN'S
Newly Invented Rail Road Carriage.

FLOOR PLAN OF MORGAN'S RAIL ROAD CARRIAGE.

The Railroad as Steamship on Rails.

In 1829, even before the first actual railroad was built in the United States, the periodical "The American Traveller" printed the design of a railroad car which was clearly reminiscent of a riverboat. This is demonstrated by the floor plan: the interior is composed of the main cabin (A), lined on both sides by cots (B), and there is even a "Captain's Office" (D). This design, which was never actually built, demonstrates how powerful the image of the steamship was in the minds of the American designers.

From: *The American Traveller,* 1829

the two decks of the car, similar to those of a steamer. Final proof for the immediacy with which steamboat concepts have been transferred to the railroad in this proposal is the fact that the locomotive is not expected to pull several of these novel cars (in other words, a train), but just a single one.

This proposal, and a considerable number of similar ones that were published in the nineteenth century,[44] was never realized, but that does not diminish its validity as proof of the persistence of the image of the steamship in American transportation consciousness. It is precisely Morgan's eccentrically literal transposition of the steamer design that casts light on the steamship's formal influence on the American railroad car, the influence being less immediately recognizable in the standardized car. Different spatial dimensions prevent the envisaged total adoption of steam forms. "Obviously the difference in clearances and functional organization of railroad cars inhibited their designers from taking a leaf bodily from the book of the river steamers," says Beebe, "but that they looked at them with longing eye and appropriated what they could is abundantly evident in the record."[45]

What the railroad car was unable to adopt from the riverboat, due to different spatial relations, it copied from another model, the canal packet, which played a far greater role in passenger traffic in the United States than it

General James Semple's Prairie Steam Car.

This design, which was also never realized (printed by the ''Scientific American'' in 1846), comes even closer to the concept of a steamship on land, because it was intended to cross the prairies of the West on large roller-like wheels rather than on rails. As the text accompanying the illustration implies, the prairie was seen as a kind of terrestrial ocean, and this spurred the intention of ''navigating the extensive prairies by steam-power, and with carriages capable of accommodating 100 passengers, besides twelve to twenty tons of merchandise...''

From: Scientific American, 1846.

The Cabin of the Canal Boat as Model for the Railroad Passenger Car.

From: Seymour Dunbar, History of Travel in America

Railroad and Canal Packet.

The connecting line between Philadelphia and Pittsburgh in the 1830's was a combined canal and railroad line. For this purpose, a curious form of canal-packet was constructed, the canal-packet in sections (usually consisting of three parts: front, center and rear). The individual parts, together with the passengers, were lifted onto a railroad chassis and transported by rail, only to be put together on the next leg of the journey to continue the trip as a boat. It is probable that the design of the American railroad car has been influenced by this canal packet.

New York Public Library, Picture Collection.

ever did in Europe, although it did not gain the spectacular eminence of the steamer. In the American Northeast, on the much-traveled stretches of the Erie Canal and on the canal network connecting Philadelphia and Pittsburgh, the packet was an integral part of the traveling experience. On the Philadelphia-Pittsburgh Canal, which was actually a combination of canal and railroad, the canal packet and the train entered into a curious symbiosis. During the journey the packets, with their passengers on board, were mounted on bearing carriages and hauled to the next stretch of canal — a combination that one can well imagine to have been part of the inspiration for Winans' car, which made its appearance shortly thereafter.[46]

The canal packet of the 1820s and 1830s provides a good model for the railroad car due to its compatible form and dimensions. Its saloon consists of a long rectangle with windows on the sides and entrances at both ends. Contemporary representations of both its exterior and interior demonstrate a similarity to the later railroad car that a comparison of dimensions corroborates with almost mathematical precision. In 1838, the English engineer Stevenson states that the main saloon cabin of a canal packet is forty feet long and eleven wide;[47] around the middle of the century, the standard railroad car is thirty to forty-five feet long and nine to ten feet wide.[48]

As we have seen, the difficulty in reconstructing the genesis of the American railroad car is based on the fact that there was no one model among prior means of transportation, such as the European coach, but two models that had to be synthesized to produce the final result. Whatever the particulars of that synthetic process, it is quite obvious that the result is a different form, and even a different mode of travel than that of the European compartment car.

Sea Voyage on Rails

The basic situation of travel in the European compartment, the immobility of the passenger, harks back to the situation in the stagecoach, which was the one means of travel that put its stamp upon Western European travel culture in the late eighteenth and early nineteenth centuries. This ascendancy of the stagecoach became possible because of the more or less developed highway network then existing in Western Europe.

The characteristics of the American transport situation at the beginning of the nineteenth century were underdeveloped traffic by land, but highly developed traffic on the inland waterways. In American travel, the river steamer was a far more important factor than the stagecoach. "The innumerable steam boats . . . are the stage coaches and fly wagons of this land of lakes and rivers," remarks Frances Trollope in 1832, and this impression of American travel recurs in contemporary reports by European visitors.[49]

Being the second mechanized means of transportation, the railroad becomes closely linked with the steamer in American transportation development and consciousness. These links are reinforced on the one hand, by the American notion of steam power as the force joining the parts of the country into a living nation, and on the other, by the reality of an underdeveloped highway system; highway building continues to be neglected after the arrival of the railroads, all the way up to the beginning of the twentieth century and the arrival of the automobile.[50] "The Americans," says a French author discussing the situation in the mid-nineteenth century, "seem to have been so entirely predestined to the exclusive use of steamboats and railroads that they have no taste for the use of carriages nor for the construction of the great roads necessary for such carriages."[51]

The social relations of the river steamer, as described by L.C. Hunter, were the very opposite of those of the class-stratified European train:

A "world in miniature" was the phrase with which literary travelers were wont to describe the western steamboat, and such in truth it was. Here all the essential processes of living went on, keyed to a higher pitch than in the ordinary course of land-bound existence. Here people laboured, ate, slept, amused themselves, suffered illness and hardship, and, not infrequently, died. Here luxury and poverty, overindulgence and deprivation, freedom and bondage were found in close proximity. Here all ranks and classes were represented: proletarian and chattel slave, frontiersman and emigrant, merchant and manufacturer, farmer and planter. Here was a society with a distinctive life and folkways of its own. Here was a freedom of intercourse among persons of different rank and from different walks of life which impressed foreign observers as symbolic of the egalitarian quality of American life.[52]

Quite apart from the democratic aspect, Europe did not have anything comparable to these "Floating Palaces" and "Moving Hotels":[53] the European counterparts of these boats were modest by comparison. "The model of this steamer is beautiful," says one American reporting on a steamer trip down the Rhine in 1844, "but the room is extremely limited."[54]

European visitors, on the other hand, find the American river steamer alien in form (for Charles Dickens, "these Western vessels are . . . foreign to all ideas we are accustomed to entertain of boats") and singular in their roominess and the attendant conviviality. Thus David Stevenson, in 1839, on the doings in the main saloon: "The scene resembles much more the coffee-room of some great hotel than the cabin of a floating vessel."[55] Or Charles Sealsfield (Friedrich Gerstäcker) in 1827, when the river steamer had a virtual monopoly on American travel:

> No one is more at home when traveling than the American, particularly when traveling in his own country. He regards the steamboat as a hostelry in which he is staying, as his temporary property, and acts quite accordingly. The citizen of the United States travels so extensively and his journeys are of such great duration that they do not present him with the notions of discomfort or fear that the European might have. His traveling facilities (I am speaking of travel by water) are far more comfortable and better equipped than those of any other nation, not excluding the English.[55a]

In our discussion of the development of design we have seen how the spaciousness of the riverboat is regarded as a desideratum for the railroad car. The earliest record of this can be found in Benjamin Dearborn's proposal of 1819, which suggests that the passenger cars of the future railroad be furnished "with accommodations for passengers to take their meals and their rest during the passage, as in packets; that they be sufficiently high for persons to walk without stooping, and so capacious as to accommodate twenty, thirty, or more passengers, with their baggage."[56]

Thus it is not only the motive power they share (i.e., steam) that causes river steamer and railroad to be seen as two manifestations of one and the same thing, but also their capacity to provide the same form of travel with ample space and mobility during the journey. "We have moving palaces on the water and the land," gushes an article in the 1840 *Merchant's Magazine and Commercial Review*, reflecting the popular notion of "saloons with gilded columns, carpeted with the costly fabrics of foreign looms, adorned with mirrors and paintings and rich tapestry. . . ."[57]

The only strange thing about this text is its date: around 1840, the spacious car was firmly established on American railroads, but only in a very sober, plain, almost primitive form not easily compared with "steamboat gothic."[58] That the figure of speech about "moving palaces on the water and the land"

*Grand Salon of a large
Riverboat, 1870's.*
In contrast to the main
cabins of the smaller
and earlier steamboats
(see illustration on
p. 106), we find here the
large dimensions and
ornamentation which
have obviously been
borrowed from
transatlantic
steamships. The salon
pictured here is a good
example of the style
which was called
"Steamboat Gothic" by
contemporaries.

New York Public Library,
Picture Collection.

could nevertheless become so popular, despite the obvious differences, demonstrates how deeply anchored the analogy of steamer and train had become in
popular consciousness.

Although the similarity between the interiors of river steamers and railroad trains is merely a figment of the imagination in 1840, it becomes a reality
twenty years later. From 1859 on, Pullman builds cars that openly allude to the
model of the "floating palace" steamer in their very name of "Palace cars": as
contemporary illustrations show), their interiors are indeed hard to distinguish
from the luxury saloon of a riverboat.

These Pullman cars reflect the nation's wealth, which becomes increasingly
apparent after the end of the Civil War. With them, a first class is introduced
into the until then classless American railroad system.[59] Otherwise they are
merely a further development of the arrangement and the functions that have
been characteristic of the American railroad car from the beginning. As the
railroads reach the West Coast, American rail journeys become even longer
than before. The need for mobility and communication during the journey
increases in direct proportion to the traveled distance: although the need was
always typical of American travel, the new distances and new wealth add a new
quality to it. The train consisting of Pullman cars looks like a steamer on rails:
"Baths, both tub and shower, barbershops, manicures, lady's maids, valet service, news tickers, libraries, current periodicals and hotel and railroad di-
rectories, smokers' accessories and, of course, the fullest possible facilities for
sluicing and gentling the patrons with wines and strong waters were taken for

114

a.

*Interiors of Pullman
Cars, 1870's and 1880's.*

If one compares the
organization of space,
the furnishings and the
social amenities of the
Pullman car, as they
appear in these
illustrations, with those
of the Grand Saloon of
a steamboat
(illustration, opposite
page), one could almost
say that one is an exact
replica of the other in
reduced format.

a. New York Public Library,
Picture Collection.
b. From: The Railway Gazette,
1887.

b.

Production of an "On-Board" Newspaper on the Transcontinental Train.

Kitchen in Transcontinental Train

From: Leslie's Magazine. 1887.

granted on all luxury trains of the era."[60] For a while, the Union Pacific Railroad published a newspaper on its transcontinental run,[61] according to which two organs had been installed on the train so that passengers were able to attend religious services and musical performances while on board.[62]

With the image of that Pullman train traversing the Western plains like a steamship on rails we end our consideration of the American railroad: no doubt, that was its finest hour. This image of a ship on land, crossing the prairie so frequently described by travelers as an ocean of land,[63] gives the American railroad's nautical associations vivid confirmation.

The American railroad's original and fundamental task was to create transportation where no natural waterways existed. This function becomes more obvious than ever on journeys through the vast dry reaches of the Great Plains: if, until then, the railroad was merely reminiscent of the waterway it was a surrogate for, the train running on it now becomes a ship on dry land in a concrete sense. In 1846, Thomas Hart Benton suggested that the two coasts of the American continent should be joined not by a railroad but by a system of waterways.[64] Although this notion, born out of the tradition of water travel, did not stand a chance against the technically superior railroad, the latter was to pay its respects to that same tradition, by crossing the continent like a steamship engaged in what Daniel Webster once called "land navigation".[65]

Postscript

The question as to why the traveling situation in the American railroad car involves so much more mobility than that in its European counterpart cannot be entirely satisfactorily answered by mere reference to that general mobility which, since Tocqueville at least, is regarded as an American national characteristic. One may assume that the "passion for locomotion" that Michel Chevalier and countless other European visitors observed in the nineteenth century applies not only to general commercial and technological dynamics in America but is also characteristic of individual American bodies. Chevalier has a passage that seems to demonstrate why Americans do not travel in a state of compartmentalized immobility: he says that the American

> is always in the mood to move on, always ready to start in the first steamer that comes along from the place where he had just now landed. He is devoured with a passion for movement, he cannot stay in one place; he must go and come, he must stretch his limbs and keep his muscles in play. When his feet are not in motion, his fingers must be in action; he must be whittling a piece of wood, cutting the back of his chair, or notching the edge of the table, or his jaws must be at work grinding tobacco. . . . He always has something to do, he is always in a terrible hurry. He is fit for all sorts of work except those which require a careful slowness. Those fill him with horror; it is his idea of hell.[66]

7. The Pathology of the Railroad Journey

> The man, for the time being, becomes a part of the machine in which he has placed himself, being jarred by the self-same movement, and receiving impressions upon nerves of skin and muscle which are none the less real because they are unconsciously inflicted.
>
> — *The Book of Health,* 1884

Until the end of the 1850s, medical science exhibits only sporadic interest in the effects that rail travel has on the health of passengers and railway personnel.[1] The first systematic study appears in 1857: it is E.A. Duchesne's *Des chemins de fer et leur influence sur la santé des mécaniciens et des chauffeurs*. (On the railroads and their influence on the health of the engineers and the firemen). It is an industrial-medical survey of the type introduced by Gaskell in England in the 1830s to study the health of factory workers. The engine-drivers and firemen, whose health Duchesne discusses, are seen as industrial workers. The locomotive is the machine they operate, and it is also the cause for the various symptoms of disease that Duchesne verifies and sums up with the term *maladie des mécaniciens* (engineers' malady). These consist in part of pseudorheumatic pains that result from the driver's and fireman's exposed working position on the locomotive and from the alternation of heat and cold.[2] Then there are the consequences of the specific mechanical vibration peculiar to the motion of the locomotive and the train. On one hand, the train proceeds so very smoothly — which is why early travelers feel they are "flying" — but, on the other, wheel and rail produce a new kind of vibration that is quite different from the jolts experienced on a coach journey on the highway. This vibration results from the exact interaction between steel rail and steel wheel, from the speed, and particularly, from the distance between the rails. What differentiates it from

118

preindustrial forms of mechanical shock is the train's velocity, which causes the jolts to be so brief and to follow in such rapid succession that they are no longer felt as individual jolts but as a condition of continuous vibration. There is an excellent description of this in a German text of 1838: "The motion of the cars is quite regular; there is no shaking or jolting whatsoever. The noise caused by the wheels resembles that of a mill mechanism and makes it impossible to conduct a conversation with one's neighbor."[3]

If this vibration is felt in the entire train, it is particularly strong in the locomotive, where the steam engine adds its own vibration to it. Duchesne's *maladie des mécaniciens*, characterized by "generalized, continuous, and persistent pains, accompanied by a feeling of weakness and numbness,"[4] is mostly due to this mechanical vibration from the engine: "Without exception, all the firemen and drivers complain about the trepidation of the machines, the regular but perpetual movements that it transmits to the entire body and to the lower extremities in particular."[5] Von Weber, in his 1860 article, *Die Abnützüng des physischen Organismus beim Fahrpersonal der Eisenbahn* (The wear and tear of the physical organism of railroad train personnel), gives a more exact account of the way in which the vibration affects the body: "In the locomotive personnel these shocks express themselves as a continuous tremor in all the joints of the body that is only interrupted by sudden vertical jolts or sideways motions: this tremor is so intense and rapid that if the engine-driver or fireman were to attempt to rest his body on its bone structure in a rigid fashion by planting his feet firmly on the floor, it would be impossible for him to stand even for a short time."[6]

Von Weber and Duchesne both describe how the locomotive workers try to counter the mechanical tremor by keeping their bodies in an elastic state. The engine-drivers do not plant their feet on the locomotive floor but stand on tiptoe, thus creating the spring suspension that the locomotive does not possess.[7] As this is very fatiguing, some drivers invent arrangements designed to cushion the shocks. Duchesne reports: "Some place a doormat under their feet, others a wooden board supported at both ends by a brace. That board thus becomes a kind of springboard on which they stand and which absorbs the shocks; still others equip the board with five metal springs or rubber buffers. Some have even designed an elastic stool on which they can sit down from time to time."[8]

Obviously, these machine tremors do not affect only the locomotive personnel but also, in somewhat lesser measure, all the people traveling in the train. Von Weber makes explicit mention of this, distinguishing between locomotive personnel and train personnel: he states that the shocks to which the train personnel is subjected "are far less intense, partly because the suspension of the cars is much closer to perfection than that of the engines and particularly the tenders; furthermore, the shocks can be considerably ameliorated by the use of seat cushions etc."[9] If locomotive and train personnel suffer from the same vibration — although to a varying degree — one must assume that the passengers, too, are subjected to it. In principle, their situation is the same as the train personnel's — that is, they are sheltered in the closed cars, resting on springs and upholstery, yet not entirely removed from the shocks caused by the machinery that is transporting them.[10]

In 1862 the leading English medical journal the *Lancet* publishes a pamphlet called *The Influence of Railway Travelling on Public Health*; here we find corroboration that the same factors apply to travelers. The mechanical vibration and tremor is said to be caused by the *inelasticity* that characterizes the railroad and distinguishes it from all earlier means of transportation:

> In animal bodies the means of motion are muscle and tendon. Tigers or cats can leap from many times their own height without damage. A railway engine or carriage would be destroyed by a very small fall. Removed from the rail to a paved road, either it or the road, or both, would be rapidly destroyed. The reason is that there is great deficiency in the mechanical appliances which should represent muscle. If a malformed man has one leg shorter than the other, he can compensate for the difference of radius by more or less of muscular action. No such compensation is found in railway vehicles. Again: a horse works over hard pavements for years, saving the jolts by the action of his muscles and tendons. After a time his tendons lose their power, and his footing becomes uncertain. The veterinary surgeon interferes and rehardens and tempers his springs or tendons by the process which is called firing. The railway carriage, even at the outset, is in the condition of a worn-out horse. It is a framework of bones without muscles.[11]

The *Lancet* pamphlet's description of the passenger's state comes up with similar results as Duchesne and Von Weber. Due to the mechanical regidity of the machine parts, i.e., the rails and wheels of the railroad, the journey becomes a "series of small and rapid concussions."[12] Inevitably, the passenger reacts to these the same way the locomotive personnel does — by trying to absorb with his own body what the suspension mechanisms are unable to absorb. According to the *Lancet* pamphlet, the passenger's body compensates for the railroad's rigidity by the elasticity of its own muscles, which are inadvertently set into motion: "The immediate effect of being placed in a vehicle subjected to rapid, short vibrations and oscillation . . . is that a considerable number of muscles are called into action, and maintained in a condition of alternating contractic effort throughout the whole journey. . . . The frequency, rapidity, and peculiar abruptness of the motion of railway-carriages keep thus a constant strain on the muscles; and to this must be ascribed a part of that sense of bodily fatigue, almost amounting to soreness, which is felt after a long journey."[13]

The muscles grow tired, and so do the individual sense organs. The rapidity with which the train's speed causes optical impressions to change taxes the eyes to a much greater degree than did preindustrial travel[14] and, the sense of hearing has to cope with a deafening noise throughout the trip.[15] Thus the traveler's entire organism is subjected to a degree of wear and tear that did not exist in preindustrial travel, not to mention the purely psychological stresses repeatedly emphasized by contemporary authors.[16]

Twenty years after the *Lancet* pamphlet, in 1884, a medical text explains this unprecedented degree of strain as an outgrowth of the new ratio between traveling time and traversed space, claiming that this multiplies the formerly known symptoms of fatigue:

There is pulling at the eyeballs on looking out of the window; a jarring noise, the compound of continuous noise of wheels, and this conducted into the framework of the compartment; with the obligato of whistle and of the brake dashing in occasionally, and always carrying some element of annoyance, surprise, or shock; there is the swaying of the train from side to side, or the jolting over uneven rails and ill-adjusted points; and the general effect of these upon the temper, the muscles, and the moral nature. Let all that is especially, or accidentally, out of the order be left out of consideration, and suppose that all is as good as it can be, and yet there are the residua that have been mentioned. There are "impressions" that are made, and that unavoidably, by the very conditions of the journey; and they involve fatigue. The eyes are strained, the ears are dinned, the muscles are jostled hither and thither, and the nerves are worried by the attempt to maintain order, and so comes weariness. (Russell Reynolds, "Travelling: Its Influence on Health," in *The Book of Health*, ed. Malcolm Morris, London, Paris and New York, 1884, p. 581.)

The symptoms that the *Lancet* pamphlet diagnoses in travelers of the first and second class as a state of fatigue specific to railroad travel are, in somewhat ameliorated form, the same as those subsumed by Duchesne as *maladie des mécaniciens*. Only the rheumatic troubles are missing, since the travelers are transported in sheltered compartments. Nevertheless even the compartment travelers are subject to the same tremors, the same noise, the same speed as the train personnel. Commuters are particularly subject to these stresses. One of the *Lancet* authors describes his impression, gained by years of observation, of daily business commuters between London and Brighton: "I have had a large experience in the changes which the ordinary course of time makes on men busy in the world, and I know well to allow for their gradual deterioration by age and care; but I have never seen any set of men so rapidly aged as these seem to me to have been in the course of those few years."[17] Let us compare the preceding description of bourgeois travelers, those of the first- and second-class carriages, with this account of the general state of health of industrial workers, given in 1836 by Peter Gaskell, who was later to be regarded by Marx and Engels as the foremost authority in the field of industrial medicine: "On the whole, it may be said that the class of manufacturers engaged in mill labour, exhibit but few well-defined diseases; but that nearly the entire number are victims to a train of irregular morbid actions, chiefly indicated by disturbances in the functions of the digestive apparatus, with their consequent effects upon the nervous system; producing melancholy, extreme mental irritation, and great exhaustion."[18]

It would seem risky to use these scant medical texts to construct a thesis according to which railroad travel in the nineteenth century was, for the bourgeois public, an experience analogous to the work experience of the industrial proletariat. The difference between the situation of the laborer, e.g., the locomotive driver, who expends his energy on a machine by the sweat of his brow, and that of the passenger sitting in his comfortable upholstered compartment is quite obvious: it is the difference between an active-productive and a passive-consumptive participation in the same industrial process of production. Yet the simultaneous nature of that participation that joins worker and traveler permits us to speak of the "industrial experience" of the latter. He, too, experiences industrial production, although from the consumer's standpoint. The railroad's industrial product is transportation, change of locality. What makes this production fundamentally different from all other industrial production is exactly that *simultaneity* of production and consumption. The consumption of industrially manufactured objects takes place at a temporal and spatial distance from their production. Their industrial character finds only indirect expression (e.g., in their uniformity, great quantity, etc.). But in the production of transportation, where the traveler is the instant consumer, the industrial character is experienced in the act of travel itself. This utility is inseparably connected with the process of transportation, which is the productive process of transportation. Men and commodities travel by the help of the means of transportation, and this traveling, this change of location, constitutes the production in which these means of transportation are consumed. The utility of transportation can be consumed only in this process of production. It does not exist as a use-value apart from this process."[19] Elsewhere, even more explicitly: "The useful effect that they [the means of transportation] create during their productive function, i.e., during their time in the sphere of production, the change of locality, becomes simultaneously assimilated in the individual consumption, as, for instance, the traveler's."[20] To which we might add that not only the change of locality, but also its material, technological, and industrial production, is assimilated in the traveler's consumption: the vibrations of the maximally exploited rolling stock and rails, the noise of the machinery at work, the interaction, characteristic of large industries, of gigantic machine complexes that make human beings appear as "mere living appendages" (Marx)[21] of themselves.

All this gives new significance to the previously mentioned complaint of bourgeois travelers of the first half of the nineteenth century that one no longer travels as a person but is transported like a parcel.[22] This figure of speech contains the implication that the railroad is to travel as industry is to manufacture. The industrial revolution, in the production of goods as well as in travel, destroys what one might call the "esthetic freedom" of the preindustrial subject. This preindustrial subject had a live interaction with its object engaging all the senses, whether as an artisan working at a craft or as a traveler participating in the "organic" motion of the vehicle through the landscape.

The "esthetic freedom" of the preindustrial subject is only discovered at the moment when the preindustrial methods of production and transportation seem threatened in their very existence by mechanization: this is a typical process of romanticization, one that even the young Marx was not entirely immune to. As long as the preindustrial methods and their forms of work and travel were the dominant ones, a Carlyle or Ruskin or Morris would never have thought of seeing them in an esthetic light. As every travel journal and every social history of artisanship demonstrates, they were quotidian and cumbersome. When industrialization suddenly causes these old forms to be seen from an esthetic and romanticizing viewpoint, this tells us less about those forms themselves than about general attitudes towards industrialization. On the other hand, the estheticization of the outworn forms brings out one of their aspects that had not been noticed before because there was no conscious need for it.

Thus "organic" travel and artisan manufacture become a conscious need, i.e., a valued esthetic quality, only at that moment when a new technology arrives and demonstrates the monotony of industry.

   Machinery, in its ever more powerful intervention, destroys that "live" connection between the producer or consumer of the product and the production process. The nineteenth-century English bourgeoisie gains no authentic experience of the reality of the great industries of Manchester and Sheffield. It becomes aware of them only indirectly, by means of the displays of world exhibitions and humanitarian fiction. Yet the railroad, the industrial process in transportation, does become an actual industrial experience for the bourgeois, who sees and feels his own body being transformed into an object of production.

Upholstery in a First-Class Compartment, France 1890's.

Archive Roger Viollet, Paris

   As incontrovertible and physically palpable as that industrial experience is, everything possible is done to reduce it. This is where upholstery originates as a central cultural-historical phenomenon of the nineteenth century. It starts out on the railway train as something merely functional: its initial purpose is simply to protect the human body from the mechanical shocks caused by machinery. The engine-drivers observed by Duchesne and Von Weber can only deal with these by means of their own muscles and a few primitive aids. Their bodies themselves bear the brunt of the problem. The first- and second-class passengers are more fortunate, being protected by the interior furnishings of their compartments. Discussing the possibility of amelioration of the railroad's "peculiar jerking vibrations" and their unpleasant effects, the *Lancet* pamphlet

Cross Section of a First-Class Passenger Car.
The steel springs in the upholstery of the seats are clearly visible.

From: *Handbuch für Eisenbahntechnik*, Leipzig, 1870.

Detail Cross Section of an upholstered first-class Seat.
The springs concealed inside of the actual upholstery, giving it a voluptuous and opulent form, serve a function analogous to that of the structural beams concealed behind the ornate facades of late nineteenth century architecture.

From: *Handbuch für Eisenbahntechnik*, Leipzig, 1870.

alludes to several prevalent means to that end and identifies the principle underlying them:

> . . . the means whereby their influence may be counteracted can be expressed in one word — elasticity — the natural antagonist of jerk. The provision of a sufficient intervention of elastic materials reduces the movement, which in a springless railway waggon is inconceivably distressing, to a gentle swaying motion. The springs of railway carriages, the horse-hair seats (and the elastic floor of cork supplied to the new royal carriage), are recognitions of the principle, which the habitual traveller may wisely extend for himself by many expedients, if he keeps in view what he has to attain — elasticity.[23]

In the course of the century, the functional purpose of that elastic upholstery falls by the wayside: it becomes an end unto itself and expands in direct ratio to the expansion of industry. Siegfried Giedion has hinted at this connection by remarking that the overstuffed furniture typical of late nineteenth-century culture arose in the Western European countries simultaneously with the rise of the new industrial bourgeoisie.[24] Such upholstery is no longer functional when it appears in realms such as the living room, where there are no mechanical-industrial jolts or jerks to be counteracted. Thus the jolt to be softened is no longer physical but mental: the memory of the industrial origin of objects, from railway stations or exhibition halls constructed out of steel, to chairs constructed out of wood. The opulent baroque and Renaissance fronts that cover the steel girders are nothing but, on a larger scale, the braided and tasseled upholstery cushions that render the true construction of the armchair or sofa invisible and thus forgettable.[25]

a.

b.

The Upholstery comes into its own.

Towards the end of the nineteenth century, upholstery, which had previously been a subordinate factor, became the predominant element in furniture construction. Many pieces of furniture, like this French armchair from the 1880's (a), "appear to the naive eye as a complex of cushions somehow miraculously held together." (Siegfried Giedion). Illustration (b) symbolically shows how the upholstery overcomes the structure: like a wave, the cushions overwhelm the structural frame.

Illustrations from: a. H. Havard, Dictionnaire de l'ameublement. b. Practical Upholstery, London 1883.

a.

b.

Architecture and "Upholstery."
Illustration (a) shows the rear facade of Garnie's Paris Opera, a richly ornamented Beaux-Art creation, behind which the structural elements are concealed or "upholstered" (b).

From: M. Steinhauser, Die Architektur der Pariser Oper, München, 1969

Excursion: Industrial Fatigue

The curves of fatigue for metals coincided in
a remarkable way with the curves of fatigue
for muscular effort.
                                    — Yearbook of the
                            Smithsonian Institution, 1911

According to the *Lancet* pamphlet of 1862, the state of fatigue that overwhelms
travelers after train journeys of some duration is due to the mechanical shocks
they experience. But these "rapid, short vibrations and oscillations" do not
affect only the human body but equally the materials of the machine transporting it. Not only the travelers suffer from fatigue, the materials do, too.

In the mid-nineteenth century the concept of fatigue acquires this additional connotation, the technical one. It was first documented in a lecture given
in 1854 to the London Institution of Civil Engineers; the lecture, entitled "On
the Fatigue and Consequent Fracture of Metals", proposes the new concept as
follows: "There are reasons for believing, that many of the appalling, and
apparently unaccountable accidents on railways, and elsewhere, are to be ascribed to that progressive action which may be termed, the 'fatigue of metals'.
This fatigue may arise from a variety of causes, such as repeated strain, blows,
concussions, jerks, torsion, or tension."[1]

It had been known for a long time that continuous concussion will cause
iron to crystallize and finally break: the phenomenon receives systematic attention only after iron becomes the mainstay of the industrial revolution. There
are several reasons why the railroad represents the spearhead of this development (as well as of so many others). In terms of machine technology, the
railroad is the most advanced industry of its time; it is also an object of public
attention to a far greater degree than the manufacturing industries; and, finally, railroad disasters rank among the most spectacular events of the
nineteenth century. On May 8, 1842, one of these disasters took place on the
Paris-Versailles line: it killed fifty-five travelers and severely maimed more than
a hundred others. It caused a European railroad trauma.. The disaster had been
caused by a broken locomotive axle, i.e., material fatigue; in 1842, that technical
term was not yet available for diagnosis. Remarkably enough, the concept of

fatigue nevertheless appears, näively as it were, in a technical publication dealing with the disaster. One of the experts assigned to the study of the causes of the accident, the engineer Laignel, sees the physiology of the travelers and the material parts of the railroad as equally subject to the same concussions, when he says that "the shocks and vibrations fatigue the travelers and destroy, in effect, all the material, and particularly the wheels and the axles."[2] Two decades later, in the 1860s, the German August Wöhler lays the foundation for modern testing of materials. He describes and quantifies the phenomenon of material fatigue as demonstrated by broken train car axles, and proposes that more stress-resistant alloys be used in the future production of railroad materials.[3]

Pre-History of Material Testing.
An illustration in Galileo's "Discorsi", on the problem of pliability of a beam.

From: Walter Ruske, Hundert Jahre Materialprüfung in Berlin.

While systematic material research begins with Wöhler, it has its historical antecedents. One of Galileo's experiments can be seen as a test of material: to calculate the resilience of a beam anchored to a wall, he attached a weight to the other end. In general, preindustrial material testing was identical with construction statics. A separate development occurred in the military realm, which once again proved to be a pacemaker for the industrial revolution. In order to regulate the Prussian army's purchases of firearms, which were far from systematic in the eighteenth century,[4] military material testing institutions were founded, such as the Prussian Office for the Testing of Materials and the Military Experimentation Office.[5]

Boiler Explosion in an American Riverboat, 1830's.

From: F. Donovan, River Boats of America. New York 1966.

The industrial application of the steam engine raised the testing procedures to a new level. From the eighteenth-century Newcomen engine to the nineteenth-century high-pressure engine, it is not only the technology that changes but also the construction material required by the machines. If the early low-pressure engines still consisted in part, of wood, the modern machines had to be constructed entirely of iron. Even that was to prove insufficient. In the United States, where Evans' high-pressure engine is mass-produced for the river steamboats, the 1830s witness a series of boiler explosions whose toll of casualties far exceeds that of the major European railroad disaster that was to occur in 1842.[6] These explosions provide a further impulse for the study of materials. In the 1830s, Alexander Dallas Bache conducts studies at the Franklin Institute in Philadelphia to determine the necessary strength of the steel out of which boilers are constructed.[7] The main attention of this research is directed toward material flaws and material resistance to pressure and temperature: thus the concept of fatigue does not yet emerge. The mechanical jolts and vibrations that further attack the material have not yet been recognized as significant.

What reveals to material research the new concept of material fatigue, is precisely that new kind of vibration to which the machine parts are increasingly subjected. It results from the working of the machine, from the interaction of its individual parts. The static element — the subject of investigation from Galileo to Bache — is now replaced by the dynamic.[8] That it is the *working* of the machine, the work performed by it, which causes its component materials to suffer *fatigue,* is no mere figure of speech: there is an obvious connection

129

a.

b.

Testing of Physiological Fatigue.
The founder of modern physiological fatigue research, Angelo Mosso, constructed this apparatus — called the "Ergograph" — to quantify the fatigue of certain muscles. The arm of the subject was firmly anchored so that a single finger would repeatedly lift a weight (a). By means of a drawing device, the declining muscle strength, i.e., the fatigue, was recorded on a slowly revolving drum (b).

From: A. Mosso, La Fatica.

between the rise of modern material testing and what Marx calls the "intensification of labor." Capitalist industry exploits, in fact, both material and human labor power. Marx describes the intensification of labor as "increased expenditure of labour in a given time, heightened tension of labour-power, and closer filling up of the pores of the working day."[9]

We find a corresponding statement in regard to machinery in a more recent standard work on metal fatigue: "The continuing trend towards higher strength/weight and power/weight ratios, more refined static design techniques, and the use of higher working stresses, increased speeds of operation, with the resultant accumulation of large numbers of cycles in a small period of time."[10]

What Taylorism does for the optimal exploitation of human labor power, material testing does for the exploitation of material labor power. The time and motion studies that Frederick Winslow Taylor instituted in American factories between 1880 and 1900 have the same functions as the studies done in by modern material researchers. In both cases the task is to find out how a given potential can be rearranged, and thus improved, to increase yield.

Chronology suggests that material research encouraged the development of Taylorism. After the most rational mode of construction had been ascertained for machines, this formulation pointed the way to investigation of how human labor could be utilized in the most rational way.[11] The manner in which the concept of fatigue migrates back and forth between physiology and technology demonstrates how the two realms exert mutual influence upon each other. At first, the physiological phenomenon of fatigue is a diffuse and scientifically negligible concept; then technology borrows it in order to name a novel condition that has been discovered in the context of the industrial revolution. After the fatigue concept has received its precise technological definition and quantification, it proceeds to migrate back to physiology. Now its physiological meaning is no longer diffuse: it gains exactitude as a concept in labor medicine. Its increasing importance can be clearly perceived in the development of medical literature dealing with physiological fatigue. The *Index Catalogue of the Library of the Surgeon-General's Office,* an authoritative international medical bibliography, lists in its 1883 edition only two dissertations and five journal articles under the heading "Fatigue." In the 1900 edition, the "Fatigue" bibliography already extends over almost two large pages of fine print. In the 1925 edition, we find three and one-half pages, in 1940, more than six pages with hundreds of titles.

130

8. The Accident

— *die Krisen des Unfalls (der unbeherrschten Dinge) werden ebenso länger bleiben wie sie tiefer lergen als die Krisen der Wirtschaft (der unbeherrschten Waren).*

... the crises of the accident (of the uncontrolled things) will remain with us longer to the degree that they remain deeper than the crises of economy (of the uncontrolled commodities).

— Ernst Bloch

Let us glance at Thomas Creevy's description of a train journey in 1829: "It is really flying, and it is impossible to divest yourself of the notion of instant death to all upon the least accident happening."[1]

Early perception of the railroad is characterized by a curious ambivalence. The journey is felt to be uncannily smooth, easy, secure, like flying. "When I closed my eyes this sensation of flying was quite delightful, and strange beyond description; yet strange as it was, I had a perfect sense of security, and not the slightest fear," relates Fanny Kemble, the famous London actress, giving her impressions of a train journey from Liverpool to Manchester in 1830.[2] At the same time, the train journey entails a sensation of violence and potential destruction. This sensation becomes concretized in the metaphor of the railroad train as a projectile shot through space and time. Thus all the ease, comfort, security that are superficial characteristics of the train journey are always accompanied by an ever-present subliminal fear: as one German author of 1845 says, there is a "certain dampening of the spirits that never quite goes away despite all the pleasant aspects of train journeys." And that anxiety is explained by the always "close possibility of an accident, and the inability to exercise any influence on the running of the cars."[3]

The ever-present fear of a potential disaster remains, however, only until

131

*Contemporary
Illustration of a
Railroad Accident on
the Paris-Versailles Line
on May 8, 1841.*

Musée Carnavelet,
Cabinet des Estampes

the railroad has become a part of normal everyday life. By the time Western Europe has culturally and psychically assimilated the railroad, that is, by the mid-nineteenth century, these anxieties have vanished, as has that turn of phrase so typical of the early period, "the annihilation of space and time." The expression has become nonsensical because the new geography created by the railroad (and first experienced as a shock) has become second nature. The same applies to the travel process itself. The new activities and forms of behavior (reading while traveling, "panoramic" perception etc.) institutionalize the new reality of the new technological standard of travel. They form a new psychic layer that obscures the old fears and lets them lapse into oblivion. These old fears are forgotten concurrently and commensurately with the preceding technology, whose replacement by the new one was the prime cause of those fears.[4]

If the normal functioning of the railroad is now experienced as a natural and safe process, any *sudden interruption* of that functioning (which has now become second nature) immediately reawakens the memory of the forgotten danger and potential violence: the repressed material returns with a vengeance. Bloch has characterized this aspect of the technological accident. He speaks of the demonic nature of the first railroads, and of its gradual metamorphosis into the quotidian, and says: "Only the accident still reminds us of it sometimes, with the crash of collision, the roar of explosion, the cries of maimed people — a production that knows no civilized schedule."[5]

132

One might also say that the more civilized the schedule and the more efficient the technology, the more catastrophic its destruction when it collapses. There is an exact ratio between the level of the technology with which nature is controlled, and the degree of severity of its accidents. The preindustrial era does not know any technological accidents in that sense. In Diderot's *Encyclopédie,* "Accident" is dealt with as a grammatical and philosophical concept, more or less synonymous with coincidence. The preindustrial catastrophes are natural events, natural accidents. They attack the objects they destroy from the outside, as storms, floods, thunderbolts, hailstones, etc. After the industrial revolution, destruction by technological accident comes from the inside. The technical apparatuses destroy themselves by means of their own power. The energies tamed by the steam engine and delivered by it as regulated mechanical performance will destroy that engine itself in the case of an accident. The increasingly rapid vehicles of transportation tend to totally destroy themselves and each other whenever they collide. The higher the degree of technical intensification (pressure, tension, velocity, etc.) of a piece of machinery, the more thoroughgoing its destruction in the case of dysfunction. The breaking of a coach axle in the eighteenth century merely interrupted a slow and exceedingly bumpy trip on the highway; the breaking of a locomotive axle between Paris and Versailles in 1842 leads to the first railroad catastrophe that causes a panic in Europe. In 1844, two years after this disaster, the *Encyclopédie des chemins de fer et des machines à vapeur* (Encyclopedia of railroads and steam

Accident in the Gare Montparnasse.

The locomotive went out of control and sped over the buffer stops, burst through the glass facade of the station and fell into the street, which was on a considerably lower level. (See title page.) Magritte's painting "Time Transfixed" alludes to this event which fascinated the surrealist movement.

Musée Carnavalet, Cabinet des Estampes

133

engines) devotes to the subject of "Accidents" a nine-page article, in which the accident is seen as a negative indicator of technological progress:

> All man-made things are subject to accidents. By a kind of compensation . . ., the more these things are perfected, the greater the gravity of the accidents that happen to them. That is why, without rigorous surveillance at all points, the most powerful and most perfected industrial means, that is, steam engines and railroad trains, can cause the most grave and fatal mishaps. The mass of the objects they set in motion, the velocity they engender, their very power, once halted or turned from its proper objective, is transformed into a terrible agent of destruction. Steam power, while opening up new and hitherto unknown roads to man, also seems to continually put him in a position best compared to that of a man who is walking along the edge of a precipice and cannot afford a single false step. It is a situation analogous to the one engineers term an unstable equilibrium, which can be upset by the least little effort.[6]

Accident and Crisis

The modern technological accident, the sudden collapse of a highly developed machinery, is a result of the management of industry according to capitalist principles, as is industrially applied technology as a whole. This technology is subject to the dictates of the profit motive. Bloch's comparison between the "crises of the accident" and the "crises of economy" is based on this interrelationship between technology and economy. The phenomenon of material fatigue has demonstrated for us how the exploitive interest affects even the molecular structure of the materials. In *Das Kapital* Marx provides a definition of economic crisis that reads like a translation of the technological accident back into the economic sphere. If the nineteenth century perceives the cause of technological accidents to be the sudden disturbance of the uncertain equilibrium of a machine (i.e., the relationship between curbed energy and the means of curbing it), Marx defines the economic crisis as the disruption of the uncertain balance between buying and selling in the circulation of goods. As long as buying and selling work as a balanced and unified process, the cycle goes on functioning, but as soon as the two become separated and autonomous, we arrive at a crisis: "To say that these two independent and anithetical acts [purchases and sales] have intrinsic unity are essentially one, is the same as to say that this intrinsic oneness expresses itself in an external antithesis. If the interval in time between the two complementary phases of the complete metamorphosis of a commodity becomes too great, if the split between the sale and the purchase becomes too pronounced, the intimate connexion between them their oneness, *asserts* itself by producing — a crisis."[7] (Italics added.)

9. Railroad Accident, "Railway Spine," Traumatic Neurosis

The destructive force of the railroad disasters manifests itself not only in the physical demolition of the technological machinery and the passengers: it has other effects as well. In many accident victims who have suffered no injuries, or only minor ones, symptoms of psychic and physical deterioration appear after some time that frequently lead to total disability and in some cases to death. The medical profession finds it difficult to diagnose these symptoms, which become an important subject of medical and legal controversy after the railroad companies have become legally liable for their passengers' safety and health. (In England this happens in 1864, in Germany in 1871.)[1] Only material, i.e., pathologically demonstrable, damage caused to accident victims qualifies them for compensation. Thus the compensation of physically injured victims provides no problems, but those victims who suffer damage without pathologically demonstrable cause create — in the period roughly between 1865 and 1885 — a legal and medical problem whose solution in the courts depends on the medical profession. The medical experts called upon in compensation cases have to determine whether the claimant's ailment is an imaginary one, i.e., simulated in order to receive compensation from the railroad company, or whether it is a manifestation of a new medical syndrome.

The medical explanations given for the new symptoms change significantly

A new Type of Insurance, Accident Insurance.

This American insurance advertisement from the 1870's vividly evokes all of the dangers that may befall the traveller in a technological world. Travel insurance developed first in England in the 1840's when the railroad became the primary means of transportation.

From: New York Public Library, Picture Collection.

during those two decades. The initial explanation is a pathological one. The experts decide on either simulation or a supposed microscopic deterioration of the spinal cord ("railway spine") due to mechanical shock caused by the accident. This explanation is based on the traditional medical view that all ailments have purely pathological causes, which is bolstered by the corresponding juridical dogma that only physical injuries qualify as cause for compensation. From the early 1880s on, the purely pathological view is superseded by a new, psychopathological one, according to which the shock caused by the accident does not affect the tissue of the spinal marrow, but affects the victim psychically. Now the victim's experience of shock is the main causative factor of the ailment. By the end of the 1880s, the concept of "railway spine" has been replaced by that of traumatic neurosis.

In terms of medical history, Esther Fischer-Homberger* has described this development in a masterful way that includes detailed sociological considerations.[2] In this work, we are interested in the story of "railway spine" and traumatic neurosis not so much as part of the history of medicine but rather as a reflection in medical science of the new reality of industrialized life, concretely exemplified by the railroad and its accidents. If the novel symptoms of the traumatized accident victims originate in the new quality of railroad accidents, studying the history of the medical explanation of those symptoms has to contribute to the understanding of the effects of the industrialization of travel on the human mind and body. Thus it is our intention to demonstrate how the original "railway spine" theory represents a first attempt to explain industrial traumata, and how the subsequent attempts finally lead us to Freud's theory of stimulation and overstimulation, and the protective mechanisms against it — an explanatory model still relevant today.

Since our main interest is not in the history of medicine but in the connection between industrialization and certain symptoms of illness, we shall restrict ourselves to the development in England, using Erichsen and Page as the two definitive authors. Fischer-Homberger does also deal with these authors, but only as a preamble to the history of the traumatic neurosis. She bases her description mainly on German psychiatric literature of the 1880s and 1890s, stating, no doubt accurately, that German research into traumatic neurosis — an originally German medical concept — was the leading research on the subject in the world at the time, comparable to Charcot's investigations of hysteria in France. For the researcher, developments in England have the advantage of beginning with the first manifestations of the problem — as in the overall history of the railroad — and of providing a manageable amount of literature. It certainly is *no* accident that medical attention to victims of railroad accidents begins in the 1860s in England — then *still* the leading industrial nation in the world — while discussion begins in Germany twenty years later, after that country has experienced its great industrial leap forward.

The phenomenon of accident shock, i.e., a traumatization of the victim without discernible physical injury, naturally existed before the English medical profession started devoting its systematic attention to it in the mid-1860s, after the passage of the liability laws.[3] There are reports about railroad accidents that describe travelers as exhibiting signs of strong psychic disruption, phobias, obsessive actions, etc., without having suffered any actual injury. Thus a newspaper report on an unhurt participant in the great disaster on the Paris-Versailles line in 1842: "We saw a woman who had been in the first compartment of the car that followed right behind the locomotives; she had not received any injury, but had experienced a commotion so extreme when confronted by this horrible disaster that she did not remember anything of it at all."[4]

The concept of the commotion, while already sounding quite psychological, is intended in a merely physical sense: a French medical dissertation of 1834 defines it as "the shock experienced by certain parts of the body on the occasion of falls or when being stricken."[5] The cause of such a commotion, the text goes on to say, is always "a shock that affects the same part or a contiguous part of the body to the one affected."[6]

Two things are constantly noticeable in reports given by traumatized accident victims. Immediately after the accident the victim feels completely normal; after one or two days he then becomes overwhelmed by the memory of the event. We have one of these reports by Charles Dickens. On June 9, 1865, he experiences a minor railroad accident and escapes entirely unscathed. Four days later he discusses it in a letter, describing how he assisted other travelers immediately after the accident occurred; then he gives a description of the scene of destruction, and continues:

Charles Dickens.

> I don't want to be examined at the inquest and I don't want to write about it. I could do no good either way, and I could only seem to speak about it to myself. . . . I am keeping very quiet here. I have a — I don't know what to call it — constitutional (I suppose) presence of mind, and was not in the least fluttered at the time. I instantly remembered that I had the MS of a number with me and clambered back into the carriage for it. *But in writing these scanty words of recollection I feel the shake and I am obliged to stop.* Ever faithfully, Charles Dickens.[7] (Italics added.)

The abrupt ending of the letter, caused by the suddenly overwhelming memory of the accident, is all the more remarkable for the fact that Dickens is not exactly known for such sudden shifts in his manner of writing. We find a further testimony for this kind of aftereffect of accidents, popularly termed "shock" in the nineteenth century, in the report of an American traveler who experienced an equally negligible accident between Manchester and Liverpool in 1835 and likewise survived it without any injury. After that event he stands on a bridge across the rails and tries once again, as in former times, to enjoy the sight of an approaching train, but finds it impossible: "As it approached the bridge on which I stood, I could not bear to look at it, and seemed inclined to run off, lest it should be carried away from under me; I shrank back involuntarily, and refused to follow it with my eye to the goal. . . . But still no accident occurred, except in my creative imagination. . . ."[8]

All these examples concern accident victims who have escaped unscathed but for the fright. They show no enduring symptoms of disease and require no medical treatment. Because of their innocuousness these cases fall below the threshold of medical attention. However harmless and finally without consequence the victims' fright may have been, its sudden and powerful return to their memories proves that it belonged to that class of accident traumata that would occupy the courts and their medical experts from the mid-1860s on.

In medical literature the new subject appears for the first time in 1866. The *Lancet* publishes a three-part article by Thomas Buzzard entitled "On Cases of Injury from Railway Accidents." In the same year, an author who had previously published papers on epilepsy and hysteria, William Camps, publishes his "Railway Accidents or Collisions: Their Effects, Immediate and Remote, Upon the Brain and Spinal Cord and Other Portions of the Nervous System." And, finally, that year also sees the publication of the "history-making book" (Fischer-Homberger, *op. cit.*, p. 21) by John Eric Erichsen, *On Railway and Other Injuries of the Nervous System.*

After the near-absence of material dealing with such accidents in the *Lancet* of preceding years, this sudden onset of a literature is remarkable — as is the fact that not one of the three authors makes any reference to any of the others or to previous publications. Nevertheless, all three works present approximately the same views on the specific nature of the railroad accident, namely, that this kind of accident does not differ from other accidents in principle but in degree of violence, with the additional observation that that degree is a new and previously unknown one. Subsequently that observation will prove to be the great contradiction with which the medical authors have to try to come to terms. Here is William Camps' description of the peculiar nature of the railroad accident:

> There is something in the crash, the shock, and the violence of a railway collision, which would seem to produce effects upon the *nervous system* quite beyond those of any ordinary injury. In some cases, we are told, the sufferer may not even have sustained any fracture, and the cuts and external injuries may be apparently slight to the visual perception of the medical man; whilst, notwithstanding this comparatively and apparently external trifling injury or injuries, yet there may be coincident with all this, such a *shock* to the system as for a time to shatter the whole constitution, and this, moreover, to such a degree, to such an extent, that the unfortunate sufferer may not altogether recover throughout the remainder of his life, which I apprehend, may, in some instances at least, be reasonably expected to be curtailed in its duration.[9]

In essence, the same view is repeated in Erichsen's book, although, as noted, neither of the authors refers to the other.

Let us now see how Erichsen describes the consequences of the accident in victims who have suffered no physical injury. His text reads like a medical paraphrase of Dickens' report on *his* experience:

> One of the most remarkable phenomena attendant upon this class of cases is, that at the time of the occurence of the injury the sufferer is usually quite unconscious that any serious accident has happened to him. He feels that he has been violently jolted and shaken, he is perhaps somewhat giddy and confused, but he finds no bones broken, merely some superficial bruises or cuts on the head or legs, perhaps even no evidence whatever of external injury. He congratulates himself upon his escape from the imminent peril to which he has been exposed. He becomes unusually calm and self-possessed; assists his less-fortunate fellow sufferers, occupies himself perhaps actively in this way for several hours, and then proceeds on his journey. When he reaches his home, the effects of the injury that he has sustained begin to manifest themselves. A revulsion takes place. He bursts into tears, becomes unusually talkative, and is excited. He cannot sleep, or, if he does, he wakes up suddenly with a vague sense of alarm. . . .[10]

According to Erichsen, these are the subsequent symptoms: fatigue, headaches, difficulty in concentration, digestive problems, forgetfulness, stammering, reduction of sexual potency, cold sweats, states of anxiety, etc. Erichsen also mentions dreams that reflect the victim's anxiety: "The sleep is disturbed, restless, and broken. He wakes up in sudden alarm; dreams much; the dreams are distressing and horrible."[11] He does not expressly state that these dreams are, in their content, repetitions of the traumatic accident — a fact that Freud later points out as important — but it can be assumed that the dreams in question are of that nature, especially since Buzzard mentions a female patient "complaining that she saw the engine coming in at the window."[12] The surprising thing about Erichsen's book is that, on the one hand, it distinguishes between two groups of accident victims — the physically injured, and those suffering from medical symptoms without physical injury — and, on the other, it recombines both of these groups in the diagnosis that they are both suffering from a concussion of the spine, caused by the violent mechanical shock of the accident. As consistent as Erichsen is in his defense of this purely pathological view, he does not at all succeed in proving an actual pathological change in the tissue of the spinal marrow. He has to content himself with the analogy of the magnet, in which similar changes occur that cannot be demonstrably proven:

> How these Jars, Shakes, Shocks or Concussions of the Spinal Cord directly influence its action I cannot say with certainty. We do not know how it is that when a magnet is struck a heavy blow with a hammer, the magentic force is jarred, shaken, or concussed out of the horse-shoe. But we know that it is so, and that the iron has lost its magnetic power. So, if the spine is badly jarred, shaken, or concussed by a blow or a shock of any kind communicated to the body, we find that the nervous force is to a certain extent shaken out of the man, and that he has in some way lost nervous power. What immediate change, *if any,* has taken place in the nervous structure to occasion that effect, we no more know than what change happens to a magnet when struck. (Italics in original.)[13]

How shaky Erichsen's belief in the pathological view is in the face of his own observations is evidenced by that surreptitious "if any" qualifying his reference to the alleged but unproven pathological change in the tissue. This internal contradiction becomes even more obvious in Erichsen's repeated implicit stress on the psychic factor in railroad accidents, i.e., on the experience of fright:

> It must . . . be obvious . . . that in no ordinary accident can the shock be so great as in those that occur on Railways. The rapidity of the movement, the momentum of the person injured, the suddenness of its arrest, the helplessness of the sufferers, and the natural perturbation of mind that must disturb the bravest, are all circumstances that of a necessity greatly increase the severity of the resulting injury to the nervous system, and that justly cause these cases to be considered as somewhat exceptional from ordinary accidents.[14]

Although Erichsen finally sticks to his pathological explanation, the passage just quoted demonstrates sufficiently that he is unable to ignore the psychological distress resulting from the relative exceptionality (i.e., violence) of the railroad accident.[15] The confusion of pathological and psychopathological explanations is caused by Erichsen's inability to distinguish between the accident's mechanical power to shock and the psychic *reception* of that shock. His definition of the "concussion of the spine" as "a certain state of the spinal cord occasioned by external violence"[16] is intended to be read in terms of pathology, but could just as well be interpreted in a psychopathological sense. In the latter case, the outside force would no longer affect the spinal cord in a direct, mechanical fashion, but would affect psyche and organism in the form of an experience of fright.

Erichsen suppresses such an interpretation of the traumatic reaction in 1866. In the considerably enlarged and revised eidtion of his book, published in 1875, he does express his recognition of it.[17] Although that recognition is intended to be secondary, it is given sufficient space to justify the supposition that Erichsen has, as it were, changed his orientation behind his own back. This is the decisive passage in the 1875 edition: "It is important to observe that a serious accident may give rise to two distinct forms of nervous shock. . . . The first is mental or moral, and the second purely physical. These forms of 'shock' may be developed separately, or they may coexist. It is most important . . . to diagnose between these two, and if co-existing to assign to each other its proper importance."[18]

Erichsen states unequivocally — thus correcting his inadequate distinction between psychic and physical concussion in 1866 — that the "mental shock" does not result from a mechanical but from a psychic blow: "It is probably dependent in a great measure upon the influence of fear."[19] This psychic blow is the *translation* of the mechanical blow into an experience of fright. In recognizing this, Erichsen furthermore arrives at a new evaluation of the specific quality of the railroad accident. In 1866, the only difference he sees between the railroad accident and any other is the merely quantitative: for example, the railway accident is more violent than falling off a horse.[20] In 1875, Erichsen sees a new, entirely specific quality in the rail accident that distinguishes it from all other kinds of accidents:

> During a hospital practice of thirty years I can scarcely recall to mind a single case in which the emotional or hysterical state that I am about to describe[21] has been met with after, or as a consequence of, any of the ordinary accidents of civil life. But I have seen many instances of it after railway concussions. Is this due to the frantic terror which often seizes upon the sufferers from railway collisions, or is it due to some peculiarity in the accident, some vibratory thrill transmitted through the nervous system by the peculiarity of the accident? I am disposed to think that terror has much to do with its production. It must be remembered that railway accidents have this peculiarity, that they come upon the sufferers instantaneously without warning, or with but a few seconds for preparation, and that the utter helplessness of a human being in the midst of the great masses in motion renders these accidents peculiarly terrible. In most ordinary accidents, as in a carriage accident from a runaway horse, the sufferer has a few minutes to prepare, is enabled to collect his energies in order to make an effort to save himself, and does not feel the utter hopelessness of his condition in his struggle for life and safety. The crash and confusion, the uncertainty attendant on a railway collision, the shrieks of the sufferers, possibly the sight of the victims of the catastrophe, produce a mental impression of a far deeper and more vivid character than is occasioned by the more ordinary accidents of civil life.[22]

The modifications that Erichsen makes in his views from 1866 to 1875 do not cause him to abandon his pathological shock theory. Nevertheless, they clearly indicate how the new technological-industrial reality, so palpably demonstrated in the railroad accident, gradually and in the face of many resistances infiltrates and ultimately transforms traditional medical thought. Erichsen's hesitations and contradictions illustrate the process that Foucault calls reorientation of medical vision. Such a reorientation occurs as medicine is forced to acknowledge the existence of new qualities created by the industrial revolution.

With Erichsen's recognition of fright as a causative factor in the traumatization of railroad accident victims, the modernization of medical thought on this subject becomes an accomplished fact, even though Erichsen himself does not want to admit to it.[23] Medical literature after Erichsen, while expanding his work and criticizing it, primarily continues along lines contained in his work. The pathological explanation is discarded and the psychological one is granted both exclusive and universal validity.[24] The first comprehensive critique of Erichsen's theory is given in 1883 by Herbert W. Page, in his "Injuries of the Spine and Spinal Cord without Apparent Mechanical Lesion and Nervous Shock, in Their Surgical and Medico-Legal Aspects." Page says that Erichsen's failure was "[not] to have separated and differentiated those symptoms which we must have recognized are much more cerebral or psychical, from those which can only find an explanation in some actual lesion of the spinal cord or of the nerves which are given off from it."[25] In direct opposition to Erichsen, Page is interested exclusively in the psychically caused symptoms; for him — and for the entire line of research begun by him — these are the only valid ones. Only the psychic fright arising out of an accident is recognized as the cause for the psychosomatic consequences, and that fright is seen as something specific to the railroad accident. According to Page, the essential difference between a person run over in the street by a carriage and a railroad accident victim is "that in the one case [railroad accident] there is an element of great fear and alarm, which has perhaps been altogether absent from what may be called the less formidable and less terrible mode of accident."[26]

Page describes the traumatizing effect of the rail accident in words that even Erichsen could have used: "The suddenness of the accident, which comes without warning . . . the utter helplessness of the traveler, the loud noise, the hopeless confusion, the cries of those who are injured . . . are surely adequate to produce a profound impression upon the nervous system."[27] The decisive difference is that these psychic concussions are now regarded as the only cause of traumatization: "The incidents of every railway collision are quite sufficient — even if no bodily injury be inflicted — to produce a very serious effect upon the mind, and to be the means of bringing about a state of collapse *from fright and from fright only.*"[28] (Italics added.)

In Page's work, the psychological theory of accident traumatization becomes the dominant one, although there still is no generally accepted term for the syndrome. Clearly departing from Erichsen's "railway spine," experts now speak of "railway brain," while also using Erichsen's concept of "general nervous shock" in a new psychological interpretation. At the end of the 1880s Hermann Oppenheim comes up with the term "traumatic neurosis," and it gains acceptance with some rapidity. In his article of 1889, "Die traumatischen neurosen" (The traumatic neuroses), Oppenheim describes himself as a follower of Page, and defines the essential character of the traumatic neruoses as consisting of the fact "that they are not based on broad anatomical nor microscopically demonstrable changes but on cerebral functional disturbances, most probably located in the neo-cortex, affecting the psyche and the centers of motility, sensibility, and sensory functions."[29] Two years later, in 1891, Page publishes a new edition of his book of 1883 and notes that his theory has found general acceptance in the intervening years. However, he himself does not adopt the concept of traumatic neurosis but calls the syndrome he describes a "fright neurosis." Subsequently, the literature on the subject grows by leaps and bounds, introducing competing and partially overlapping terms like traumatic neurosis, fright neurosis, hysterical neurosis, libidinal neurosis, and (with World War I providing new realities) war neurosis.[30]

Let us recall the starting point of this chapter of medical history. We began with the question that arose from the legal liability of the railroad companies and had to be resolved in courts of law: were physically undamaged, traumatized victims of railroad accidents mere malingerers, or was their suffering genuine? Even after medical science had struggled through to the notion that mere psychic fright could indeed deteriorate a person's health, it took a long time before there was any change in the legal concept of injury. Even after the turn of the century, legal handbooks deny recognition to psychic shock. Thus Street's *Foundations of Legal Liability*, 1906: "Simple nervous shock and consequent injury to the mind, considered alone do not as a matter of law supply a ground of action. Bodily injury necessarily involves mental suffering. Being bound together the law refuses to separate one of these elements from the other and allows compensation for both."[31] In *Mayne's Treatise on Damages*, 1899, reference is made to a precedent of the 1880s that states, similarly, "that damages resulting from mere sudden terror or mental shock, could not be considered the natural consequence of the negligence complained of."[32]

Thus it seems that Erichsen's pathological explanation of accident traumata was more helpful to physically undamaged accident victims seeking compensation than the later psychological theories that recognized psychic trauma as a legitimate syndrome. (We can, however, only assume this on the basis of the legal handbooks referred to, as it was not possible to go into a study of the transcripts of compensation lawsuits.)

In Anglo-American common law, the recognition of psychic trauma as an actual malady that is eligible for compensation occurs as late as the middle of the twentieth century — more than fifty years after its recognition by medical science. A legal handbook published in 1963 states this general principle: "Nervous shock is a form of personal injury for which damages may or may not be recoverable according to the circumstances of the particular case." The handbook cites a decision made in 1943: "The crude view that the law should take cognizance only of physical injury resulting from actual impact has been discarded, and it is now well recognized that an action will lie for injury by shock sustained through the medium of the eye or the ear without direct contact. The distinction between mental shock and bodily injury was never a scientific one, for mental shock is presumably in all cases the result of, or at least accompanied by some physical disturbance in the sufferer's system."[33]

The specific character of the railroad and its accidents, from which the discovery of psychic trauma emanated, is no longer present in the above example of the further evolution of law and medicine. The importance that the concept of trauma gains in Freud indicates how the final reminiscences of the material-mechanical explanation of the causation of trauma gradually wear away. As Freud concentrates his attention increasingly on the psychoneuroses of sexual origin (as distinct from the actual neuroses), the patient's disposition becomes the decisive element, and the traumatic event itself loses objectivity. Fischer-Homberger calls this Freud's "psychologization of the trauma and its subsequent dissolution as an etiological factor."[34] Similarly, Laplanche and Pontalis find that "psychoanalytical investigation leads to a questioning of the concept of traumatic neruosis: by, on one hand, stressing its relativity in regard to the subject's tolerance, and on the other, integrating the traumatic experience in the subject's specific history and organization, it negates the determinative function of the traumatic event."[35] Psychoanalysis tends to "equate trauma that triggers neurosis with what Freud has elsewhere called 'refusal' (Versagung)."[36]

Yet Freud sees more than the psychological aspect of trauma. While he does abstract it into a psychological function within the framework of the sexual causation of neuroses, he later develops a renewed interest in the kind of neurosis that is brought about in an actual fashion, by means of violent events from outside. The stimulus response theory he develops in *Beyond the Pleasure Principle*, which Walter Benjamin has used in his reconstruction of a specifically modern structure of perception,[37] involves a recapitulation of the original concept of traumatic neurosis.

Freud's preoccupation with what he himself calls the "old, naive theory of shock" significantly occurs soon after the end of World War I. The drastic change in the quality of warfare (i.e., a new technology of battle materiel) caused medicine to renew its interest in mass psychic phenomena. This time, the mass phenomenon was shell shock, or war neurosis. Shell shock can certainly be seen as a successor to the railroad shock of the nineteenth century. In both cases the victims are psychically traumatized by a sudden and violent release of energy, without being demonstrably damaged in the physical sense.[38] As before, medical experts are called in to decide on the question of simulation, only this time the objective is not to see who deserves to be awarded damages, but to see who is a malingerer and should be sent back to the front lines, and who is a genuinely sick person requiring treatment.

If one recognizes the new quality of military technology in World War I as the cause of the "gigantic epidemics of neuroses" (Fischer-Homberger), and this mass phenomenon of shell shock as the reason for Freud's new interest in the old concept of shock,[39] it is possible to establish a relatively direct connection between that novel technical quality and Freud's reorientation. One might say, perhaps a little too loosely, that the period of peace in which Freud developed the sexual etiology of neurosis favored the psychologization and attendant abstraction of trauma concept, and that it took the very real mass experience of trauma of the World War to recall the original concept and render it interesting again. Without the experiential background of that war, Freud's theory of the destruction of the stimulus shield by great amounts of energy would be as hard to imagine as the nineteenth-century theories of "railway spine" and traumatic neurosis would be without the railroad and its accidents.

That Freud's new orientation is essentially based on a novel quality in warfare technology is not surprising, considering the important effects that military technology has had on civilian life, economy, and the human psyche in the last five hundred years. The emergence of the shock concept from military life, and its subsequent application to civilian cases, parallel the way in which the military developments of early modern Europe repeatedly anticipate forms and symptoms that later reappear in the civilian life of the period of the industrial revolution.

Excursion:
The History of Shock

That Freud in his later years developed his concept of shock and his theory of the stimulus shield on the basis of the mass phenomenon of shell shock during World War I, would seem a direct continuation of the history of *shock,* as such, which is, in large measure, part of military history.

According to the Oxford English Dictionary, the word *shock* carries since the seventeenth century the connotations of blow, strike, concussion, in a material-physical as well as a borrowed psychological sense. The original meaning, first noted in the sixteenth century, is a military one. "First adapted as a military term," says the OED, it denotes "the encounter of an armed force with the enemy in charge or onset; also, the encounter of two mounted warriors or justlers charging one another."

The French word *choc* receives the same meaning about the same time. Hans Delbrück quotes Field Marshal Blaise Monluc describing the encounter of the opposing troops in the battle of Ceresole, 1544: "Tous ceux des premiers rangs, soit du *choc* ou des coups, furent portés par terre." (All those in the front lines had fallen to the ground, either from *shock* or blows.)[1]

Before the word receives this military meaning in English and French, it denotes, in the Germanic languages, "a pile of sheaves," later the exact number sixty; but even then *Shock* is "used more generally, as a concept of indefinite amount . . . mostly in regard to crowds of people and hordes of soldiers." (Grimm, *Deutsches Wörterbuch.*)

According to Trübner,[2] the word *shock* entered the Romance languages via the Middle Dutch *schokken,* meaning to collide. A possible explanation for the process by which this general concept of colliding became a specifically military form can be found in the work of Lynn White, who describes the

145

New Combat Capability through the Stirrup.

"The stirrup, by giving lateral support in addition to the front and back support offered by pommel and cantle, effectively welded horse and rider into a single fighting unit capable of a violence without precedent." (Lynn White).

From: Max Jähns, *Atlas zur Geschichte des Kriegswesens von der Urzeit bis zum Ende des 16. Jahrhunderts.* Berlin 1878.

evolution of a new mode of battle, "mounted shock combat," as the result of the technical innovation of the stirrup in the first half of the eighth century:

> The stirrup, by giving lateral support in addition to the front and back support offered by pommel and cantle, effectively welded horse and rider into a single fighting unit capable of a violence without precedent. The fighter's hand no longer delivered the blow: it merely guided it. The stirrup thus replaced human energy with animal power, and immensely increased the warrior's ability to damage his enemy. Immediately, without preparatory steps, it made possible mounted shock combat, a revolutionary new way of doing battle.[3]

Here we have the beginning of that development toward the consolidation of energies that will later become the military phenomenon of shock. The nature of that shock consists in creating a situation where it is no longer the individual muscular force of the single combatant that counts, but the fusion of his individual power with one extraneous to it.

If the fusion of the energies of horseman and steed into a powerful new force behind the lance is the first decisive step towards the development of military shock, the second step occurs with the rise of modern armies, at the

146

From: Leonhart Fronsperger, *Von Kayserlichen Kriegsrechten Malefitz und Schulhandeln/Ordnung und Regiment/sampt der selbigen und anderen hoch oder niderigen Befelch, etc.* Frankfurt am Mayn 1565.

beginning of the modern age. Sombart, who calls these armies one of the most important motive forces behind the early development of capitalism, gives an excellent description of the differences between companies of knights on horseback and modern mass armies, demonstrating therein how the military shock is no longer executed by the rider-horse unit, but by the new mass unit of the army. Sombart says that the modern army is characterized by "its working by means of its size, being a large band of warriors combined into one tactical unit. When you had a thousand knights in the field, they still did not constitute one unified mass: they were a thousand individual warriors, fighting together. But a thousand modern cavalrymen collaborate to deliver *one blow,* when they charge."[4] (Italics added.)

The basic principle of this new tactical organization is that the warriors no longer do battle individually but as parts of the new combat machine; the squadron (Geviert Haufen), developed in the fourteenth century, is frequently compared to a machine.[5] As Delbrück says, it "forms the self-contained tactical body whose parts are used to finding and understanding their strength in exactly that containment and cohesion."[6] Sombart, who sees in this new military form an analogy to other modern capitalistic forms of the division of labor, recognizes that it puts an end to the personal development of the individual warrior, because the individuals now joined into one military body are merely

Square formations in 16th century combat.

The precise rectangle formed by lances is characteristic of this contemporary representation. There is no correspondence between the number of lances in this "forest of lances" and the number of soldiers who carry them. These formations actually look like square shocks of grain: in Germanic, "shock" means sheaf or bundle of grain. Looking closely at the illustration, we see that in positioning, the soldiers are not at all disciplined but seem to be strewn at random. The order and discipline of the formation is depicted solely by the lances.

147

the executive organ of an authority exterior to themselves: "Thus the functions of (spiritual) leadership and (physical) action have become separated and are performed by different persons, while they had previously been conjoined in one and the same person."[7]

In the single combat of warriors of the era of chivalry, the combatants relate to each other so intensely that the event can be seen as a form of dance:[8] while it ends with the death of one of these warriors, it creates a highly animated relationship between the participants, and also a series of functional body motions. By contrast, the modern body of soldiers functions according to an abstract discipline that has nothing to do with the fighting *per se,* but merely serves the cohesion of that body. Its function, according to Sombart, "is to create, by mechanical means, the connection between leading and executive organs."[9]

Thus we see how in the creation of the modern military, there is a mechanization of the "human material" analogous to the mechanization in the more or less simultaneously emerging process of mass manufacture. Sombart: "I believe that we have not yet given sufficient credit to the influence that the development of the modern army has had on the entire culture and on its economic life in particular. During the decisive seventeenth century we experience the fragmentation and demolition of that natural man who still dominated the years of the Renaissance."[10]

As significant as the analogy between military and economic organization is, we are mainly interested in the fundamental difference that exists between the two. In the economic realm, the new mechanized collectivity of manufacture, and later of industrial production, appears, as it were, peacefully. It is productive and it reproduces itself linearly. In the military, on the other hand, the purpose of the mechanical organization is the annihilation of the enemy, the performance of the military clash — the initial meaning of *shock.* The new military organization concretizes the entirely specific sense of the word: the clash of two bodies of troops, each of which represents a new unified concentration of energy by means of the consolidation of a number of warriors into one deindividualized and mechanized unit. What is new in this military clash is its unheard-of violence (due to the concentration of energy) as well as the degree of attrition of its elements; the latter occurs in direct proportion to the degree of energy concentration. Again, we encounter what we have called, in the context of technical accidents, the "falling height" of a mechanical apparatus: the greater the degree of concentration/mechanization of the two colliding bodies of troops, the more violent the shock of their clash, the greater the attrition of the elements that constitute the whole. The definition of *shock* in the OED relates to this military clash situation: "A sudden and violent blow, impact, or collision, *tending to overthrow or produce internal oscillation in a body subjected to it.*" (Italics added.)

The modern organization of armies, i.e., the gathering of deindividualized warriors into a single body, caused the concept of shock to become identified with an event involving the discharge of violence.

The initial development of the new military form began within the framework of traditional weapons technology. In the seventeenth century, the standard weaponry of armies did not yet consist of firearms but of pikes and halberds. Only in the course of the eighteenth century do hand firearms become standard issue in the European armies. They do not only strengthen the tendency to mechanize the military units but raise that mechanization to a new level. This role of the hand firearms can be compared to the one played by the steam engine in the industrial revolution: it is the continuation of existing developments on a new technical level. The use of simple offensive weapons such as pikes required certain craftsmanlike skills on the part of their users, whereas the new firearms were easily mastered mechanical tools. They are the technical counterpart to the already firmly established mechanics of troop organization. "This reform of warfare," Feld comments on the transition from pikes and halberds to firearms in the eighteenth century, "was analogous to the change, in industrial production, from a craft to an assembly line mode."[11]

Kunstibibliotek Berline, Sammlung Lipperheide.

The new quality of combat with hand firearms consists of the final loss of a "personal" relationship between combatants such as was still inherent in battle waged with pikes. The characteristic trait of the new method of fighting is the *salvo,* the collective, unaimed discharge of firearms by the entire unit. Delbrück discusses this new tactic of the eighteenth century: "Due to the great inaccuracy of the single shot, the decision was made to forego taking aim or training soldiers in marksmanship: effectiveness was sought by means of collective fire repeated as rapidly as possible, the salvo, delivered on command. While Frederic, [II, of Prussia] still ordered his troops not to fire too hastily — "because the fellow has to look and see what he's shooting at" — later orders even *prohibited* such deliberate taking of aim. The main stress now was as on split-second timing of the salvo so that it would sound like one shot."[12]

Mechanized Warfare: Firing Salvos.

The emphasis is not on aiming at individuals — the troop formations make this impossible — but on the psychological shock produced when many soldiers fall from formation at once. Mechanical synchronization is the principle of the salvo, which, according to military handbooks of the eighteenth century, should sound as a single shot.

The salvo tactic already presages the later psychological significance of the shock concept. The desired effect of the salvo, the *simultaneous* slaying of as many soldiers as possible within the closed ranks of the enemy unit, is seen quite consciously as a psychological one leading to the demoralization of the enemy. In paragraph 178 of Scharnhorst's *Taktik* the salvo is preferred over single fire "because ten men falling to the ground at the same time will cause a battalion to retreat sooner than fifty that drop at different times and in different places."[13]

We see how the original military concept of shock changes its meaning after the introduction of hand firearms. The force of the clash loses its concrete physical manifestation. The collision is no longer performed directly by the participating military units but occurs at a distance, by means of the salvo.

Quite obviously connected with this military-technical and tactical change is the additional significance the concept of shock receives in the eighteenth century. It no longer applies only to the military clash but also to the consequences it causes, by means of the use of firearms, in the organisms of the affected soldiers. In Henri-François Le Dran's *Treatise, or Reflections, on the Use of Firearms* (1743), an English translation of the French military surgeon's account, we find this: "The Bullett . . . thrown by the Gun Powder acquires such rapid force that the whole Animal Machine participates in the Shock and Agitation."[14] Groeningen, in *Über den Shock* (1885), describes this alteration or enlargement of the concept, although he does so without mentioning the initial military meaning of the word: "Towards the middle of the eighteenth century the common demotic English word for blow, strike, etc., the word shock . . . had acquired next to its active meaning a passive one, and even in medical nomenclature shock no longer describes only the blow but also its consequence, the concussion, and the pathological general state of the victim caused by it."[15]

The fact that a certain state that occurs after being wounded by a firearm is discovered in the eighteenth century and described by the word shock would seem to indicate that this state has to do with the evolution of army organization and military technology. One can assume that the mechanization of combat, which gives the individual combatant a consciousness different from that involved in medieval modes, does not only make that individual behave differently while engaged in combat but also causes different reactions in him when he receives a wound. A wound caused during a medieval duel is essentially different from one caused by a salvo of firearms. The intense relationship between the duelists may be seen as one of alert expectation. The individual combatants can see from exactly which direction the possible wound may be caused: they are, as it were, well prepared for it. From the eighteenth century on, such a state of readiness no longer exists. The wound caused by mass fire occurs suddenly, invisibly; it comes "out of nowhere." (The earlier specific state of readiness should be distinguished from the generalized readiness of a soldier who is aware that he is in a war and that he can get wounded or even killed: the latter is not an alert expectation but a dull routine state of mind.)

The wound shock discovered by military medicine in the eighteenth century is obviously not only a consequence of the lesion itself but is equally a result of the specific situation involved in receiving wounds caused by firearms, i.e., from the lack of effective readiness. Observations made by military surgeons in the nineteenth century seem to confirm this conclusion. "The wounded man," says Pirogoff, "does not experience the wounding as such but rather feels the concussion or a shock similar to an electric one."[16] The receptive situation can even be so unexpected and diffuse that the wound is not noticed at first. Groeningen gives an example: "McLeod tells us about an officer who had lost both his legs below the knee and only noticed it as he was trying to get up."[17] Rose clarifies the connection between lack of expectation and "unnoticed" firearm wounds: "Most warriors do not feel their wounds at all, not only because of the rapidity of the damage but rather because of the total exertion of all their psychological powers towards other goals. Every sensation requires a degree of attention, however small."[18]

It would be outside of the framework of this discussion to try to ascertain whether the mechanization of the modern military, and the introduction of firearms in particular, has actually altered human organic reaction upon the receipt of a serious wound so that the new reaction is a more serious wound shock than was previously the case.[19] Within our context, the main interest lies in the psychic state of receptivity before getting wounded, and this state obviously has changed radically due to the organizational and technical innovations of the military in the past five hundred years.

The lack of readiness is what connects the military-medical concept of shock with the later psychological concept of shock developed in the wake of railroad accidents and makes the earlier concept the forerunner of that later one. The history of shock, its origin in military innovations (e.g., stirrup, mass army, firearms), conveys its own modernity: this consists of the fact that *shock* no longer describes any simple blow or strike but a violent act compounded from the concentration of many individual elements. *Now* shock *describes the kind of sudden and powerful event of violence that disrupts the continuity of an artificially/ mechanically created motion or situation, and also the subsequent state of derangement.* The precondition for this is a highly developed general state of dominance over nature, both technically (military example: firearms) and psychically (military example: troop discipline). The degree of control over nature and the violence of the collapse of that control, in shock, are proportionate: the more finely meshed the web of mechanization, discipline, division of labor, etc., the more catastrophic the collapse when it is disrupted from within or without.

The history of modern armies demonstrates this proportional relationship between control of nature and shock so clearly because the destructive application of productive energy is an integral part of military history, as opposed to the situation in manufacture and industrial production. Not only did the new capitalistic productivity manifest itself first in the European armies but it also manifested itself most clearly there, in the negativity of destruction. The level that the development of the productive forces had reached became visible as "falling height" in the military clash. In a sense, the technical and organizational development of the military is a paradigm for the simultaneous or immediately subsequent analogous development of the civilian productive forces, and the military shock is a paradigm for what threatens man in the event of the collapse of those productive forces.

10. Stimulus Shield; or, The Industrialized Consciousness

These discoveries [i.e., the new technical devices such as the railroad] ... bend our senses and our organs in a way that causes us to believe that our physical and moral constitution is no longer in rapport with them. Science, as it were, proposes that we should enter a new world that has not been made for us. We would like to venture into it; but it does not take us long to recognize that it requires a constitution we lack and organs we do not have. [1]

G. Claudin, 1858

It is now easy to perceive why the originally military and military-medical concept of shock experienced a revival in the nineteenth century in the context of the railroad and its accidents. The railroad relates to the coach and horses, as the modern mass army relates to the medieval army of knights (and as manufacture and industry do to craftsmanship). In the railroad journey, the traditional experience of time and space is demolished the way the individual experience of battle of the Middle Ages is abolished in the modern army (and the individual craft activity is abolished in manufacturing and industrial production). The early descriptions of the train journey as an experience of being "shot" through space (with the train as projectile) no longer seem merely accidentally associated with the military realm. Structurally, the train passenger is analogous to the soldier in the mass army in being conditioned by the unit in which he functions as an integral part. The conditioning of the individual in a military context can now be seen as the earliest model of all subsequent and similar conditioning in the civilian economic world. In the modern army individuals are for the first time mechanized, or even subsumed, into an organizational scheme that is completely abstract and exterior to them. In the further history of the modern age, this condition becomes increasingly common in all spheres of life.

We have seen how the nineteenth-century travelers gradually get accustomed to what at first seemed frightening: the demolition of traditional time-space relationships and the dissolution of reality. The travelers develop new modes of behavior and perception, forms in which the new experiential content extends itself. "Panoramic vision" is one of these innovations, as is the new general consciousness of time and space based on train schedules, and the novel activity of reading while traveling.

These new modes of behavior and perception enable the traveler to lose the fear that he formerly felt towards the new conveyance. The process by which human beings get accustomed to new technical means that initially evoke mistrust and fear can be characterized as a process of repression of fear, or, more neutrally, as a diminution of fear. In the early descriptions of the railroad, open fear or subliminal apprehension is evident as a fear of derailment, of velocity, of collisions. People used to the more leisurely technology of the previous era were still unable to comprehend that it was now possible to travel safely in something that seemed like an enormous grenade. These fears have an actual technological base, as railroad technology in its first phase still suffers from "gaps," or infantile maladies, which are real enough sources of danger. In that phase, technology still has one foot in the realm of obsolete forms and the other in that of the new form of production. This interim situation is conducive to fear, but it does not last long. The conveyance is perfected, it works ever more smoothly, and its disquieting idiosyncrasies are, if not abolished totally, at least ameliorated, or "upholstered".[1a] The sinister aspect of the machinery that first was so evident and frightening gradually disappears, and with this disappearance, fear wanes and is replaced by a feeling of security based on familiarity. The traveler who sits reading his newspaper or novel instead of worrying about the ever-present possibility of derailment or collision no doubt feels secure. His attention has become diverted from the technological situation in which he finds himself and directed to an entirely independent object. One might say that he feels secure because he has forgotten how disquieting the technological conveyance still is, how tremendous and potentially destructive are the amounts of energy it contains. This forgetfulness becomes possible because the technology itself helps it along by eliminating or obfuscating all its initially anxiety-producing manifestations (vibration, mechanical jolts, etc.).

Every airplane traveler experiences this process today, and reremembers it, while anxiously and attentively observing the mighty vibrations of the machine in its takeoff phase, then relaxing entirely during the flight, and then again, when it comes time to land, attentively listening to the technological noises to detect any irregularity that might herald catastrophe.

In their empirical psychological study "Zur Psychologie des Sicherheitsgurtes" (On the psychology of the safety belt), H. J. Berger, G. Bliersbach, and R. G. Dellen pursue the question why the introduction of the safety belt in automobiles meets with considerable resistance on the part of the driving public. In contrast to all the other manual motions required to start and drive the car, the one of fastening the seat belt has not so far been assimilated by the drivers of automobiles: ". . . for the majority of drivers of private vehicles, the safety belt appears as an *unsafety* belt. Instead of reducing anxiety, it actualizes a great deal of it simply by the fact that it has to be fastened time and again" (italics in original).

This is so because the latent danger is permanently present in the safety belt, so very visibly that it cannot be repressed: "The safety belt *confronts* the driver with the actual dangers of traffic on the road, and he has to come to terms with them whether he wants to or not. Feeling the safety belt against his body, the driver is constantly reminded of the possibility of an accident, since that is what the belt is for" (italics in original). "Most persons tested, when asked for spontaneous associations with the belt, came up with the images of injury or death."

While the safety belt thus inherently perpetuates the fear of accident, which makes it impossible to get used to, the air bag is a popular safety device. The reason is its invisibility. This enables the driver to forget/repress the danger of accident. Thus it appears to be a modern version of train upholstery: while the seat upholstery in nineteenth-century first-class compartments ameliorates the technological vibrations and thus aids the travelers in forgetting their fear of the technology, the air bag serves an analogous function without even being visible. It provides actual safety from the results of a collision, and by its invisibility it ensures that the fear of an accident is not perpetuated.[1b]

It is obvious how closely such a feeling of safety is joined to the technology upon which it is based. The technology creates an artificial environment which people become used to as a kind of second nature. If the technological base collapses, the feeling of habituation and security collapses with it. What we called the "falling height" of technological constructs (destructivity of accident proportionate to technical level of construct) can also be applied to the human consequences of the technological accident. The web of perceptual and behavioral forms that came into being due to the technological construct is torn to the degree that the construct itself collapses. The higher its technological level, the more denaturalized the consciousness that has become used to it, and the more destructive the collapse of both.

In the technological accident and the shock released by it, the fear that has been repressed by the improvement in technology reappears to take its revenge. It becomes obvious that the original fear of the new technology has by no means dissolved into nothingness during the period of habituation, but that it has only been forgotten, repressed, one could even say, reified[2] as a feeling of safety. It then appears in a new form — as it were, from behind the victim's back — as fright. If the original anxiety anticipated the imagined or actual danger that emanated from the new technology, and protected people to a certain degree from actually occurring accidents by creating an attitude of readiness, the later fright works in the opposite direction. The disposition that has enjoyed a sense of security which is then proven to have been spurious is attacked suddenly and unexpectedly by that fright.

Freud deals with this distinction between anxiety and fright and proceeds to draw far-reaching conclusions from it. It is particularly interesting that Freud discusses these in connection with his theory of the stimulus shield, in *Beyond the Pleasure Principle,* the work in which he develops the theory which originated in his immediate reponse to the context of World War I and its neuroses.

"Anxiety," says Freud, "describes a particular state of expecting the danger or preparing for it, even though it may be an unknown one. . . . 'Fright', however, is the name we give to the state a person gets into when he has run into danger without being prepared for it; it emphasizes the factor of surprise. I do not believe anxiety can produce a traumatic neurosis. There is something about anxiety that protects its subject against fright and so against fright-neuroses."[3] The precondition for fright, Freud specifies, "is the lack of any preparedness for anxiety."[4] Thus he can be seen as working in the tradition of the *psychological* explanation of the traumatic neurosis: for him, too, the moment of fright is decisive, that sudden, violent, and unexpected accident *experience* that the psyche finds itself unable to deal with.

Yet Freud goes far beyond the traditional explanation, in his theory of the stimulus shield. This theory, an explanation of the conditions necessary for the development of traumatic shock, is described by Freud himself, very cautiously, as "speculation, often far-fetched speculation." Walter Benjamin, in his writings on Baudelaire, has demonstrated that we can find in it a very useful suggestion for the understanding of what modern civilization does to human consciousness.[5]

After we have described what kinds of traces the railroad has left on the actual and psychic landscape of the nineteenth century, we can elevate these observations to a more general level by applying Freud's theory. It provides a possible answer to the question how the industrialization of travel is reflected in the traveler's psychic structure — or, more broadly speaking, as in one of Marx's well-known formulations, how "production not only creates an object for the subject but also a subject for the object."[6]

To illustrate the relationship between consciousness and the outside world, Freud reduces the elements of the relationship to the highest possible degree of abstraction:

> "Let us picture a living organism in its most simplified possible form as an undifferentiated vesicle of a substance that is susceptible to stimulation. Then the surface turned towards the external world will from its very situation be differentiated and will serve as an organ for receiving stimuli. . . . It would be easy to suppose, then, that as a result of the ceaseless impact of external stimuli on the surface of the vesicle, its substance to a certain depth may have become permanently modified, so that excitatory processes run a different course in it from what they run in the deeper layers. A crust would thus be formed which would at last have been so thoroughly 'baked through' by stimulation that it would present the most favourable possible conditions for the reception of stimuli *and become incapable of any further modification.*"[7] (Italics added.)

What Freud develops here with his model of the small vesicle, we can imbue with historical concreteness in tracing the history of the development of railroad perception. One of the essential new *stimuli* of the train journey is its speed, which expresses itself as dispersed perception of foreground objects, as the feeling of the annihilation of space and time. This new stimulus at first merely irritates the traveler, who is still accustomed to the old velocity of the coach. Yet gradually everything connected with the new velocity becomes psychically assimilated: as Freud would say, the stimuli burn their way into the skin layer of consciousness and "its substance to a certain in depth may . . . become permanently modified." The train passenger of the later nineteenth century who sits reading his book thus has a thicker layer of that skin that the earlier traveler who cannot even think about reading because the journey still is, for him, a space-time adventure that engages his entire sensorium. (When the later traveler stops reading and looks out the compartment window, he does so with a gaze that is quite different from his predecessor's. The development of what we have called the panoramic vision perhaps demonstrates most clearly how the "baking" of the stimuli into the skin layer of consciousness changes it. A comparison between the traditional and the panoramic vision demonstrates which technological developments the latter has assimilated.)

Freud's conclusion that the skin layer modified by the impact of stimuli "has become incapable of any further modification" seems an important one. It indicates that the stimuli, once they have been psychically assimilated, determine consciousness and perception to the extent that stimuli of a quality entirely different from the assimilated ones no longer register, or at least not adequately. Once the traveler has reorganized his perception so that it becomes panoramic, he no longer has an eye for the impressions of, say, a coach trip, no more than preindustrial travelers like Ruskin are capable of panoramic vision, as their skin layer has been similarly conditioned, once and for all, and is "incapable of any further modification." (An analogy from military history: the skin layer/consciousness of the soldier in the modern mass army has been so deeply conditioned by the stimuli specific to modern battle organization that this soldier would find himself totally helpless in the battle situation of the chivalrous duel — not for reasons of weapons technology, but for psychic ones.)

The creation of this skin layer by the effects of outer stimuli is, indeed, the development of what Freud calls the stimulus shield. It exemplifies a function of consciousness that is, according to Freud, just as vital as the reception of stimuli: the ability to ward off stimuli. Freud says of the small vesicle:

This little fragment of living substance is suspended in the middle of an external world charged with the most powerful energies; and it would be killed by the stimulation emanating from these if it were not provided with a protective *shield against stimuli*. It acquires the shield in this way: its outermost surface *ceases to have the structure proper to living matter, becomes to some degree inorganic* and thence-forward functions as a special envelope or membrane resistant to stimuli. In consequence, the energies of the external world are able to pass into the next underlying layers, which have remained living, with only a fragment of their original intensity; and these layers can devote themselves, behind the protective shield, to the reception of the amounts of stimulus which have been allowed through it. By its death, the outer layer has saved all the deeper ones from a similar fate — unless, that is to say, stimuli reach it which are so strong that they break through the protective shield."[8] (First italics in original; second italics added.)

Freud's explanation of the traumatic neurosis assumes such a possibility, an onslaught of stimuli powerful enough to pierce the shield: "We describe as 'traumatic' an excitations from outside which are powerful enough to break through the protective shield. It seems to me that the concept of trauma necessarily implies a connection of this kind with a breach in an otherwise efficacious barrier against stimuli."[9]

Thus relating trauma to a prevention mechanism that becomes shattered in the traumatic event, Freud advances the theory of traumatic neurosis by an important step. The concept of the stimulus shield proves to be a suitable model for what one might call the formation of *an inorganic protective layer due to civilization.* The strength or density of the stimulus shield indicates the strength or density of the stimuli that it receives, and, again, the strength or density of these stimuli is an indicator of the prevailing historical stage of civilization.

Although Freud's vesicle model was intended as a pure abstraction for the demonstration of psychic processes, its vocabulary does have immediate, specifically modern connotations. An outside world "charged with the most powerful energies" cannot be all that timeless. That Freud's model is based on an experience of modernity, even if that experience is not subjectively known to the author, can be demonstrated by a glance at Georg Simmel's essay, written around twenty years earlier, "The Metropolis and Mental Life." Describing the fate of the psyche in metropolitan life, Simmel arrives at conclusions that are remarkably similar to Freud's. One only has to substitute concepts — Freud's "stimulus shield" for Simmel's "intelligence", Freud's "deeper psychic layers" for Simmel's "heart" — to realize that the description concerns the same event. The urban dweller distinguishes himself from the small-town or rural person in that his intelligence — according to Simmel — is more developed due to the many impressions/stimuli that it has to deal with. The intelligence, however, "has its locus in the transparent, conscious, higher layers of the psyche; it is the most adaptable of our inner forces." And furthermore: Thus the metropolitan type of man — which, of course, exists in a thousand individual variants — *develops an organ protecting him against the threatening currents and discrepancies of his external environment which would uproot him.* He reacts with his head instead of his heart. In this an increased awareness assumes the psychic prerogative. Metropolitan life, thus, underlies a heightened awareness and a predominance of intelligence in metropolitan man. The reaction to metropolitan phenomena is shifted *to that organ which is least sensitive and quite remote from the depth of the personality.*[10] (Italics added.)

Freud's model is so well suited to the description of the psychic process of civilization because it demonstrates the relationship between subject and outside world to be a synthesis of both. The stimulus shield is subject as well as outside world in that it *is* outer world (i.e., stimuli of that world) assimilated into the subject, absorbed and interiorized by it.[11]

On the other hand, the stimulus shield model is so abstract that it can be applied to all possible kinds of stimuli: to technically caused ones (i.e., velocity) as well as cultural ones (laws, customs, etc.). Thus the "civilizing process" described by Norbert Elias can be understood as the formation of a stimulus shield, just as we have understood the process of travel by rail to be one. The "stimuli" that the individual becoming civilized in Elias' sense absorbs during the civilizing process are the social rules that are interiorized by the courtly upper strata in the seventeenth and eighteenth centuries. A violation or breaking of these rules is commonly described as "shocking": it is the shattering of a stimulus shield of convention — an analogous event to "shock" in military clash or railroad accident, with the sole difference that the tissue torn in the former consists of interiorized forms of social intercourse and not of interiorized technically caused stimuli.

Thus we have to distinguish between two different formations of stimulus shields or psychic civilizing processes, occurring at different levels: on one hand, interiorization of social rules, on the other, interiorization of technologically caused stimuli. As qualitatively different as the sources are, their stimulus effect on the psychic structure is comparable. Social rules and technologically produced stimuli structure the individual in a similar manner, regularizing, regulating, shaping him according to their inherent laws.

Conceptually, we can comprehend the distinctness and the similarity of both these sources of the civilizing process by describing them as external and internal domination of nature. Technology is an expression of external domination: by means of technological constructs (machines) nature's powers and materials become disciplined to produce cultural, i.e., economic achievements. The social rules are constructs designed to serve internal domination: they structure the individual in such a way that he fits into the social context and performs constructively within it.

The technological constructs affect the natural forces in the same way social rules affect the individuals; furthermore, the constructs of external domination themselves demonstrate progress in terms of increasing self-discipline, as do the individuals who internalize the social rules. Let us compare how Elias describes the process of human self-discipline to Franz Reuleaux's description of the corresponding process in the development of machines. Elias: "The behavior of an increasing number of people has to be co-ordinated, the web of actions organized ever more precisely and rigorously, in order for the individual action to perform its social function within that web. The individual is forced to regulate his behavior in an ever more differentiated, ever more regular and stable fashion."[12]

According to Reuleaux the progress of machine technology consists in the increasing elimination of *play*. Play signifies the relation of the elements of a machine to each other. The more primitive the technology, the less attuned the parts of the machine to each other, the greater the degree of play. The more perfected the technology, the less play the individual parts have in regard to each other. "I am convinced," says Reuleaux in 1875, "that the cogwheel working entirely without play will be the rule within a few years."[13] Creating an almost poetic image, Reuleaux describes how the increasing density of the machine grasps the forces of nature ever more firmly: "As waterwheels have become perfected, the water jets left to the free play of forces have disappeared; the Strauber wheel [which Reuleaux previously says is technically so deficient that the propelling stream of water still washes over it like a natural waterfall] has developed into the smoothly and quietly running turbine, which hardly produces any of that spray and diffusion of small water particles. . . . The cosmic freedom of the natural phenomenon becomes transformed by the machine into an order and law that outside forces of an ordinary kind are unable to disrupt."[14]

Medieval Machinery.
Design of a sawing machine, designed on the principle of perpetual motion (thirteenth century). The individual components of the apparatus are so loosely connected, so poorly synchronized, that we can hardly speak of a machine in the modern sense at all. The parts are not only constructed from wood, but they also clearly show the natural contours of the tree.

From: Franz Maria Feldhaus, *Die Maschine im Leben der Völker*, Stuttgart 1954

Machinery in the Seventeenth Century.
Although the mechanical saw pictured here is still built of wood, it no longer betrays the traces of natural growth, but is used as a neutral and disciplined construction material. Compared to the medieval apparatus, the "play" of the individual parts has been significantly reduced. The water wheel transmits the force of the millstream to the actual saw by means of a system of *gears* which was already very complex.

From: Heinrich Zeising, Theatri Machinarum, Leipzig 1613-58.

We return to the civilizing process understood as the formation of a stimulus shield. After making the distinction between culturally and technologically caused stimuli and relating it to the distinction between internal and external domination of nature, we still have to demonstrate why, in our opinion, the technological stimuli deserve at least as much attention as agents in the civilizing of psychic life as the cultural "stimuli" of social forms, which Elias has described in such a magnificent manner. The answer is simple. The technologically produced stimuli, as signals emanating from the external domination of nature, are *more immediate* expressions of the productive forces than are the social rules; like all ideological forms, the latter develop as functions of producttive forces, but only through a complex process. It might not be equally useful in regard to all periods of human history to describe the civilizing process of consciousness in terms so closely related to the development of technology; however, it does seem appropriate to an epoch as permeated and even overwhelmed by technology as that of the industrial revolution. Marx's remark that production not only provides an object for the subject but also provides a subject for the object would appear applicable, and it ought to be possible to describe what an "industrialized consciousness" is.

11. The Railroad Station: Entrance to the City

We find ourselves in the gigantic vestibule of
a large city, with millions streaming into and
out of it. The space encloses thousands of
people in any single minute, and then dis-
perses them in all directions in the next.
— Richard Lucae, 1869

In the preindustrial era, overland traffic was confined to the space of the
landscape through which it proceeded, and this remained the case even at its
destination, i.e., the city. The stagecoach related to the city in exactly the same
way that it related to the open country. The stagecoach depot was located in the
center of the city, usually adjacent to an inn that was named after it (e.g., Zur
Post, The Coach and Horses etc.), and thus was practically indistinguishable
from the surrounding buildings in architectural terms. The stagecoach was
completely integrated into urban life.

The railroad, however, terminates that intimate relationship between the
means of transport and its destination. The railroad depots and stations are as
different from the old coach depots, as the train from the coach and the rails
from the highway. The railroad station is not an integral part of the city: it is
located outside the traditional city walls, and for a long time it remains an alien
appendage. The immediately adjoining parts of the city soon are stigmatized as
being industrial and proletarian: they become the disreputable "railroad district" (the "wrong side of the tracks"). There is a remark in Perdonnet's handbook — in its third edition (1865), not in the first edition of 1855 — which
shows that this was an unexpected development. The rubric is, "La Répulsion
des habitants des villes par les gares" (The repulsion felt by the city dwellers

161

Stagecoach Station and Hotel, Early Nineteenth Century.

New York Public Library, Picture Collection.

towards the railroad stations): "It was long assumed, erroneously, that the railroad stations would become points of attraction for the city dwellers. Far from it; today we see them trying to stay as far away as possible from those noisy centers. Only rarely do the hotels located too close to the stations prove successful."[1]

If the surroundings of the railroad station appear tainted by industry, then the station itself must have an extremely noticeable industrial character. As an architectural type, it clearly and exclusively belongs to the category of typically nineteenth-century steel and glass edifices that have been termed "traffic buildings."[2]

The *traffic* function finds its architectural expression in a far more immediate way in the railroad station than it does in the other types of steel and glass architecture. In the market halls, exhibition pavilions, arcades, department stores, etc., the traffic of goods takes place in a stationary fashion, in the form of storage, display, etc; in the railroad station, the human traffic literally flows through actively, in the form of travelers streaming in and out of the trains. Unlike the other "traffic buildings" of this period, the railroad station appears as a palpably industrial building, in which the railroad's transportation industry is perceptible to all the senses.

Nevertheless, the industrial aspect is only one of the railroad station's characteristics. The metropolitan passenger terminal that we are exclusively considering is not merely a utilitarian industrial construct of steel and glass. The total installation is curiously dual: first we have the actual train hall, built out of steel and glass, and then the reception building, erected out of stone.

162

Arrival of A Stagecoach in the American West, 1870's.

New York Public Library, Picture Collection.

The former faces the open country, the latter, the city. This division into two entirely different realms, once aptly apostrophized as *mi-usine, mi-palais* (half factory, half palace)[3], is, as Alfred Gotthold Meyer notes, a novelty in the history of architecture: "Architecturally, these are two entirely separate worlds. Heretofore, architecture has failed to create another species of building in which one single edifice combines two main parts that are formally totally different as is the case in our great railroad stations that conjoin the stone-built reception buildings with the steel and glass halls of the actual *railroad terminal*."[4]

This two-facedness of the metropolitan railroad station is the result of two decades of railroad expansion. The train halls are not built out of steel and glass until the early 1850s; when this finally happens, it is, no doubt, partly due to the European success of London's Crystal Palace of 1851, which generally furthered the cause of commercial glass architecture.[5] The decisive factor, however, arose out of the development of the railroad itself, which demanded new technical solutions even for the terminals. In the 1830s, when railway traffic was still restricted to bilateral connections between cities, the dimensions of the stations were modest. Most stations consisted of a single train platform, separate buildings for arrivals and departures, and an overall roofing that was often a plain wooden structure.[6]

As the railroad network grew denser in the 1840s, traffic put greater demands on the terminals. A greater number of tracks now converged on them, requiring a greater number of platforms. These had to be connected with each other in order to enable the passengers to transfer from one train to

163

a.

the next. And finally, the entire, now considerably enlarged, structure had to be roofed. The solution is a new type of building with a midway connecting the platforms and with a train hall constructed out of steel and glass.

From the mid-nineteenth century on, this kind of station becomes a characteristic feature of the great European cities. Situated on the periphery of the inner city, these stations, as Meyer describes them, "receive traffic from the city in their vestibules, conduct it to the midway in the main building, and thus distribute it by means of individual access platforms to the trains. Simultaneously, an equally intense volume of traffic proceeds in the opposite direction, from the rails to the city, at first cohesive, then divided and dispersed."[7]

Thus, the station functions as a kind of gateway which has to connect two very different kinds of traffic and traffic space with one another: the traffic space of the city, and that of the railroad. One part of it, the neoclassical stone building, belongs to the city; the other part, the steel and glass construct, is a pure function of the railroad's "industrial" side.

By means of this two-facedness, the railroad station's function as a gateway finds its architectural expression. As the departing traveler proceeds from the city, through the reception building, to the train hall, traversing these qualitatively different spaces, he experiences a process of expansion of space, one might even say, of industrialization of space. He leaves the urban space of the city (in the 1850s, still relatively reassuring) and enters the station's space, which in turn prepares him for the actual industrial space of the railroad. Conversely, the arriving traveler goes through a process of spatial reduction. The boundless and shapeless space of the railroad journey is first delimited by the hall in which the train arrives, and then reduced further in the traditional stone architecture of the reception building which provides a continous transition to the urban spaces of the city.

This function of the station as a spatial gateway is what Richard Lucae has in mind when he describes the different effects that the train hall has on departing and arriving passengers. Lucae says that the space of the train hall,

b.   c.

"with one of its sides wide open to the world, may, by contrast with the closed buildings of the city, create an unpleasant or perhaps even frightening impression. But to one who arrives from outside, the gigantic hall with its solid stone enclosure and its wide-spreading protective roof, may, despite the enormous dimensions, seem positively cozy after the limitless space through which the train wheels have been carrying him for miles and miles."[8]

The neoclassical character of the facades of the station buildings is quite certainly another expression of the typical nineteenth-century desire to disguise the industrial aspect of things by means of ornamentation.[9] And yet, unlike, say, the exhibition halls of the Second Empire, whose stucco facades had no other purpose than concealment of the steel and glass constructions they covered, the stone fronts of these railroad station buildings exercise a real function, that of a kind of stimulus shield: they are there to connect two fundamentally different realms, city space and railroad space. The stone reception building that obscures the train hall from view remains necessary as long as the city itself remains essentially preindustrial in character. Through the 1850s, an abrupt entry of the industrial apparatus of the railway into the city, not ameliorated, not "filtered" in some way, would be far too shocking.[10] But very soon thereafter, and helped along by the railway in a crucial sense, the city loses its medieval character and assumes an industrial character determined by modern traffic. This transformation renders both reception building and train hall redundant.[11]

The change, simplification, and acceleration of the process of transition from the city realm to the railroad realm becomes apparent in an interesting modification that takes place in the interior spatial arrangement of the railroad station around 1860. Before that time, there is no direct access between reception area and station platforms: the latter can be reached only by moving

Farewell Scenes on the Railroad Platform.

This is based on the painting by Frith, 1866. We can clearly see the enlargement of the terminal building in comparison to the earlier buildings seen in previous illustrations. We can hardly avoid making a pictoral comparison between this mass farewell and the one depicted in the following illustration.

Science Museum, London.

A Farewell at the Stagecoach, Paris, ca. 1820.

Kunstbibliotek Berlin, Sammlung Lipperheide

American Country Station

Harper's Weekly, 1869.

The Railroad Right in the Middle of Town.

This is a situation unheard of in Europe, in America a common occurance, an expression of differing attitudes toward technology.

From: George Shumway, *Conestoga Wagon.*

through the waiting rooms. In these, the passengers, (like air travelers in our day) have to congregate and wait until the doors to the midway are opened, shortly before the train's departure. This regulation prevents the travelers from reaching their trains in an uncontrollable individual fashion: especially in continental Europe, which at that time has not yet achieved a high degree of industrialization, there are doubts as to the general public's ability to deal with industrial machinery in the absence of precise regulations.[12] But that changes in the 1860s, and the reception building and the train hall become directly connected. Thus, the waiting rooms lose their function as gateways and become peripheral to the main stream of traffic. The reception hall assumes the function of both waiting rooms and midway and becomes a "concourse" (Meeks), a "vast mixing chamber . . . serving as a self-adjusting traffic center."[13] "Once the function of the concourse was comprehended," says Meeks in his summary of this development, "it became possible to abandon the midway altogether and to provide separate quiet waiting areas while all moving traffic was handled in the concourse."[14]

The new spatial arrangement quite obviously reflects a speeding-up of the process of spatial transition. The travelers' sojourn in the waiting room, that hiatus in the passage of traffic from city to railway, is perhaps the clearest indication of the station's function as a gateway. One might say that the pause was necessary to enable the traveler to cope with the change in the quality of space. However, now the change of space can be mastered in a continuous motion by merely walking through the reception hall (now the "concourse") and out onto the platforms — a further indication of the rapprochement between city space and railroad space. Direct access from the city to the railroad has become possible because the city itself, to paraphrase Lucae, has become as "frightening" (i.e., industrialized) in its aspect as the train hall.

12. Tracks in the City

The Attila of the straight line.
— Victor Fournel, speaking of
Georges Haussmann, 1865

The transformation of the still largely medieval aspect of the European city in the nineteenth century; the explosion of its spatial enclosures; its horizontal expansion of urban space, with the creation of specialized districts (residential, business, and industrial; bourgeois and proletarian, etc.) — all are results of the industrial revolution in general, and of the railroad's transportation revolution in particular. Where this development is not caused directly by the railroad, the latter nevertheless functions as an accelerating factor for existing tendencies. Kellett, who has researched the railways' influence on urban development in nineteenth-century England, gives a summary that is fundamentally applicable to developments in all the other Western and Central European countries as well: "... it was the influence of the railways, more than any other single agency, which gave the Victorian city its compact shape, which influenced the topography and character of its central and inner districts, the disposition of its dilapidated and waste areas, and of its suburbs, the direction and character of its growth; and which probably acted as the most potent new factor upon the urban land market in the nineteenth century."[1]

The railroad makes its most immediate and visible impression on those parts of the city which it interacts with physically, i.e., the districts immediately adjoining the tracks and the stations. Here, the railroad changes the physiognomy of the old cities with bold strokes. "The plans of British towns, no matter

170

how individual and diverse before 1830," says Kellett, "are uniformly super-inscribed within a generation by the gigantic geometrical brush-strokes of the engineers' curving approach lines and cut-offs, and franked with the same bulky and intrusive termini, sidings, and marshalling yards."[2]

These changes do not affect the actual heart of the city. Apart from some exceptions,[3] the railroad lines are drawn merely to the peripheries of the old centers, and that is where the terminals are built. This is not so much due to reverence for the historical architecture of the centers — although that may well have something to do with it, considering the century's generally ambiguous relationship to machinery and industry — but to the high cost of real estate in the middle of town. The railroads, requiring considerable space for their actual tracks, stations, storage halls and other technical installations, locate themselves in a part of the city that meets the requirements of optimal location in terms of traffic and of optimal (i.e., minimal) real estate prices. Perdonnet, commenting on the location of passenger terminals: "The passenger stations are not located close to the centers of the cities unless the expenditure involved in such close location, which is mostly a considerable one, is justified by the advantages gained."[4]

A glance at the city plans of the European metropolises in the 1850s demonstrates in exactly what zone of the city the terminals are located, in each

The Railroad in the City.

The London-Greenwich Line blazes a trail through the city like a modern expressway. However, only those areas of the city with low real estate prices are afflicted in this way, like the East End of London, for example. The West End has been largely spared.

Columbia University, Parsons Collection.

171

Railroads and Stations in London, around 1845.

We can clearly see how the three main eastern lines intrude deeply into working class neighborhoods, while the western lines come to a halt at the outskirts of the city. The different routes are the result of the variation in real estate values between eastern and western London.

New York Public Library, Map Division.

instance. The terminals of Paris are sited between the inner and outer rings of the boulevards. In London, the social difference between the East End and the West End is demonstrated by the fact that the western terminals are located on the outskirts of the city, while the eastern lines penetrate deep into the industrial-proletarian region.[5] A map of Berlin from 1846 shows the terminals on the periphery of the old city; later maps demonstrate how, starting about 1860, this old inner city grows around and beyond the terminals, becoming a new, expanded inner city. This explains the quite central situation of the terminals in typical European city development.[6]

The railroad does not only influence those parts of the city that are in its immediate vicinity. More generally, it increases the volume of traffic, and this increase finally leads to the demolition of the city's traditional interior structure. The effects of increased traffic volume become apparent as soon as a city is attached to a railway network: the streets in the environs of the station change character overnight. "Walking along the Leipziger Strasse that leads to the railroad, one has difficulty recognizing it," observes a newspaper article after

172

Railroads and Stations in Paris, 1851.

The northern lines end in the districts between the inner and outer boulevards (Gare du Nord, Gare de l'Est), an area that is neither the center nor the periphery of the city.

New York Public Library, Map Division.

the opening of the railroad between Berlin and Leipzig. "There is a constant stream, in both directions, of pedestrians, coaches, cabs, and other vehicles; the solid, massive buildings reverberate from the continuous shocks, and inhabitants who formerly thought to find here a quiet, beautiful street, with its advantages of proximity to the countryside, green trees, and fields, are now moving back into the city to find their lost serenity. In the future, the great Leipziger Strasse will most probably be a thoroughfare of factories. . . ."[7]

Thus, even the volume of traffic that the railroads direct into the cities becomes most clearly apparent in the vicinity of the stations. These are the bridgeheads of the new traffic that will now spread, from here, over the entire city. The first main arteries are those between railroad station and city center, as well as those between the various main terminals of a metropolis. Around 1855, London's daily traffic on these thoroughfares amounts to seventy-five thousand vehicles.[8]

The street system of the old cities cannot cope with the new volume of traffic, and thus modernization and modification become necessary. "The

173

Baron Haussmann, ca. 1870.

The Boulevard as a Continuation of the Railroad Line.

One of the first new traffic arteries which Haussmann cut through Paris was the Boulevard de Strasbourg, which is a linear continuation of a railroad line. Plan (a) shows how far this continuation of the railroad by other means was realized by 1855: the Boulevard de Strasbourg ends abruptly among the tangles streets of the old quarter. Only a few years later, the final stretch, the Boulevard de Sebastopol, is completed (b). In this way, an imposing straight line was drawn from the station into the heart of the city.

Musée de la Ville de Paris.

greatly increased internal circulation of people and goods, by day and night, in the expanding cities, had to be accommodated by expensive street re-alignments and improvements."[9]

Baron Haussmann's renovation of Paris is an exemplary case. In a mere fifteen years the physiognomy of that city undergoes a complete transformation, a *régularisation* (Haussmann) that is unique in European history. In London, where traffic certainly was as pervasive a problem as in Paris, the accommodation of the city to the needs of modern traffic occurred during a longer period of time and in more "civilized" forms. The authoritarian, highly structured, even brutal methodology with which Haussmann "renewed" old Paris is often seen only as a modification of the city to make it conform to the counterrevolutionary strategic needs of the Second Empire. It is obvious that the avenues and boulevards were designed to be efficacious army routes, but that function is merely a Bonapartist addendum to the otherwise commercially oriented new system. The form and methodology of Haussmann's street plan is authoritarian and military; its purpose, like the overall intention of the Bonapartist regime, is the advancement of the bourgeoisie's business interests.[10]

Thus, the underlying authoritarian intentions do not entirely explain the drastic obviousness of Haussmannism. In the preparation and realization of his work, Haussmann uses the railroad as his technological model, not subjectively, but objectively. Describing the straight lines of Haussmann's avenues, Victor Fournel cannot think of a better parallel than the railway line: "To avoid any curve invisible to the eye and unnoticeable to the foot, cuts are made across the terrain, as in the case of tunnels for the railroad."[11] Haussmann approaches Paris as a railroad engineer approaches a terrain through which a line has to be laid. He begins his labors by surveying the city; until 1853, no complete street map of Paris existed, but only partial maps, indicative of the mutual isolation of the individual *quartiers*.[12]

The survey produces a complete street map, upon which the envisaged new thoroughfares are inscribed. Before the actual street construction begins, there is "a general levelling of Paris, to eliminate the minor humps and hillocks which could play havoc with a road intersection or a long perspective."[13] Finally, the completed thoroughfares are ceremonially opened, not so much as memorials (as Walter Benjamin assumes)[14] but, in the manner of new railway lines.

The first thoroughfare thus completed, the Boulevard de Strasbourg, becomes, as André Morizet notes in his history of Paris, "much more essential . . . as the rapid development of the railroad network shakes the Parisians out of

a.

*Opening of the
Boulevard de
Sebastopol, 1858.*

Musée Carnavalet,
Cabinet des Estampes

their old homebody habits and revolutionizes their circulation."[15] The
Boulevard de Strasbourg not only begins at a terminal, the Gare de l'Est, its
arrival and departure gate to the inner city,[16] but it then runs as a direct
continuation of the rails, mathematically parallel and just as linear. Like the
railway line in the open terrain, the boulevard strikes across the cityscape,
heedlessly cutting through whatever is in its way. Thus, the Gare de l'Est, which
receives the railroad on one side and permits it to continue on the other,
transformed into a thoroughfare, would see the most exemplary of all European city terminals. As a clearly recognizable direct continuation of the railroad
line in the city, the Boulevard de Strasbourg is unique: but even Haussmann's
other main thoroughfares can be perceived as complements to rail traffic. They
either connect the terminals with the center of the city, or with each other.[17] In
Paris, as well as in all the other European metropolises, the terminals function
as bridgeheads for the new traffic that slowly expands from them over the
entire city. The farther this expansion of traffic proceeds, the more it becomes

b.

emancipated from its points of origin, the railroads and the terminals. What finally characterizes the new streets is no longer any specific reminiscence of the railroad but their general function, which now is mere subservience to the flow of traffic. Françoise Choay says:

> Problems of traffic flow were given priority. Haussmann's first step was to conceive a network of through streets which have no significance in themselves but are essentially a means of connection. They form new lines of communication, general ones between districts (east, west, north, south), specific ones between certain old or new key points such as railway stations or market places. . . . This overall network of arterial connections constituted what Haussmann described as a kind of "general circulatory system", which he subdivided into hierarchized tributary systems, each organized around a plaza, which is no longer a place in itself but a traffic node, or what the Prefect [Haussmann] termed *nodes of relation*.[18] (Italics in original.)

The streets that Haussmann creates serve only traffic, and this distinguishes them from the medieval streets and lanes that they destroy, whose function was not so much to serve traffic as to be a forum for neighborhood life; it also distinguishes them from the boulevards and avenues of the baroque, whose linearity and width was designed more for pomp and ceremony than for mere traffic.[19] It is not even necessary to go back as far as the baroque to recognize the "modernity" of the traffic function of Haussmann's streets. Even Pierre Patte's Enlightenment-oriented proposal of 1765 demonstrates the difference between a type of city planning that is primarily traffic-oriented and one to whom management of traffic does not yet exist as a task. Patte's plan envisages modernizations such as water supply, removal of cemeteries to the outskirts of town, and even traffic improvements between individual districts — so that one might assume, as Pinkney does, that "he might be easily taken for a nineteenth-century urban reformer or city planner." This impression, however, is deceptive: "when he came to recommendations of specific improvements in the city's streets he remained a man of his age." According to Pinkney, Patte's plan remained "a work of embellishment; the needs of communication were forgotten."[20]

With the remodeling of Paris for flowing traffic, with the construction of streets, "which have no significance in themselves but are essentially means of connection," the inhabitants familiar with the old Paris experience a situation similar to that of the first railroad travelers. As the latter, accustomed to the space-time perceptions of coach travel, experience the railroad journey as a destruction of space and time, the former see the new traffic-oriented city of Paris as a destroyed one — in a double sense: physically demolished as well as demolished in its spatial and historical continuity. The railroad puts an end to the lyricism of old modes of travel; the new thoroughfares signal the end of the poeticism of Paris. (Contemporaries do not recognize the fact that, in both cases, the old appears "poetical" only at the very moment when the new technology announces its termination.)[21]

Haussmann's work, observes Victor Fournel in 1865, causes Paris to lose "the picturesqueness, the variety, the unexpectedness, that charm of discovery

Hausmannism in Action, 1860's, a vision which anticipates Dresden.

Musée Carnavalet, Cabinet des Estampes

which made a walk in old Paris an exploratory voyage through always new and always unknown worlds, that multiple and living physiognomy that gave each great district of the city its special traits like those on a human face."[22] The spatiotemporal disorientation of the first railway passengers is caused by the collision of two space-time relationships, the traditional with the new; similarly, a comparable disorientation of the Parisians of the 1850s and 1860s can be understood as a result of their seeing, with their own eyes, one Paris intersecting and colliding with another in the process of demolition and reconstruction.

"Buildings arise in place of old roads; new roads make their way across the debris of demolished houses. From all sides, the avenues advance as if to attack, overturning, bulldozing, flattening everything in their way," says Fournel, that implacable critic of Haussmann.[23] This obliteration of the old Paris and its subsequent replacement with a new city must have seemed as unreal and as speedy to the contemporaries as a change of stage scenery. The new avenues, now spreading out where only a short while before there were vacant demolition lots, and before that, part of a medieval city, try to compensate for their lack of historicity by means of pompous opening ceremonies and organizational and technological perfection. They are given over completely to traffic, and, as if to conceal it, stagily adorned with thirty-year-old trees planted by means of a machine specially invented for this purpose.[24]

If contemporaries attached to the old Paris, such as Fournel and Adolphe Thiers,[25] no longer feel at home in this new Paris of flowing traffic, others do, nevertheless, arrive at a consciousness adequate to the new cityscape. The broad, tree-lined streets are seen as providers of light and air, creating sanitary conditions in both a physiological and a political sense — the latter favorable to the rule of Napoleon III. Gautier, who unlike other apologists for Napoleon[26]

177

The Paris of the New Boulevards, a city re-organized for traffic. Illustration (a) shows the new twin boulevard Strasbourg-Sébastopol with the Gare de l'Est at the vanishing point, Illustration (b) the new Avenue de l'Opéra; here the traffic artery is the focal point around which the rest of the city is organized. It is not only the center of the picture, but it also distorts all dimensions. The buildings look like doll houses, completely out of proportion to the vehicles.

Musée Carnavelet, Cabinet des Estampes

a.

b.

is not quite able to suppress a feeling of melancholy in the face of the destruction of the old Paris, sees the avenues as indices of civilization: "Civilization, which needs air, sun, and space for its frenzied activity and constant motion, advances along great avenues into the dark labyrinth of narrow streets, squares, and deadends of the old city; it strikes down buildings the way the American pioneer fells trees. In its own way, it also opens up new territory."[27]

In Zola's *La Curée*, we find a description of the new Paris and its appropriate consciousness, in which there no longer is a trace of reminiscence of the bygone city. Renée and Maxime, relatives of the unscrupulous speculator Saccard, ride along one of the new boulevards:

> While gliding along in their carriage, they observed, amicably, the endless, broad, grey bands of sidewalks with their benches, multi-colored advertising kiosks, scrawny trees. This bright channel, stretching, growing ever narrower and ending in a square of blueing emptiness, all the way to the horizon; the uninterrupted double row of the great stores . . .; the flowing masses of people, the noise of their footsteps and intermingling voices, slowly filled the two women with unconditional, unadulterated joy, with an impression of the excellence of this street life. . . . They drove on and on, and it seemed to them that the carriage was rolling over carpets stretching along this straight and endless highroad that had been expressly constructed to save them from the sight of the small dark streets. Each boulevard became a hallway in their own house. The gaiety of sunlight smiled at them out of the new housefronts, made the windowpanes light up, rebounded from the awnings of the stores and cafes, warmed the asphalt under the busy footsteps of the crowd.."[28]

Paris as a Street Palimsest.

The old Paris, through which traffic arteries have been built, looks like a jungle with trails cut through it. The new volume of traffic in the nineteenth century required streets which were many times broader than the narrow old lanes, and the new streets were straight as railroad tracks.

Musée Carnavalet, Cabinet des Estampes

13. Circulation

While Haussmann transforms the old Paris into a new city of flowing traffic, a similar change starts taking place in the realm of retail business. In 1852, Aristide Boucicaut opens the first Parisian department store, the Bon Marché. The simultaneity is not coincidental: the department store, as a new form of retail merchandising, is predicated on a well-developed intraurban traffic system. "It only became possible to exploit such large retail outlets after the development of the omnibusses during the following decades and the appearance of the first horse-powered tramways in the period between 1850 and 1860."[1] As Haussmann's traffic arteries are connected to the rail network by means of the railway stations, and thus to all the traffic in its entirety, the new department stores, in turn, are connected to these new intraurban arteries and their traffic. The *Grands Magasins* that arise during the second half of the nineteenth century are concentrated on the grand boulevards that supply them with goods and customers.

There are three fundamental differences between the department store and the traditional retail business. The department store makes its profit by means of high turnover at a low rate of profit: the prices are low, but fixed, and the customers are encouraged to enter the store without any obligation to buy. Retail business becomes industrially revolutionized by means of these cheaper prices based on mass turnover. From the beginning of the nineteenth century there have been attempts to bring retail merchandising in line with the new industrial productivity; such as the *Magasins de Nouveauté,* and the arcades, in which several independent retail businesses join to form a kind of bazaar. However, those new arrangements consist merely of a collection of autonomous businesses — there is no new quality to the organization of retail merchandising. In the traditional retail shop, buyer and purchaser still confront one another in person: when a customer enters, this presages, if not necessarily a transaction, at least a conversation between him and the shopowner.

The department store puts an end to that sales conversation, as travel by rail puts an end to verbal exchanges among travelers. The latter are replaced by travel reading; the former, by a mute price tag. This change results from the increased turnover of goods. The increase in quantity requires new forms of distribution and behavior in travel space as well as in commercial space.

Not only does the department store change the relationship between seller and buyer, it also changes the buyer's attitude toward the goods. In the transition from the traditional retail shop to the department store, the customer's

Millinery, Paris ca. 1820.

Kunstbibliotek Berlin, Sammlung Lipperheide

181

Parisian Department Store, 1860's to 1880's. The modern department store is to the traditional retail shop as the railroad station is to the coach station (see illustration on pages 162-63). The accelerated volume of sales made possible by the railroad has found its characteristic expression in the department store. "The loud noises from outside now drowned out the din of activity inside of the building; neither the rolling of the cabs could be heard, nor the slamming of carriage doors; nothing could be heard but the busy murmur of the market . . . In the still air . . . a thunder swelled up from all the noises, the continuous clatter of feet, the unending repetition of the same phrases around the sales counters, and the ring of gold on the brass cash registers . . . (E. Zola, *Au Bonheur des Dames*).

New York Public Library, Picture Collection.

perception of the goods changes in a manner analogous to the traveler's perception during the transition from coach to train, and to the Parisian's perception in the process of his city's Haussmannization. The department store encourages the development of the kind of perception that we have called panoramic. To recapitulate its essential characteristics as seen in the context of the train journey: as speed causes the *foreground* to disappear, it detaches the subject from the space that immediately surrounds him, that is, it intrudes itself as an "almost unreal barrier" between object and subject. The landscape that is seen in this way is no longer experienced intensively, auratically (as by Ruskin, the critic of rail travel), but evanescently, impressionistically — panoramically, in fact. More exactly, panoramic perception is one which finds the objects attractive in their state of dispersal. That attraction is generated by the motion that creates this perception of the objects in the observing subject. We have observed a similar process at work in the kind of perception that esthetically enjoys Haussmann's new thoroughfares as much as it loathes the old Parisian streets: here, the attraction lies in the width, the lightness, the continuous traffic of those new streets. We called this perception panoramic, by contrast with the traditional one that involves a static, intensive relationship with the objects observed.

We can call the appearance of the goods in the department store a "panoramic" one — in distinction from their appearance in shops of the old type — because those goods participate in the same acceleration of traffic which generated the new mode of perception on the railways and boulevards. In the department store, this means an acceleration of turnover. This acceleration changes the relationship between customer and goods to the same degree that the railroad's accelerated speed changed the traveler's relationship with the landscape. In both cases, the relationship becomes less static, less intensive, less auratic, and more mobile.

The price-tag system introduced by the department stores does not only silence sales conversation, it also transforms the appearance of the goods. No longer does this appearance speak for itself, as it did in the traditional retail store, where the price of goods was determined by their visible and tangible qualities, as evaluated by the customer and shopkeeper in the sales conversation; that intrinsic quality, the use value, becomes obscured by the price tag. (The price tag interposes itself between goods and customer as the railroad's speed interjects itself between traveler and landscape.) On the side of the goods, the price tag corresponds to money as carrier of exchange value; on the side of the buyer, it indicates the degree to which that exchange value has become a dominant part of the appearance of the goods. From now on, the goods are perceived primarily in terms of price, while they formerly presented themselves as concrete, individual objects whose price only emerged in the give-and-take of the sales conversation.

This change strips the goods of their former, immediate, individual presence and sensuous quality, and provides them with a new one. The attractiveness of an item no longer consists in its individuality (its use value) but results from the totality of *all* the goods assembled in the salesroom. The gathering of a mass of heterogeneous goods under one roof, and its arrangement according to a concept, produces that "extraordinary power of attraction to the public,"[2] i.e., the motive power of the accelerated turnover, and thus leads the department stores to triumph over the traditional shops.

Zola's carefully researched department store novel, *Au Bonheur des Dames,* casts light on the sales dynamics and sales psychology of the last third of the nineteenth century that are based on this new relationship between customer and goods. *Motion* appears in this book as the foundation of that relationship. Motion originates in the actual street traffic that leads in and out of the department store, and thus the steady expansion of the department store proceeds apace towards one of the main traffic arteries. "As long as the main entrance fronted onto the Rue Neuve-Saint-Augustin, a dark street of ancient Paris, his work remained mere dilettantism and lacked consequence," begin the musings of Zola's department store tycoon. "He wanted to flaunt it in the face of the new Paris, by one of these newly constructed avenues, where the noisy throngs of the second half of the century paraded by in broad sunlight."[3] One of this protagonist's fantasies involves not only situating the story *by* that artery but even incorporating it: "Had he seen his way of doing it, he would have liked to let the thoroughfare run right through his store."[4]

If the connection with street traffic is necessary to ensure the numbers of customers and goods required by accelerated turnover, it is also true that that turnover itself depends on motion. The influx from the street is of a new kind: it is channeled by means of a carefully manipulated display of goods. Zola's tycoon knows this: "He made it a law that not one far-flung corner of the Bonheur des Dames should remain tranquil. There had to be noise, commotion, life everywhere, because life, he said, attracts life, bears new life, and multiplies quickly."[5]

The customer is kept in motion; he travels through the department store as a train passenger travels through the landscape. In their totality, the goods impress him as an ensemble of objects and price tags fused into a pointillistic overall view:

> Mrs. Desforges saw everywhere only the great big signs with enormous numerals whose garish colors contrasted with the bright calico, the radiant silk, the muted wool materials. People's heads almost disappeared behind piles of ribbons; a wall of flannel protruded like a headland; everywhere around, mirrors made the salesrooms seem even huger, reflecting displays and parts of the public, appraising heads, half-glimpsed shoulders and arms; while to the right and left, the side corridors allowed glimpses of the snowy bays of white goods, the mottled deeps of knitted things, of remote worlds illumined by a beam of light from some part of the glass roof, where the crowd became merely human dust motes."[6]

The motion in the department store is a part of the general motion of traffic that generated the panoramic perception of railroad and boulevard landscapes. However, in the department store, the panoramic eye is not dealing with landscapes or boulevards but with goods. This calls for another perspective on the panoramic concept. The department store customer's new relationship to the goods proves to be less a result of his own physical motion (although this, too, is occurring) than the result of the new economic relationship that has found its expression in the form of the department store. In the department store, the goods achieve more of their character *as* goods — their appearance as items of exchange value; one might say that their "commodity-esthetic" aspect becomes ever more dominant.

It seems questionable to describe two widely differing subjects such as the appearance of goods in a department store and the appearance of the landscape seen from the train compartment by the same term, "panoramic," one being the result of actual, i.e., physical speed, the other a reflection of an economic relationship. Yet the problem solves itself as soon as we look at the railway journey, no longer in its aspect of physical motion, but in economic terms: economically speaking, the railway journey is a commodity, a service performed, transportation purchased in the form of a ticket.[7] Thus the panoramic view from the compartment window can be understood not only as a result of physical acceleration but also, and simultaneously, as a consequence of the new economic relationships, which have made the railroad journey a commodity, to a qualitatively new extent.[8] The fragmentation and panoramic reconstruction of the railway journey's landscape *does* correspond, structurally, to the fragmentation and pointillistic reconstruction of the appearance of the goods in the department store. The city names on the station buildings are evidence of the same process that attaches price tags to the commodities.

We have to recognize both of the sources that feed the panoramic perception — physical speed, and the commodity character of objects — to an equal degree. They are intimately connected in that the physical speed achieved by means of a vehicle of transportation is merely the base for the economic circulation of the commodities: that circulation increases the commodity character of the goods with a rapidity that is in direct proportion to the physical rapidity of the vehicles. To recognize such a close interaction between commodity character and change of location would, finally, seem to be quite in accord with the previously cited observation by Marx which states that "this moment of locality" may be assumed to be the "transformation of the product into a commodity." We also gain further insight into that turn of phrase so well liked by the railroad's critics — the claim that this form of travel transforms the traveler into a parcel. The realization that one no longer feels like a person but like a parcel, i.e., a commodity, indicates some awareness that one has been assimilated not only by physically accelerated speed but also by the generally accelerated process of the circulation of goods.

It now becomes possible to define panoramic perception in more general terms. It is perception based on a specific developmental stage of the circulation of commodities, with corresponding specific stages of technology in general, traffic technology in particular, retail merchandising, etc. Panoramic perception of objects, panoramic ways of relating to objects, make their appearance in connection with, and based upon, the accelerated circulation of commodities — as distinct from the traditional mode of perception, which, being still attuned to a prior development stage of circulation, finds it difficult to deal with the now accelerated objects.

It is a corollary of the above that it makes sense to speak of "panoramic perception" only as long as the archaism of such a traditional, old-fashioned perception still exists. As soon as a society's overall perceptions have reorganized themselves after a qualitative change of the production-circulation complex, the new normality is what was formerly the panoramic.[9]

By the end of the nineteenth century, the capitalist world's recomposition on the basis of modern traffic has been completed. From then on, traffic determines what belongs where. The preindustrial contexts of location and space-time relations are no longer valid. Only the general context of traffic assigns and dictates positions to the singular elements. The nineteenth century is very aware of this achievement, the conquest of space; this can be seen in the relatively high value it assigns to the means of communication and transportation in its official self-perception: the triad of railroad, steamship, telegraph, is evoked time and again as representative of industrial progress. The world exhibitions (which in their very definition presuppose modern world traffic) give prominent displays to the communication and transportation industries.[10] In a salute to the 1867 exhibition, Victor Hugo urges the French to disband as a nation and to join humanity.[11]

The nineteenth century's preoccupation with the conquest and mastery of space and time has found its most general expression in the concept of circulation, which was central to the scientistic social notions of the epoch. Its origin is obviously biophysiological, but it is equally obvious that it reflects the process of modern traffic. The reality of traffic is contained in the biologization of social processes and institutions that is so typical of nineteenth-century thinking. The century's social organisms are replicas of events in both the biological and the traffic sphere. In other words, when the nineteenth century sees the health and vitality of social institutions and processes as dependent on a functioning circulatory system (e.g., Jean Baptiste Say: "One imagines that the social body will be the livelier and healthier the more general and rapid the circulation of values is"),[12] it bases this view on a biophysiological notion of society and economy; yet the notion itself is merely a reflection of the actual traffic conditions.[13] This complex meaning of the circulation concept in the nineteenth century becomes quite explicit in French, where *circulation* refers to the actual movement of traffic as well as to the circulation of the blood and the circulation of goods.

In this complex sense, the circulation concept serves as a key to unlock the open triumphs as well as the hidden anxieties of the nineteenth century. The formula is as simple as can be: whatever is part of circulation is regarded as healthy, progressive, constructive; all that is detached from circulation, on the other hand, appears diseased, medieval, subversive, threatening. Haussmann's public works can now be seen in a new light. His bold thoroughfares reveal themselves as designed not only for traffic, but also for the city's physiology. (Du Camp's book on Paris, frequently reprinted during the Second Empire, bears the title *Paris, ses organes, ses fonctions, sa vie* [Paris, its organs, its functions, its life].) Haussmann's street system has been aptly characterized as based upon "the dual concept of a circulatory and respiratory system."[14] The streets have the function of connecting the old, i.e., diseased, city districts to the circulatory system that is already pulsing through modern France. Their adornment with trees merely underlines that physiological/biological intention, which cannot be separated from the traffic-oriented intention anymore than from the counterrevolutionary military one. In a rare formulation, Haussmann successfully summarizes these complex motives: he says that it is his intention "to insure public tranquility by the creation of great boulevards that allow the circulation not only of air and light but also of military units and, by means of

187

this ingenious combination, to render the people both healthier and less disposed to revolt."[15]

The same notion of circulation, light, air, life on one hand, and isolation, stagnation, darkness, death on the other, can be found in the work of Zola, albeit with a liberal, not an authoritarian slant. In his department store novel, what remains isolated from circulation are the small shops that become unable to turn over their wares. The mold that grows on those goods, the humidity and darkness of the shops themselves, whose owners die off one after another, demonstrate what it means to be cut off from the circulation of commodity turnover — seen in the novel as light radiating off the facade of the neighboring department store. The list of examples could be lengthened *ad libitum*. Harking back to a previous topic discussed in this book, the threatening nature of the train compartment, we will present only one more example. The bourgeois passenger finds the compartment frightening because it is not connected to permit traffic between the parts of the train. The side corridor, which finally provides that connection, does for the compartment what Haussmann's boulevards do for the isolated old city districts of Paris: each shines a light into the threatening darkness by providing a connection to the general traffic. The threat disappears as soon as the bourgeois traveler knows that his compartment and the possible events taking place in it are controlled by the appropriate authority. The conductor, who can view the compartments from the side corridor, is the civilian equivalent of the prison guard who controls the cells from his central tower.[16]

The notion that communication, exchange, motion bring humanity enlightenment and progress, and that isolation and disconnection are the obstacles to be overcome on this course, is as old as the modern age. The bourgeois cultural development of the last three centuries can be seen as closely connected with the actual development of traffic. In retrospect, it is easy to see what significance the experience of space and time had for bourgeois education when one considers the grand tour, which was an essential part of that education before the industrialization of travel. The world was experienced in its original spatiotemporality. The traveling subject experienced localities in their spatial individuality. His *education* consisted in his assimilation of the spatial individuality of the places visited, by means of an effort that was both physical and intellectual. The eighteenth-century travel novel becomes the *Bildungsroman* (novel of education) of the early nineteenth century. The motion of travel, that physical and intellectual effort in space and time, dominates both.

The railroad, the destroyer of experiential space and time, thus also destroys the educational experience of the grand tour. Henceforth, the localities are no longer spatially individual or autonomous: they are points in the circulation of traffic that makes them accessible. As we have seen, that traffic is the physical manifestation of the circulation of goods. From now on, the places visited by the traveler become increasingly similar to the commodities that are part of the same circulation system. For twentieth-century tourism, the world has become one big department store of countrysides and cities.

Postscript

In describing the historical-anthropological type of the *flâneur*, Walter Benjamin has found the one final straggler in the lineage of the old-time grand tourist: The *flâneur's* leisurely experience of the city has not yet been absorbed by circulation, which was, according to Benjamin, still possible in pre-Haussmann Paris. A precondition for this possibility was the stage of traffic which Benjamin describes as follows: "Ferries were still crossing the Seine at points that would later be spanned by the arch of a bridge . . . it was still possible for some entrepreneur to cater to the comfort of the well-to-do with a fleet of five hundred sedan chairs circulating about the city. Arcades where the *flâneur* would not be exposed to the sight of carriages that did not recognize pedestrians as rivals were still enjoying undiminished popularity."[17]

The artificiality of the *flâneur's* existence within this context becomes apparent in the fact that the arcades already are refuges from the vehicular traffic on the regular streets. Benjamin mentions the Parisian fad of the 1840s that involved walking turtles on a leash in these arcades;[18] he conjectures that this was the *flâneur's* way of asserting his eccentrically unhurried way of life, but it is, more likely, a sign of the general alienation from slow speeds. The *flâneur* using such a pacesetter, if only ironically, is no longer a true one. In 1843, with the opening of the first great lines, the railroad era begins in France.

Notes

Chapter 1: The Mechanization of Motive Powers

1. Werner Sombart, *Der Moderne Kapitalismus,* vol. 2, p. 1138. (first ed. München, 1902).
2. Lewis Mumford (following the Scottish sociologist Patrick Geddes) has coined the terms *eotechnology* and *paleotechnology* to describe this epoch-making change in materials and energy: "The eotechnic phase is a water-and-wood complex; the paleotechnic phase is a coal-and-iron complex." (L. Mumford, *Technics and Civilization* [New York, 1963], p. 11.)
3. Daniel Defoe, *A Tour Thro' the Whole Island of Great Britain* (first ed., 1724–27; reprint ed. in 2 vols., London, 1968), vol. 2, p. 659.
4. Conrad Matschoss, *Geschichte der Dampfmaschine* (Berlin, 1901), p. 55.
5. Thomas Ashton, *Iron and Steel in the Industrial Revolution* (first ed., 1924; reprint ed., Manchester, 1951), pp. 99–100.
6. Matschoss., op. cit., p. 77.
7. Concise information on the history of the English Corn Laws can be found in: Eric Hobsbawm, *Industrie und Empire* (Frankfurt, 1969), vol. 1, pp. 98–99; (German translation of *Industry and Empire: From 1750 to the Present Day,* Pelican Economic History of England, vol. 3 (London and New York, 1968); Asa Briggs, *The Age of Improvement, 1783–1867* (New York, 1959), pp. 202, 312; R. K. Webb, *Modern England* (New York and Toronto, 1970), pp. 153, 185–86.
   The corn legislation after 1815 can be seen as a temporarily effective skirmish conducted by the land-owning class against the rising industrial bourgeoisie. No later than 1828 the pressure of free-enterprise interests caused the law of 1815 to be modified, and by the mid-1840s it had been abolished entirely, after the industrial bourgeoisie and the working class (i.e., the Chartists) had joined, in 1838, to form the Anti-Corn-Law League.
8. Thomas Grahame, *A Treatise on Internal Intercourse and Communication in Civilised States* (London, 1834), p. vi.
9. Thomas Gray, *Observations . . .,* 3rd ed. (London, 1822), p. x.
10. P. S. Girard, foreword to the French edition of Freidrich von Gerstner's *Mémoire sur les grandes routes, les chemins de fer, et les canaux de navigation* (Paris, 1827), pp. cxxv–cxxvi.
11. C. Fohlen, in *Charbon et sciences humaines: Colloque international de l'Université de Lille en mai 1963* (Lille, 1963), p. 148.
12. Op. cit., pp. 141–42.
13. Traditionally, traffic on waterways has been greater than overland traffic. From the early fifteenth century to the end of the nineteenth century, sailing-ship technology was sufficient for the transportation needs of capitalism in all its phases of expansion. Fifty years after the mechanization of land traffic by means of the railroad, sailing-ship technology (i.e., the clipper) still dominated ocean traffic.
14. Nicholas Wood, *A Practical Treatise on Rail-Roads, and Interior Communication in General,* 2nd ed. (London, 1832), p. xii. Within the mail system, there are attempts to increase physical capacity from the sixteenth century on: letters are no longer carried long distances by means of only one courier, but from one station to the next, "with either changes of horses, or of couriers, *relays,* in any case, consisting of runners or riders or drivers." (Sombart, op. cit., vol. 2, p. 382.) This subdivision of the formerly unified effort causes the process to become intensified, but the system remains subject to the limits of physical capacity, even though this is now the sum of the physical capacities of all the individual relays. This intensification also intensifies costs, and thus only the mails employ this mode of transportation.
15. James Adamson, *Sketches of Our Information as to Rail-Roads* (Newcastle, 1826), pp. 51–52.
16. Thomas Gray, *Observations . . .* (London, 1822), p. 39.
17. Charles Babbage, *On the Economy of Machinery and Manufacture* (Philadelphia, 1832), p. 27. An application to the motion of sailing ships, the text goes on to say, would mean that "the quantity of motion given by them [the sails] is precisely the same as that which is destroyed in the atmosphere." (Op. cit.)

18. Report in *New York Magazine* (1790), quoted in Seymour Dunbar, *A History of Travel in America*, 4 vols. (Indianapolis, 1915), vol. 1, pp. 256–57.
19. W. Heimann, *Über Dampfmaschinen, Dampfwagen und Eisenbahnen* (Frankfurt, 1836), p. 2.
20. *Quarterly Review*, vol. 63 (1839), p. 23.
21. Gray, op. cit., p. 55.
22. Thomas de Quincey, *The Collected Writings*, ed. David Masson (London, 1897), vol. 13, pp. 283–84. (First published in 1849 in *Blackwood's Magazine*.)
23. *The Roads and Rail-Roads, Vehicles, and Modes of Travelling, of Ancient and Modern Countries . . .* (London, 1839), p. 279.
24. "In the manual on the art of driving published by the president of the Four-in-Hand Driving and Coaching Club, which was revived in 1870 by the Duke of Beaufort, there is a chapter titled 'the coaching revival' that deals exclusively with the club members' new practice of driving coaches on busy routes (e.g., to Brighton, Dover, Tunbridge Wells) and racing the railway trains to those destinations; this activity made the long-abandoned inns of the coaching era come alive again with the neighing of horses and the cracking of whips." (P. D. Fischer, *Betrachtungen eines in Deutschland reisenden Deutschen* [Berlin, 1895], pp. 43–44. Fischer also mentions the following coaching titles published in the 1880s: Stanley Harris, *Old Coaching Days;* W. Outram Tristram, *Coaching Days and Coaching Ways.*)
25. W. B. Adams, *English Pleasure Carriages* (London, 1837), pp. 198–99.
26. *The Fingerpost; or, Direct Road from John O' Groat's to the Land's End,* 3rd ed. (London, 1825), pp. 24–25.
27. John Gore, ed., *The Creevy Papers* (New York, 1963), p. 256.

Chapter 2. The Machine Ensemble

1. Quoted in Peter J. Wexler, *La Formation du vocabulaire des chemins de fer en France, 1778–1842* (Geneva and Lille, 1955), p. 31.
2. G. T. Poussin, *Examen comparatif de la question des chemins de fer en 1839 en France et à l'étranger* (Paris, 1839), pp. xi–xii.

   English literature does, of course, offer corresponding definitions, e.g., Lardner (see note 20 below). The French definitions are attractive in their clarity, which is partly based on the French consciousness of language, and partly on the fact that these definitions are, essentially, descriptions of something that is still unknown to the French reading audience in any immediate sense. Thus it is amusing to read a French report from England, written in 1820, that apparently corrects erroneous notions arising from the words *chemin de fer*: "Il y en a qui croient que ces routes sont pavées avec des plaques de fer, mais ce n'est pas cela du tout, ce ne sont que des ornières en fer fondu." ("There are those who believe that these are roads paved with sheets of iron, but that is not the case at all, it is merely a matter of cast-iron rails.") (Quoted in Wexler, op. cit., p. 44.)
3. In Wexler, p. 99. On pp. 107–8 Wexler notes how hesitantly the adjective *locomotif* becomes the noun *locomotive*. Generally, Wexler provides an excellent account of the railroad vocabulary's slow development from its initial "descriptive period" to the later stage when it has become a new technical vocabulary (p. 128). The process can be demonstrated more easily in French than in English: in the latter, the development of a railway vocabulary took a much longer time. Yet it is possible to see the corresponding trend in English, as in the simplification of the initially descriptive term *iron rail-way* to *rail-way* and finally to *railway*.
4. D. Lardner, *The Steam Engine*, 3rd American ed. from 5th British ed. (Philadelphia, 1849), p. 161.

   Even Lardner, who sees the cogwheel episode as a historical mistake, based on the erroneous notion that smooth rails and wheels could not provide traction, is still able to comprehend without difficulty how it was possible to arrive at this erroneous conclusion, on the basis of theories of physics derived from the tradition of Galileo and Newton. He explains the notion as follows: "If the face of the wheel and the surface of the road were absolutely smooth and free from friction, so that the face of the wheel would slide without resistance upon the road, then the effect of the force thus applied would be merely to cause the wheel to turn around, the carriage being stationary, the surface of the wheel would slip or slide upon the road as the wheel is made to revolve." (Op. cit., p. 160.)

5. Franz Reuleaux, *Theoretische Kinematik: Grundzüge einer Theorie des Maschinenwesens* (Brunswick, 1875), p. 231.

6. See the last few pages of Chapter X of this work.

7. Reuleaux, op. cit., p. 234.

8. C. H. Greenhow, *An Exposition of the Danger and Deficiencies of the Present Mode of Railway Construction* (London, 1846), pp. 5–6.

9. The technical principle of the railroad is a practical demonstration of Newton's law of motion; Newton's law, on the other hand, is based on the technical realities of its own time (i.e., shipbuilding, machine construction, and arms technology, especially ballistics), being, as it were, the theoretical sum of that technology. These connections are discussed brilliantly in B. Hessen's *The Social and Economic Roots of Newton's "Principia"* (New York, 1971). (Originally an address to the International Congress of the History of Science and Technology in London in 1931.)

10. D. Lardner, *The Steam Engine, Steam Navigation, Roads, and Railways,* 8th ed. (London, 1851), pp. 315–16.

11. Lardner, op. cit., pp. 339–40.

12. Nicholas Wood, *A Practical Treatise on Rail-Roads,* 3rd ed. (London, 1838), p. 136.

13. *The Railway Companion* (London, 1833), p. 40.

14. Thomas Roscoe, *The London and Birmingham Railway, With the Home and Country Scenes on Each Side of the Line* (London, 1839), pp. 67–68.

    The Liverpool-Manchester Act actually requires the isolation of the railroad from the surrounding countryside, highways, etc. Cohn points out while summarizing the edicts, "a railway shall at no point intersect with another road, but shall proceed separately from all other thoroughfares by means of viaducts etc." (Gustav Cohn, *Die Entwicklung der Eisenbahngesetzgebung in England,* Untersuchungen über die englische Eisenbahnpolitik, vol. 1 [Leipzig, 1874], p. 34.)

15. It is true that the highway and the vehicle moving on it also constitute a machine ensemble, because of their interrelationship. Yet that unity is, in practical terms, a very loose one, as the vehicle is individually maneuverable and mobile on the road.

16. William Nicholson' *Journal of Natural Philosophy, Chemistry, and the Arts* (London, 1802), p. 222.

17. Op. cit., p. 223.

18. Even the very first edition of Gray's *Observations* (1820) contains a map of England, Scotland, and Wales, on which the national railroad network has been drawn in as a series of *straight* connecting lines between the major cities. In the subsequent editions we find an increasingly strong emphasis on the idea that this would have to be a transportation network of an entirely novel kind. Thus, for instance, in the fifth edition, Gray speaks of the "absolute necessity of an entirely new system of national intercourse." (P. 1.)

19. Gray, 5th ed. (London, 1825), p. 12.

20. D. Lardner, *Railway Economy* (London, 1851), pp. 421–22.

21. W. T. Jackman, *The Development of Transportation in Modern England* (first ed., 1916; reprint ed., London, 1962), p. 573. Jackman deals with the entire complex on pp. 572–79. Cohn quotes the clause of the Liverpool-Manchester Act which guarantees free access to all vehicles: "All persons shall have free liberty to use with carriages all roads, ways and passages for the purpose of conveying goods or passengers or cattle" (op. cit., p. 36). Cohn continues: "For this to be possible, the carriages used by the freight entrepreneurs have to conform to those regulations that the railroad company deems practicable and advertises in every station. Furthermore, the owners of adjoining property receive the right to construct branch lines to the Liverpool-Manchester line" (op. cit., pp. 36–37).

22. Op. cit., pp. 573–74.

23. Op. cit., p. 574; see also Cohn, p. 45.

24. That institution is the Railway Clearing House, based on the Clearing House of English Banks. The best description of its genesis and function can be found in Philip S. Bagwell, *The Railway Clearing House in the British Economy, 1842–1922* (London, 1968).

25. The notion of the railroad as a great machine spread out over the land appears implicitly in the early definitions of the railroad as a machine ensemble. There is a vivid example of it in Governor Everett's speech at the opening of the Boston-Albany Line (quoted in J. S. Buckingham, *The Eastern and Western States of America* [London, 1842], vol. 1, p. 51): "Let us contemplate the entire railroad, with its cars and engines, as one vast machine! What a portent of art! its fixed portion a hundred miles long; its moveable portion flying across the State like a weaver's shuttle."

26. Cooke and Wheatstone introduce it from Germany to England, in the early 1830s. (Karl Zetsche, *Geschichte der elektrischen Telegraphie* [Berlin, 1877], p. 157.)
27. In Dolf Sternberger, *Panorama, oder Ansichten vom 19. Jahrhundert,* 3rd ed. (Hamburg, 1955). The passage comes from the posthumously published volume *Vom rollenden Flügelrade* (1882). The phrase "flying muscles" refers to the railroad's trademark, or symbol, the winged wheel. Sternberger quotes the passage while discussing the mutual influence exercised by technological and organic metaphors in the nineteenth century. (Also: New York & Oxford 1978 under the title Panorama of The Nineteenth Century).
28. A prosaic footnote to the poetic perception of telegraph poles can be found in an anonymous work of 1848, *Railway Appliances in the Nineteenth Century; or, The Rail, Steam, and Electricity* (London, 1848), p. 32. It is a proposal to determine the speed of the train (which could not yet be determined directly due to lack of technical "instinct") by means of close observation of the telegraph poles, i.e., by measuring the time that the train needs to pass from one pole to the next. "These [the poles] are generally erected about sixty yards apart, or thirty in the mile, so that the speed of the train is easily found by counting the number of poles passed in a minute and multiplying by two, which, of course, gives the rate per hour."

   Thus the telegraph poles act as a kind of gauge for determining an element of the journey, i.e., velocity, that can no longer be experienced in an immediate way. This is a factor that contributes to the traveler's alienation from the landscape.
29. Paul Verlaine, *Oeuvres poétiques complètes* (Paris, 1951), p. 106. The cycle "La bonne chanson" was written in the winter of 1869–70.

   Translation by Gertrude Hall, in *Baudelaire, Rimbaud, Verlaine: Selected Verse and Prose Poems,* (New York: Citadel Press, 1947).

Chapter 3: Railroad Space and Railroad Time

1. D. Lardner, *Railway Economy* (London, 1850), p. 35.
2. According to H. G. Lewin, *The Railway Mania and its Aftermath, 1845–52* (London, 1936), the average speed, up to 1845, was "between 20 and 30 miles per hour" (p. 95). The Great Western Express, the fastest English train, reached a speed of 46 mph (op. cit.). Lardner says the speed of the stagecoaches was a little less than 8 mph (*Railway Economy,* p. 36), whereas Lewin claims that the fastest coaches achieved 10 mph.

   The actual speed of English trains in the 1840s, i.e., their top speed, was, according to Lardner, frequently 60 to 70 mph (*Railway Economy,* p. 170).
3. *Quarterly Review,* vol. 63 (1839), p. 22.
4. Constantin Pecqueur, *Économie sociale* (Paris, 1839), vol. 1, p. 26.
5. Op. cit., p. 36.
6. Émile Durkheim, *The Elementary Forms of the Religious Life* (Glencoe, Ill., 1947), pp. 10–11, p. 440.
7. Erwin Straus, *The Primary World of the Senses* (New York and London, 1963), p. 385.
8. Pitrim A. Sorokin, *Sociocultural Causality, Space, and Time* (Durham, N.C., 1943), p. 197.
9. Heine, *Lutezia,* part 2, lvii, Elster ed., vol. 6, p. 360.
10. Charles Dunoyer, *Esprit et méthodes comparés de l'Angleterre et de la France dans les entreprises de travaux publics et en particulier des chemins de fer* (Paris, 1840), p. 104.
11. Stéphane Mallarmé, *Oeuvres complètes,* Pléiade ed. (Paris, 1970), p. 843.
12. Op. cit., p. 774.
12a. *Remembrance of Things Past,* vol. II, *Within a Budding Grove,* I; translated by C. K. Scott Moncrief (New York, 1934, pp. 489–90).
13. Karl Marx, *Grundrisse, Foundations of the Critique of Political Economy* (London, 1973), p. 534.
14. Op. cit., pp. 34–35.
14a. *Illuminations* by Walter Benjamin (New York, 1973, p. 222).
14b. Ibid., p. 220.
14c. Ibid., p. 221.
15. William Wordsworth, *The Prose Works,* ed. A. B. Grosart, (London, 1876, vol. 2, p. 326).

15a. J. A. R. Pimplott, *The Englishman's Holiday* (London, 1947, p. 118).
15b. Benjamin, ibid., p. 223.
15c. Philip S. Bagwell, *The Transportation Revolution from 1770* (London, 1974), p. 124.
16. Op. cit., p. 125.
17. Greenwich time is the time kept at the Royal Observatory in Greenwich, founded in 1675. "The precise standardization of time measurement dates from the foundation of the Royal Observatory in 1675." (G. J. Whitow, *The Nature of Time* [London, 1972].) Like the later standard time, the original Greenwich time was created to meet the needs of expanding traffic, i.e., shipping, in the seventeenth century. Vessels carried Greenwich time with them on their chronometers, as it was necessary for orientation and navigation. However, it was *not* used as a generalized norm for the division of the day: Greenwich time was still restricted to the walls of the cabinet that contained the chronometer during the voyage.
18. John Stover, *American Railroads* (Chicago, 1961), p. 157.

Excursion: The Space of Glass Architecture

1. Alfred Gotthold Meyer, *Eisenbauten: Ihre Geschichte und Ästhetik* (Esslingen, 1907), p. 11.
2. Op. cit., p. 184.
3. Op. cit., p. 64.
4. Siegfried Giedion, *Space, Time and Architecture* (Cambridge, Mass., 1962), p. 255.
5. Lothar Bucher, *Literaturhistorische Skizzen aus der Industrieausstellung aller Völker* (Frankfurt, 1851), pp. 10–11 (also quoted by Meyer and Giedion).
6. Richard Lucae, "Über die Macht des Raumes in der Architektur," *Zeitschrift für Bauwessen*, vol. 19 (1869), p. 303. A similar comment is made by the French architect Boileau in regard to the Galerie des Machines of the Paris World Expo of 1878: "The spectator is not aware of the weight of the transparent surfaces. These surfaces are to him air and light, that is to say, an imponderable fluidity." (Quoted in Giedion, op. cit., p. 265.)
7. Max Raphael, *Von Monet zu Picasso* (Munich, 1913), p. 59.
8. Giedion says that Turner's painting *Simplon Pass* "uses a humid atmosphere to dematerialize landscape and dissolve it into infinity. The Crystal Palace realizes the same intention through the agency of transparent glass surfaces and iron structural members. In the Turner picture the means employed are less abstract, but an equivalent insubstantial and hovering effect is produced." (Op. cit., p. 253.)
9. The general economic base for this evanescence of perception is the fact that less and less labor (i.e., value) is invested in the individual product. Natural organic materials are increasingly replaced by synthetic surrogates; mass-produced objects are given built-in obsolescence; and "surface finish" is emphasized.
10. M. Luckiesh, *The Lighting Art* (New York and London, 1917), p. 210.
    Luckiesh is still aware that the price paid for such controllability is monotony. "In fact, the most striking feature of daylight is its variability and, although this is often annoying, the lack of monotony is one of the attractive features of daylight." (Op. cit.)
11. Op. cit., p. 3.
12. Op. cit., p. 85.
13. However, such radical changes occur only in the U.S. A German engineering work (Hefele, *Das Fabrik-Oberlicht* [Berlin, 1931]) presents a critical view of American efforts to eliminate the use of daylight in buildings. This argument is an excellent example of how the different developmental stages of any given industry (e.g., its degree of productivity) influence the engineering consciousness. In the Germany of 1931 an engineer can still make a case for the use of daylight because the German electrical industry is not yet as productive and dominant as the American; because artificial light has not yet been made available *en masse* and cheaply; and because there are traditional and cultural reasons for using daylight.

Chapter 4: Panoramic Travel

1. *Werke,* East Berlin ed., vol. 15, pp. 348 ff.; the complete journal of the Swiss journey in *Werke,* Sophia ed., vol. 2, sec. 3.
2. Erwin Straus, op. cit., p. 319.
3. Op. cit., p. 320.
4. D. Lardner, *Railway Economy,* p. 179.
5. C. H. Greenhow, *An Exposition of the Danger and Deficiencies of the Present Mode of Railway Construction* (London, 1846), p. 6.
6. H. G. Prout, "Safety in Railroad Travel," in *The American Railway,* ed. T. M. Cooley (New York, 1889), p. 187.
7. *Horse-Power Applied to Railways At Higher Rates of Speed than by Ordinary Draught* (London, 1844), p. 48.
8. "It [the railway] transmutes a man from a traveller into a living parcel." (Ruskin, *The Complete Works,* vol. 8, p. 159.) Manfred Riedel provides the two following quotes from lesser authors. For Ida Hahn-Hahn, the traveler "demotes himself to a parcel of goods and relinquishes his senses, his independence" (Manfred Riedel, "Vom Biedermeier zum Maschinenzeitalter," *Archiv für Kulturgeschichte,* vol. 43, (1961), fascicle 1, p. 119). And, according to Joseph Maria von Radowitz: "For the duration of such transportation one ceases to be a person and becomes an object, a piece of freight." (Op. cit., p. 120.)
9. Ruskin, vol. 36, p. 62; this is essentially echoed by a French medical author: "He [the traveler] hardly knows the names of the principal cities through which he passes, and only recognizes them, if at all, by the steeples of the best-known cathedrals which appear like trees by some faraway road." (A. Aulagnier, in *L'Union médicale de la Gironde* [Bordeaus, 1857], p. 525.)
10. Great Britain, *Parliamentary Papers,* "Report from the Select Committee on Railways," vol. 5 of the section "Transport and Communications" (reprint ed., Shannon, Ireland, 1968), p. 125.
11. From Manfred Riedel, op. cit., p. 112.
12. G. Muhl, *Die westeuropäischen Eisenbahnen in ihrer Gegenwart und Zukunft* (Karlsruhe, 1838), p. 18.
13. Op. cit., p. 19.
14. *The Influence of Railway Travelling on Public Health,* (London, 1862), p. 44. (This is a compendium of articles previously published in the journal the *Lancet*).
15. *The Sociology of Georg Simmel,* ed. Kurt M. Wolff (Glencoe, Ill., 1950), p. 410.
16. Joseph von Eichendorff, *Werke* (Munich, 1970), vol. 2, p. 895.
17. Ruskin, vol. 5, p. 370. Elsewhere, Ruskin speaks of the travelers "who once in their necessarily prolonged travel were subjected to an influence, from the silent sky and slumbering fields, more effectual than known or confessed." (Vol. 8, p. 246.)
18. *Correspondance* (Paris, 1929), vol. 5, pp. 153–54.
19. Op. cit.; Letter dated 30 October 1873, quoted in Marc Baroli, *Le Train dans la littérature Française* (Paris, 1964), p. 201. People sleep in their train compartments not only out of boredom; an equally strong motivation is the need to escape from the tiring influx of stimuli by means of sleep: "There are people, hurried by their business, who . . . in the course of one day have to cast their eyes upon the panoramas of several hundreds of places. They arrive at their destination overwhelmed by a previously unknown fatigue. Just ask these victims of velocity to tell you about the locations they have traveled through, to describe the perspectives whose rapid images have imprinted themselves, one after another, on the mirror of their brain. They will not be able to answer you. The agitated mind has called sleep to its rescue, to put an end to its overexcitation." (Gustave Claudin, *Paris* [Paris, 1867], pp. 71–72.)
20. Francis Lieber, *The Stranger in America* (London, 1834), vol. 2, pp. 1–2.
21. Henry Booth, *An Account of the Liverpool and Manchester Railway* (Liverpool, 1830), pp. 47–48.
22. Matthew E. Ward, *English Items; or, Microcosmic Views of England and Englishmen* (New York, 1853), pp. 71–72.
23. Benjamin Gastineau, *La Vie en chemin de fer* (Paris, 1861), p. 31.
24. Jules Clarétie, *Voyages d'un parisien* (Paris, 1865), p. 4.
25. Dolf Sternberger, *Panorama, oder Ansichten vom 19. Jahrhundert,* 3rd ed. (Hamburg, 1955), p. 57.

26. Op. cit., p. 50.

26a. Heins Buddemeier, *Panorama, Diorama, Photographie: Entstehung und Wirkung neuer Medien im 19.* Jahrhundert (Origin and effect of new media in the nineteenth century) Munich, 1970, p. 41.

26b. Ibid., p. 45.

26c. Ibid., p. 48.

26d. Ibid., p. 78.

27. *Congrès médical de France, troisième session tenue à Bordeaux* (Paris, 1866), p. 828.

28. *Quarterly Review,* vol. 42 (1830), p. 384.

29. Michael Alexander Lips, *Die Unanwendbarkeit der englischen Eisenbahnen auf Deutschland und deren Ersatz durch Dampffuhrwerk auf verbesserten Chausseen* ... (Marburg, 1833), p. 4.

30. John W. Dodds, *The Age of Paradox* (New York and Toronto, 1952), p. 374.

31. Jean Mistler, *La Librairie Hachette de 1826 à nos jours* (Paris, 1964), p. 123.

32. Op. cit., p. 299.

33. Dodds, pp. 374–75.

34. Mistler, p. 124.

35. P. D. Fischer, *Betrachtungen eines in Deutschland reisenden Deutschen* (Berlin, 1895), p. 31.

35a. Constantine Pecqueur, *Economie Sociale,* vol. 1, p. 349.

36. Op. cit., p. 830.

37. *The Influence of Railway Travelling on Public Health,* p. 44. A French author even posits a connection between mental affliction and travel reading, claiming that the latter causes a "congestion of the retina": "An eminent Parisian alienist, with whom I recently discussed this pernicious influence of reading while traveling on trains, told me that he not only admitted it to be true, but that an English physician, the head of a great private hospital, had told him that he had treated several patients suffering from general paralyses whose initial phenomenon, or determining cause, had been cerebral congestion brought about by those conditions that I have described." (Legrand de Saulle, in *Bulletin de la Société de Médecine pratique,* (1863), p. 9.)

38. Op. cit., p. 830.

Chapter 5: The Compartment

1. *Économie sociale,* vol. 1, pp. 335–36.

2. Op. cit., p. 338.

3. Op. cit., p. 338.

4. *Moderner Kapitalismus,* vol. 2, p. 262.

5. Op. cit., pp. 110 ff.

6. G. A. Thrupp, *The History of Coaches* (London, 1877), p. 48: "Sedan chairs came into fashion in England in 1634, and were in general use by the middle of the century. The alteration in the form of the coach, from the long barge shape of Charles I's time to that of Charles II was, no doubt, suggested by the shape of the sedan chair, in London as well as in Germany."

7. *L'Union médicale de la Gironde* (Bordeaux, 1857), pp. 524–25.

8. Georg Simmel, *Soziologie* (Leipzig, 1908), pp. 650–51. This passage is partially quoted in Walter Benjamin, "On Some Motifs in Baudelaire," in *Illuminations,* ed. Hannah Avendt, tr. Harry Zohn (New York, 1969), p. 191.

    Erving Goffman defines visual contact between persons unknown to each other as a disruption of the "territory of the self," i.e., one's "personal space." Goffman proceeds, interestingly enough, to give an example of a situation on a train journey: "This is nicely illustrated in Eastern seaboard parlor cars designed with a wide, longitudinal aisle and single seats at intervals on either side, the seats arranged to swivel. When there is crowding, travelers maximize their 'comfort' by turning their seats to exactly that direction that will allow the eyes, when oriented in the direction of the trunk, to gaze upon the least amount of passenger flesh. ... In ordinary railway or bus seating in America, passengers who feel overcrowded may be able to send their eyes out the window, thereby vicariously extending their personal space." (*Relations in Public* [New York, 1972], p. 30.) It would obviously be useful to know if and to what extent average "personal space" has changed in the last 150 years, i.e., whether it has grown larger or smaller. It would be equally interesting to determine the national and cultural differences between Europe and the United States with regard to "personal space."

9. Max Maria von Weber, *Schule des Eisenbahnwesens* (Leipzig, 1857), p. 178.

10. *The Railway Times,* vol. 1 (1838), p. 46.

11. "La petite chose" (1866), quoted in Baroli, p. 151.

12. In Baroli, p. 153.

13. Op. cit., p. 152.

14. Freud: "The shaking produced by driving in carriages and later by railway-travel exercises such a fascinating effect upon older children that every boy, at any rate, has at one time or other in his life wanted to be an engine driver or a coachman. It is a puzzling fact that boys take such an extraordinarily intense interest in things connected with railways, and, at the age at which the production of phantasies is most active (shortly before puberty), use those things as the nucleus of a symbolism that is peculiarly sexual. A compulsive link of this kind between railway-travel and sexuality is clearly derived from the pleasurable character of the sensations of movement. In the event of repression, which turns so many childish preferences into their opposite, these same individuals, when they are adolescents or adults, will react to rocking or swinging with a feeling of nausea, will be terribly exhausted by a railway journey, or will be subject to attacks of anxiety on the journey and will protect themselves against a repetition of the painful experience by a dread of railway-travel." Freud, Sigmund: *The Complete Psychological Word,* op. cit., vol. 7, p. 202.

15. *Psychoanalytische Studien,* vol. 2, p. 102.

16. The flying metaphor has received its pictorial expression in the symbol of the winged wheel, adopted by numerous Continental railway companies as their trademark. The descriptions of rail travel in terms of "flying" are too copious to enable one to make a sensible selection.

17. *Zeitung für Eisenbahnwesen, Dampfschiffahrt und Maschinenkunde,* vol. 1 (1845), pp. 114–15.

18. Peter Lecount, *A Practical Treatise on Railways, Explaining Their Construction and Management* (Edinburgh, 1839), p. 196.

19. "The Globe" (1863), quoted in Ivor Smullen, *Taken for a Ride* (London, 1968), p. 131.

20. *Annales d'hygiène publique et de médecine légale,* vol. 15 (1861), p. 224.

21. "Report of Captain Tyler," Great Britain, House of Commons, *Sessional Papers,* vol. 50 (1865), p. 6. An entire series of *Punch* cartoons renders similar situations.

22. Baroli points to the murder in Gide's "Les Caves du Vatican," where "isolation in the compartment almost provokes the crime." (Baroli, p. 450).

23. Ernest Dapples, *Le matériel roulant . . .* (Lausanne, 1866), p. 8.

24. Heusinger von Waldegg, ed., *Handbuch für spezielle Eisenbahn-Technik* (Leipzig, 1870), vol. 2, p. 298.

25. This has to be qualified: initial attempts were made to transfer the principle of individual traffic to the railroads, before the transportation monopolies became established. Yet the contemporary realization that the railroad differed from the old highways is reflected in the fact that the Canal Acts, not the Turnpike Acts, were chosen as the organizational model for railroad law.

26. Charles MacLaren, *Railways Compared with Canals and Common Roads . . .* (Edinburgh, 1825), pp. 45–46.

27. Morgan in *The American Traveller,* vol. 4 (1829), no. 83. We will also deal with the subject extensively in the next chapter of this book.

28. For a long time, toilets did not exist on trains. As soon as the train was in motion, the travelers had to curb their bladders. As soon as it pulled into a station, they could race each other to the facilities. Perdonnet's handbook (*Traité élémentaire des chemins de fer* [Paris, 1855–56], vol. 2, p. 34) states that "especially on the arrival platforms we have to install urinals of large dimensions." Commenting on the later on-train toilets, Waldegg's handbook says that these "have the drawback that the traveler using them has to remain in them from one station to the next, and this, at least in the case of express trains, can be a more or less unpleasant experience." (*Handbuch für spezielle Eisenbahn-Technik,* vol. 2, p. 342.)

29. In Württemberg, in Switzerland, and in Austria, on short-distance lines there was a kind of overland bus traffic.

30. Dapples, op. cit., p. 11.

31. "Report of Captain Tyler," p. 12.

32. In England, these were soon called "Muller's Windows," after the name of Briggs' murderer. See cartoons in *Punch,* e.g., issue of November 25, 1865.

33. *Handbuch . . .,* vol. 2, p. 303.

34. Initially, Waldegg does not discuss a side corridor, but a gallery mounted on the *outside* of the carriage. (*Zeitung des Vereins Deutscher Eisenbahn-Verwaltungen,* No. 25 (1863), p. 354.)

Chapter 6: The American Railroad

1. *Vom rollenden Flügelrade* (Berlin, 1882), p. 66.
2. "The revolution in the mode of production of industry and agriculture specifically required another revolution in the general conditions of the social production process, i.e., in the means of communication and transportation." (Marx, *Capital*, op. cit., pp. 404–05.)
3. *The Process of Economic Growth* (New York, 1962), p. 262. George R. Taylor: "The American economy of the early nineteenth century might best be described as extractive-commercial in character. It is true that the beginnings of industrial growth were already discernible. But in this land of continental expanses only revolutionary developments in the techniques of transportation and communication would make possible that almost explosive rush of industrial expansion which characterized the later decades of the century." (*The Transportation Revolution, 1815–1860* [New York, 1968], p. 3.)
4. "The lands were unoccupied, and so valueless. By the building of the railroads a market would be created, and by the doubling of the price of the sections reserved the government would be reimbursed for the amount given away. The grant would therefore assume the nature of a commission from the government to the railroads as agents for placing the unoccupied lands upon the market." (*Railroad Promotion and Capitalization in the United States* [first ed., 1909; reprint ed., New York, 1966], p. 246.)
5. Henry Nash Smith, *Virgin Land* (Cambridge, Mass., 1973), pp. 158, 162. A typical example can be found in Charles Fraser's article "The moral influence of steam" (*Hunt's Merchant Magazine*, vol. 14 [1846], p. 509): "Without the steamboat, ages might have passed without such a development of her [America's] resources as is now exhibited. The enterprises and industry of the West would have been unrewarded; the progress of civilization would have been slow; the trees of the forest would have still overshadowed the sites of flourishing villages; silence and solitude would have prevailed, where now the busy hum of men resounds, and the inheritance of the hardy pioneer would have been ignorance and barbarism." Henry Adams: ". . . while the United States were commercial allies of England, and needed steam neither for mines nor for manufactures, but their need was still extreme. Every American knew that if steam could be successfully applied to navigation, it must produce an immediate increase of wealth." (*History of the United States* [first ed., 1891–96; reprint ed., New York, 1962], vol. 1, p. 66.)
6. *The Machine in the Garden* (London, Oxford, and New York, 1972), p. 238.
7. Leo Marx, op. cit., especially chapter 5.
8. H. J. Habakkuk, *American and British Technology in the Nineteenth Century* (Cambridge, 1967), p. 32.
9. *Railroad Promotion and Capitalization* (New York, 1909), p. 28.
10. G. R. Taylor, op. cit., pp. 15–16.
11. In the colonial period, settlement occurs along the Atlantic Coast and the nearby river estuaries. "A study of the spread of settlement up to 1775 shows that the immigrant population ran up the river valleys as far as the fall-line, and there generally stopped." (Balthasar Henry Meyer, ed., *History of Transportation in the United States before 1860* [first ed., 1917; reprint ed., Washington, D.C., 1948] p. 4.)

    After the waterways that connect directly with the Atlantic have been opened, the settlement expands by leaps and bounds: big pockets of settlement appear by the Great Lakes and in the Ohio Valley, and these are no longer directly connected to the ocean. That connection is then either created artificially (Erie Canal to Great Lakes) or made by using natural detours (Ohio River — Mississippi River — Gulf of Mexico — Atlantic Ocean). The same process repeats itself on a grand scale in California, where settlement begins along the Pacific Coast, and traffic mainly proceeds via Cape Horn or the Isthmus of Panama until the completion of the transcontinental railroad.

    The development of settlement and transportation in the U.S. is not unique in its initial reliance on waterways — in fact, every colonization begins from these — but it is unique in terms of the brief and concentrated span of time in which settlement takes place. European settlement also began by the water (Mediterranean, great rivers), but in the course of centuries and millennia, an infrastructure of European overland routes developed which obscured the initial pattern of aquatic connections. In the U.S. the foreshortening of that process to less than a century causes a kind of prolongation in consciousness of the initial settlement and traffic phase (i.e., the one based on waterways): in other words, American traffic consciousness in the nineteenth century still bears the imprint of the categories established by the waterways. We find a good example of this in Henry Nash Smith's discussion of the plan for a *transcontinental* waterway connection proposed by Thomas Hart Benton as late as 1846, after the railroad had been firmly established as a means of overland transportation in the U.S.: "The reason why Benton showed such a monumental inability to understand the revolution in transport that was under way was that he thought in terms of a tradition, a century of preoccupation with the network of natural waterways overspreading the Mississippi Valley." (*Virgin Land,* pp. 30–31.)

One of the essential differences between the European and the American railroads is that they establish connections of a different nature. In Europe, these connections are mainly between cities; in America, the railroad connects entire areas of settlement that could previously be reached only by means of great detours on the natural waterways. Thus the American railroad first appears as a complement to the waterway network. The first explicit recognition of this appears in an article in the *North American Review* in 1829 dealing with the projected Baltimore and Ohio Railroad: "Not only do our great rivers and lakes already afford to the vast surface which they drain, an extensive carriage of their products to some market or other, but it is found that, by means of the frequent connexion of their headstreams, this advantage may be very greatly increased and diffused." (Pp. 166–67.)

The customary notion that the American railroads simply struck out into the wilderness is not entirely correct; they were, indeed, built through extensive wilderness areas, but in order to reach another, already existing, region of settlement that could previously be reached only by water.

12. C. W. Ernst, "Boston and Transportation" (*Proceedings of the Bostonian Society* [January, 1888], pp. 22–23) cites a few more concepts borrowed from nautical terminology. See also the concept of "land navigation," a term which Daniel Webster coined for the railroad (*The Writings and Speeches* [Boston, 1903], vol. 4, p. 113).

13. G. T. Poussin, *Amerikanische Eisenbahnen* (Regensburg, 1837), p. 13.

David Stevenson provides a typical example of the European travelers' astonishment at finding a waterway culture of almost maritime dimensions in the middle of the continent. He describes the view of the Ohio River at Pittsburgh: "Here, in the very heart of the continent of North America, the appearance of a large shipping port, containing a fleet of thirty or forty steamers moored in the river, cannot fail to surprise him." (*Sketch of the Civil Engineering of North America* [London, 1838], p. 76.)

14. "A Sketch of a Journey through the Western States of North America" (1827), quoted in Reuben Gold Thwaites, ed., *Early Western Travels, 1748–1846* (Cleveland, 1905), vol. 19.

15. *History of the United States,* vol. 9, p. 173.

16. J. Mak and G. Walton, "Steamboats and the Great Productivity Surge in River Productivity," *The Journal of Economic History,* vol. 32 (1972), pp. 619–40.

17. Louis C. Hunter, *Steamboats on the Western Rivers* (New York, 1969), p. 33.

18. Op. cit., p. 61.

19. *Atlantic Monthly,* vol. 2 (1858), pp. 644–45.

20. Franz Anton Ritter von Gerstner, *Berichte aus den Vereinigten Staaten von Nord-Amerika, ihrer Eisenbahnen, Dampfschiffahrten, Banken, und andere öffentliche Unternehmungen* (Leipzig, 1839), pp. 15, 60. The figures relate to the Liverpool-Manchester Line and include not only the actual expenditure for constructing the line itself, but also expenditures for buildings, rolling stock, administration, etc.

21. Captain Douglas Galton's "Report to the Lords of the Committee of Privy Council for Trade on the Railways of the United States," (London, 1857; p. 11) gives 10,000 to 12,000 pounds sterling versus 35,000 pounds. Toward the end of the century, Arthur T. Hadley quotes the following figures: 204,000 dollars per mile in England versus 61,000 in the U.S. (*Railroad Transportation* [New York and London, 1897], p. 260.)

22. Minus Ward, *Remarks, Propositions and Calculations, Relative to a Rail-Road and Locomotive Engines . . . from Baltimore to the Ohio River* (Baltimore, 1827), pp. iv–v.

23. Stephen H. Long, "On the Principles Which Should Govern the Location and Construction of Rail-Roads," *Journal of the Franklin Institute,* vol. 6 (1830), p. 183.

The construction of curving stretches of rail, an adaptation to natural obstacles, merely presents a possibility of capital savings. As European experts unanimously note, and American engineers openly admit, the railroads are built as cheaply as possible, i.e., in a very primitive manner. This is justified by the necessity to first establish transport connections, which can be improved later on. Galton: ". . . as in a new country it is impossible to foresee at the opening of a railway where the main centres of traffic will eventually be, it would have been a mere waste to invest more capital in the construction of a railway than would render it efficient for the work immediately before it." (Op. cit., p. 10.)

This "predisposition toward impermanence" (Marvin Fisher, *Workshops in the Wilderness* [New York, 1967], p. 71) is a characteristic trait of American industrial development and one that is recognized early on. "At first view, one is struck with the temporary and apparently unfinished state of many of the American works," observes David Stevenson in 1838, "and is very apt, before inquiring into the subject to impute to want of ability what turns out, on investigation, to be a judicious and ingenious arrangement to suit the circumstances of a new climate . . ." (*Sketches of Civil Engineering of North America* [London, 1838], p. 192).

In the U.S., industrial machinery is exploited according to the same principle, "substitution of nature for capital," as are natural resources. It is constructed inexpensively, quickly, and in accordance with the latest technological developments; later it is junked with equal speed. Habakkuk says that "American manufacturers were readier than the English to scrap existing equipment and replace it by new, and they therefore had more opportunities of taking advantage of technological progress and acquiring know-how"; his remark that "the English inclination was to repair rather than to scrap" indicates that America's and England's differing attitudes towards machinery may be explained, not only by the obvious economic motivations, but also in terms of differing traditions: on the one hand, Europe's still-active heritage of careful craftsmanship; on the other, the American vision of an infinitely disposable nature, which even includes the machines. (Habakkuk, pp. 56 ff.)

24. Elias Derby, *Two Months Abroad* (Boston, 1844), p. 8.
25. "Letters Patent of Ross Winans" (October 1, 1834), Library of the Association of American Railroads, Washington, D.C.
26. C. F. Dendy Marshall, *A History of Railway Locomotives down to the Year 1831* (London, 1953), pp. 62 ff.
27. Unlike the American type of car, the "bogie" gains instant recognition by European railway experts. Lardner calls it "a simple and effectual arrangement" (*Railway Economy*, p. 338). And Gerstner notes: "There is considerably less wear and tear on both rails and carriages, and the repair costs of both carriages and locomotives are far lower than in Europe" (*Berichte*, p. 19). Toward the end of the nineteenth century, as European long-distance trains equipped with Waldegg's side corridor achieve American dimensions, the "bogie" is introduced there as well.
28. August Mencken, *The Railroad Passenger Car* (Baltimore, 1957), pp. 9 ff.
29. Galton, op. cit., p. 15.
30. C. Hamilton Ellis, *Railway Carriages in the British Isles from 1830 to 1914* (London, 1965), p. 22.
31. *De la puissance Américaine* (Paris, 1845), vol. 1, p. 157. Similarly L. Simonin thirty years later: "A day spent on the railroad in one of these cars . . . passes quickly and effortlessly because the traveler enjoys a great number of comforts and is not imprisoned in it. He is able to move at will . . . to come and go anywhere throughout the train. . . . (*Le Monde Américain* [Paris, 1875], p. 366.)
   The adjustability of backrests, Simonin notes, makes it possible to have various seating arrangements, depending on the situation: "If three or four people are traveling together, they can face each other in a kind of relative privacy" (p. 364). This statement tacitly implies that solitary travelers or those in pairs usually adjust their seats so that they do *not* face anybody; thus there is no inevitable "confrontation," as there is in the European compartment.
32. E. B. Dorsey, "English and American Railroads Compared," *Transactions of the American Society of Civil Engineers*, vol. 15 (1887), p. 1.
33. Robert S. Minot, *Railway Travel in Europe and America* (Boston, 1882), pp. 11–12.
34. Thomas L. Nichols, *Forty Years of American Life* (first ed., 1864; reprint ed., New York, 1969), vol. 2, p. 8.
35. Great Britain, *Sessional Papers* (House of Commons), vol. 50 (1865), p. 6.
36. *Voie, matériel roulant, et exploitation technique des chemins de fer* (Paris, 1873), vol. 2, p. 17.
37. Mencken, p. 5 ff.
38. Couche, p. 25.
39. *Handbuch . . .*, vol. 2, p. 5.
40. Galton, p. 16.
41. E. Lavoinnel and E. Pontzen, *Les chemins de fer en Amérique* (Paris, 1882), vol. 2, p. 1.
42. Ellis' monograph on the English railway carriage, and Mencken's on the American, range from the anecdotal to the technically detailed, with Mencken stressing the latter, Ellis the former aspect. In addition, there are scattered essays of a semiscientific, almost folkloristic nature, such as E. G. Young, "The Development of the American Railway Passenger Car" (*The Railway and Locomotive Historical Society Bulletin*, no. 32 [1933]), as well as more or less

accessible pictorial volumes with varying amounts of text, such as Lucius Beebe, *Mr. Pullman's Elegant Palace Car* (New York, 1961), which mentions the river steamboat as the model of the Pullman car (pp. 279 seq.).

43. *Victorian Comfort: A Social History of Design from 1830–1900,* (New York, 1973, p. 139, 142).

44. Benjamin Dearborn's proposal of 1819 for a shiplike rail carriage. General James Semple's illustrated proposal for a "Prairie Steam-Car," a vehicle that looks like a river steamboat and locomotes across the plains on rollers, not on rails. (*The Scientific American,* March 12, 1846.)

45. *Mr. Pullman's Elegant Palace Car,* p. 280.

46. In Ezra Reed's patent application of April 6, 1833, the sectional canal boat is described as follows: "This canal boat is to be built in parts, or sections, each having its four sides, and bottom. Of these sections there may be six, or more; the two forming the stem and the stern may differ in shape from the others, which may be nearly, or quite, alike. The separate parts are to be united by two pieces of plank on each side, extending from stem to stern, fastened by spikes, or bolts, to the bow and stern sections; the intermediate ones to be kept in their place by chains." (*Journal of the Franklin Institute,* vol. 12 [1833], p. 235.) In this separation and reassembly of interchangeable parts we recognize, once again, the Colt-Whitney principle characteristic of American technology and also expressed in the "bogie."

47. D. Stevenson, *Sketches . . . ,* p. 197.

48. Galton, p. 15; Mencken, pp. 12 seq.

49. *Domestic Manners of the Americans* (first ed., 1832; reprint ed., New York, 1949), p. 15. On the ubiquitousness of ships even in the heart of the country: "I hardly remember a single town where vessels of some description or other may not constantly be seen in full activity" (op. cit., p. 303).

50. "The great development of traffic [in the U.S.] skipped the era of highways and began, in contrast to all European countries, immediately with the construction of the most rapid and profitable means of transport, the railroad. Especially after the union of all the states it became necessary to master the enormous space they covered. Only the railroad could answer this need. Thus the promising beginnings of a highway network, particularly in New England and in the vicinity of great cities, were inhibited or even thwarted. Thus a gap was created in the development of overland traffic that remained open until the beginning of the twentieth century. Only then, after the introduction of the automobile, that gap was slowly closed," (Hans Kicia, "Die Landstrassen in den Vereinigten Staaten von Nord-amerika," *Zeitschrift für Verkehrswissenshaft,* vol. 6 [1928], p. 109.)

Discussing the development of highways in the latter half of the nineteenth century, an American publication of the year 1896 goes so far as to state that, due to the exclusive attention paid to the railroads, the highways were "in a poorer state than they were fifty years ago" (N. S. Shaler, *American Highways* [New York, 1896], p. 242).

The early nineteenth century's neglect of the highways is only one side of the matter. After the automobile becomes the mode of mass transportation, highways are built again, but now their mode of construction breaks away from its own ancient tradition and acquires a new orientation based on the railroad. (The German *Autobahnen* (highways) of the 1920s and 1930s are associated with the *Eisenbahn* (railroad), not only in name, but are even administered by the national railway corporation.) The highway constructed exclusively for automotive traffic no longer integrates urban and rural traffic, stationary and moving traffic, but, like the railroad, only serves *moving* traffic. Benton MacKay, proponent of the "limited access highway," justifies his demand for an exclusively automotive highway that no longer runs through the cities by stating that the automobile is, in fact, a locomotive. "By a similar transfer we have until recently looked upon the motor road as a fitting frontage for our home lot, instead of regarding it realistically as a causeway, as much to be shunned as a railroad. Once these conventional prejudices are abolished, we see that the motor road is a new kind of railroad. . . ." (Benton Mackay, *The New Exploration* [Urbana, Ill., 1962], p. 231.)

51. "L'Illustration," *Journal Universel,* July 22, 1848, p. 316.

52. L. C. Hunter, p. 391.

53. "Floating Palace" and "Moving Hotel" are popular nicknames for the steamboats on the Ohio and Mississippi rivers. (See Hunter, p. 390.)

54. Derby, *Two Months . . . ,* p. 32.

55. *Sketches . . . ,* p. 136.

55a. Charles Sealsfield, *Die Vereinigten Staaten von Nord Amerika* (The United States of North America), Stuttgart and Tübingen, 1827, two volumes in one, vol. 2, p. 136).

56. Report of the Committee on Commerce and Manufactures, quoted in William M. Brown, *The History of the First Locomotives in America* (New York, 1874), p. 73.

57. Lanman, in *Merchant's Magazine and Commercial Review,* vol. 3 (1840), p. 274.

58. "Steamboat gothic" is the popular term for what becomes a stylistic concept in the nineteenth century. (For a detailed description, see Hunter, pp. 396 ff.)

59. Pullman cars have a dual function, transportation and comfort. They permit the passengers to stay in the car while it is being shunted from one line to another, and as the railroad network expands, such shunting becomes increasingly frequent. They are operated by the Pullman company, which enters into cooperative contracts with the individual lines. The travelers using these cars pay an additional fare.

60. Beebe, p. 285.

61. The paper was called the *Trans-Continental.* It appears for the first time in May, 1870, on the occasion of a special trip arranged by the Union Pacific for a group of Boston businessmen. I do not know if further issues appeared.

62. *Trans-Continental,* May 26 and 30, 1870.

63. Thus, Charles Dickens calls the prairie "a tranquil sea or lake without water" (quoted in D. A. Dondore, *The Prairie and the Making of Middle America* [Cedar Rapids, Iowa, 1926], p. 290). An 1871 German text remarks: "No land in sight. As far as one can see, this ocean. . . ." (Alexander Friherr von Hübner, *Ein Spaziergang um die Welt* [Leipzig, 1882], p. 53.)

64. See note 11 above.

65. *The Writings and Speeches* (Boston, 1903), vol. 4, p. 113. A curious similarity between railroad train and steamboat appears in their relative speeds at the time. According to Gerstner, the steamers reached 12 mph, the trains 12–15 mph (*Berichte . . .,* p. 44). Even later on, American rail velocities differ considerably from the European ones. In 1864, the average speed of American express trains is 32 mph (*Appleton's Railway Guide,* quoted in John H. White, *American Locomotives, 1830–1880* [Baltimore, 1968], p. 74). English trains had already reached that figure in the 1840s.

66. *Society, Manners, and Politics in the United States* (Ithaca, New York, 1961), p. 270.

Chapter 7: The Pathology of the Railroad Journey

1. The index of the leading English medical journal, the *Lancet,* does not mention the word *railway* time in the 1830s. In the 1840s it appears in connection with accidents, but only in passing. In the mid-1830s, several physicians, discussing the projected London-Brighton line, concern themselves with the problems of smoke, sudden changes of temperature, noise, etc. Those problems, however, do not specifically relate to the actual process of rail travel. Medical views on the latter — i.e., on the effects of the novel velocity, vibration, etc. — vary and contradict each other to an extent that makes it impossible to consider them as serious scientific investigations of the new mode of transport. For instance, in 1835 Bavaria's *Obermedizinalkollegium* predicts that rail travelers would succumb to brain damage, or "delirium furiosum." (Cf. Gisela Koch and M. Hoffman, "Geschichte der Verkehrsmedizin für den Verkehr mit Landfahrzeugen von den Anfängen bis zum ende des 2. Weltkrieges," *Zentralblatt für Verkehrsmedizin, Verkehrspsychologie, Luft- und Raumfahrt-Medizin,* vol. 15, fascicle 4, p. 193). Here we quote several contrary evaluations of the effects of the vibration experienced on the train. In 1836, in C. W. Hufeland's medical journal, the swaying motion of coach travel is described as salutary, whereas "this great advantage of continuous beneficial vibration . . . entirely disappears in railway travel." (*Neües Journal der praktischen Heilkunde . . .,* vol. 75 [1836], p. 119.) Then, the exact opposite, in the *Medico-Chirurgical Review, and Journal of Practical Medicine:* "The vibratory, or rather oscillatory motion communicated to the human frame, is very different from the jolting and swinging motions of the stage-coach, and is productive of more salutary effects. It equalized the circulation, promotes digestion, tranquilizes the nerves." (Quoted in the *American Railroad Journal,* vol. 6 [1837], p. 689.)

2. "At the beginning of railroad traffic, the train personnel had no shelter from the weather. The train conductors and brakemen stood on the open carriage platform or huddled on top of the carriages on uncovered seats." (Koch and Hoffmann, op. cit., p. 198.)

3. Georg Kuhl, *Die westeuropäischen Eisenbahnen in ihrer Gegenwart und Zunkunft* (Karlsruhe, 1838), p. 21.
4. E. A. Duschesne, *Des chemins de fer et leur influence sur la santé des mécaniciens et des chauffeurs* (Paris, 1857), p. 183.
5. Op. cit., p. 146.
6. *Wieck Deutsche Illustrirte Gewerbezeitung*, vol. 25, (Leipzig, 1860), p. 228.
7. Duchesne, pp. 145–46; Von Weber, p. 228: "In order to ameliorate the jolts and to react to the engine's motions with greater ease, these people spend almost all their time standing on the front part of their feet, raising their heels up from the floor."
8. Op. cit., p. 146.
9. Op. cit., p. 228.
10. Only travelers in the two higher classes enjoy the shelter of closed and roofed cars; the situation of the third- and fourth-class passengers, riding in open quasi-freight cars, is almost identical to that of the locomotive personnel. "People sat on crowded benches, with the wind roaring over them so that they were unable to talk, the smoke stinging their eyes and nostrils; when it rained, they had to open up their umbrellas. . . . One can see how they endure, patiently, hour by hour, and how they then clamber down from the cars, literally racked, sooty, covered in dust." (E. Stich, "Über die Massnahmen zur Erhaltung eines gesunden Eisenbahnpersonals," *Verhandlungen des Verbandes deutscher Bahnärzte* [Cologne, 1889], quoted in Koch and Hoffmann, op. cit., p. 200.)
11. *The Influence of Railway Travelling on Public Health* (London, 1862), pp. 23–24. This is a pamphlet from the medical journal, the *Lancet*. It will be referred to hereafter as the *Lancet* pamphlet.
12. Op. cit., p. 41.
13. Op. cit., pp. 40–41.
14. Op. cit., p. 44.
15. "No less detrimental to the human organism than the shocks are the powerful noises that literally inundate the locomotive personnel; most of these are of an intensity and pitch that are truly damaging to ears and nerves. The volume of noise experienced while riding in the locomotive (and, at times, even in the carriage) is uncommonly great. . . . Thus any attentive person has noticed that when he rides on a train and passes large groups of people who are engaged in some festive occasion and *shouting*, the latter fact can only be perceived visually, not *heard* at all." (Von Weber, op. cit., p. 229.) See also *Lancet* pamphlet, op. cit., p. 45.
16. The *Lancet* pamphlet discusses "an often experienced condition of uneasiness, scarcely amounting to actual fear, which pervades the generality of travellers by rail. The possibility of collision is constantly present to such persons, and everyone knows how, if by chance a train stops at some unusual place, or if the pace be slackened, or the whistle sounds its shrill alarm, a head is projected from nearly every window, and anxious eyes are on the look-out for signs of danger. . . . The pace, also, prevents the traveller from that observation of natural objects and sights of interest on the road, which made coach travelling a source of mental relaxation and a pastime. The passenger is forced into subjective sources of mental activity; and where the tendency to excitement exists, this also, *quantum valeat*, must be esteemed an undesirable feature belonging to this manner of locomotion." (Op. cit., p. 43.) Another psychic strain is caused by the fear of missing the train. Thus, an article of 1855 in the *Journal of Public Health and Sanitary Review:* "The causes of the evil are not to be found in the noise, vibration, and speed of the railway carriage . . . but in the excitement, anxiety, and nervous shock consequent on the frequent efforts to catch the *last* express; to be in time for the fearfully punctual train." (Vol. 1, p. 425.) The frequent mention of this aspect demonstrates the generality of such anxiety in the 1850s and 1860s. In 1868, there even is a monograph dedicated mainly to this subject: Haviland's *Hurried to Death.*
17. Op. cit., p. 53.
18. Peter Gaskell, *Artisans and Machinery: The Moral and Physical Condition of the Manufacturing Population Considered with Reference to Mechanical Substitutes for Human Labour* (London, 1836), pp. 237–38.
19. *Capital,* (Chicago, 1906–1909), vol. 11, p. 62.
20. Op. cit., p. 164.
21. *Capital,* vol. 1 (164), p. 455; identical or similar formulations can, of course, be found in almost any text by Marx. Gaskell's characterization of the industrial worker is very similar: ". . . he will have lost all free agency, and will be as much a part of the machines around him as the wheels or cranks which communicate motion." (Op. cit., p. 338.)
22. Cf. chapter IV, note 8 above. The Ruskin quote reads in full: "The whole system of railroad travelling is addressed to people who, being in a hurry, are therefore, for the time being, miserable. No one would travel in that manner who could help it — who had the time to go

THE RAILWAY JOURNEY

leisurely over hills and between hedges instead of through tunnels and between banks: or at least, those who would, have no sense of beauty so acute as that we need consult it at the station. The railroad is in all its relations a matter of earnest business, to be got through as soon as possible. It transmutes a man from a traveller into a living parcel."

23. Op. cit., p. 137.
24. *Mechanization Takes Command* (New York, 1969), p. 365.
25. Siegfried Giedion, in the section of *Mechanization* entitled "The Reign of the Upholsterer," gives the following description of Second-Empire lounge furniture: "The skeleton of the chairs and sofas has retreated deep into the cushions: a process that the French have called 'la victoire de la garniture sur le bois' (the victory of the trimmings over the wood). Every and any means are used to make the armchairs, sofas, divans, ottomans, as heavy and as bulky as possible. Foot-long fringes sometimes veil even the stumps, all that remain of the legs. The furniture increasingly tends to suggest bloated cushions." (Op. cit., p. 366.) Compare this with Erich Schild's description of Garnier's Paris Opera: "The entire structure consists of constructions of iron girders and pipes that have been covered up with masonry, marble, and stucco, and transmuted into forms that all but obliterate the skeleton. . . . There is no rivalry here between construction and form. The outward shape is everything, the underlying structure merely a helpmeet, subordinated into service." (*Zwischen Glaspalast und Palais des Illusions* [Frankfurt, Berlin, and Vienna, 1967], p. 92.)

What the interior, invisible, steel girders are to Beaux-Arts architecture, the steel spring is to upholstered furniture. The spiral spring, until then used only "for purely technical purposes" (Giedion, op. cit., p. 382), now facilitates the unprecedentedly lavish upholstery that rests upon and around it, concealing it from view just as the Paris Opera conceals its girders.

In France, the Second Empire marks the full flowering of the upholstery principle in both architecture and furniture. For all of Europe, the reign of upholstery extends from approximately 1855 to 1890. Between 1850 and 1855 the principle of free and unconcealed construction prevails in the utilitarian architecture of exhibition buildings, railroad terminals, market halls, etc., in the wake of the success of London's Crystal Palace of 1851. But in 1855, a reaction sets in, signaled by the Parisian World Expo building of that year. "A sharp shift in taste at this time, leading to a predominant preference for the massively plastic in architecture, made unfashionable both the delicate membering suitable to iron and the smooth transparent surfaces provided by large areas of glass." (Henry Russell Hitchcock, *Architecture: Nineteenth and Twentieth Centuries* [Baltimore, 1958], p. 115.). And, on the Paris Expo building of 1855: "The great iron-and-glass arched interiors were all but completely masked externally by a very conventional masonry shell." (Hitchcock, op. cit., p. 128).

From around 1890 on, construction starts to emancipate itself again, most notably in Dutert's famous hall of machines at the Paris World Expo of 1889, a steel construction without any masonry shell at all. Roughly at the same time, the furniture industry manifests tendencies to reduce upholstery. Thus we find the following in an article published in August, 1897, in *Furniture and Decoration and the Furniture Gazette:* "It is necessary now that the system of thin stuffing has become prevalent to pay more careful attention to the frames of our couches than was commonly done a few years ago. The frames of some of the old-fashioned thickly-stuffed Chesterfield sofas bore little or no relation to the finished piece of upholstery. The lines of the wood formed merely a skeleton which was padded out and completely extinguished in an envelope of horsehair, flock, alva, shavings. . . . The construction of the article was completely hidden from the lay eye. . . ." (Quoted in John Gloag, *Victorian Comfort* [New York, 1973], pp. 70–71.) Gloag points out that the simplification of furniture is an expression of the same tendency toward functional construction manifested in architecture, roughly simultaneously, by Wright, Sullivan, van de Velde (op. cit., p. 72).

The final and general rejection of the upholstery principle in both furniture and architecture can certainly be connected with World War I, the destructive culmination of Europe's Industrial Revolution: the Bauhaus was born in 1919.

204

Excursion: Industrial Fatigue

1. Lecture by Frederick Braithwaite, *Proceedings of The Institute of Civil Engineers* (Great Britain), vol. XIII (1854), p. 463.
2. B. Laignel, *Quelques mots et remarques sur les chemins de fer, à l'occasion de l'événemant du 8 mai* (Paris, 1842), p. 2.
3. Wöhler's essays in the *Zeitschrift für Bauwesen:* "Versuche über Biegung und Verdrehung von Eisenbahnwagenachsen während der Fahrt" (vol. 8 [1858], pp. 461 seq.); "Versuche über die einwirkenden Kräfte und die Widerstandsfähigkeit bei Eisenbahnwagenachsen" (vol. 10 [1860], pp. 583 seq.). Wöhler: "Versuche über die Festigkeit von Eisenbahnwagenachsen" (vol. 13 [1863], pp. 233 seq.); "Versuche über die relative Festigkeit von Eisen, Stahl und Kupfer" (vol. 16 [1866], pp. 67 seq.).
4. In a contract between firearms manufacturers and the Prussian army, 1722: "The rifles will be received by an officer who has the barrels tested by shooting and, if they are found to work well, has those barrels stamped with an eagle; he likewise examines and tests each rifle lock." (Quoted in Walter Ruske: 100 Zahre Materialprüntüng in Berlin. Ein Beitrag Für Technikgeschichte. Berlin-West, 1971, p. 217.
5. Almost a quarter (about 100 pages) of the *festschrift* of the German Federal Institute of Material Testing is devoted to the history of military testing institutions.
6. According to an estimate made in 1848, between 1816 and 1848 there were 233 boiler explosions on American river steamboats, and these caused 2,563 deaths (John G. Burke, "Bursting Boilers and the Federal Power," in *Technology and Culture,* ed. M. Kranzberg and W. R. Davenport [New York, 1972], p. 109). The year 1838 witnessed 14 explosions and 496 deaths (op. cit., p. 98). The explosion on the *Moselle,* in 1838, took the lives of all 151 passengers and crew members; another, the lives of 140. (Op. cit., p. 106.)
7. Ruske, p. 29.
8. Braithwaite gives a clear description of the distinction between statically and dynamically stressed material: "Metal, in a state of rest, although sustaining a heavy pressure, or strain, as in a girder, and exhibiting the deflection due to the superposed weight, will continue to bear that pressure, without fracture, so long as its rest is not disturbed, or the same strain is not too often repeated, but, if its rest is too frequently disturbed, the metal becomes deteriorated, and worn out, at the part subject to the reiterated strain, and fracture will, ultimately, ensue." (Op. cit.)
9. *Capital,* vol. 1 (Chicago), 1906–09, p. 448.
10. J. Y. Mann, *Fatigue of Metals* (London and New York, 1967), p. 3.
11. Cf. Marx's comment on Descartes' understanding of animals as machines: "It may here be incidentally observed, that Descartes, in defining animals as mere machines, saw with eyes of the manufacturing period, while to eyes of the middle ages, animals were assistants to man." *Capital,* vol. I, op. cit., p. 426.)

Chapter 8: the Accident

1. Cf. Chapter 1, note 27.
2. Quoted in Cyril Bruyn Andrews, *The Railway Age* (London, 1937), p. 31.
3. *Zeitung für Eisenbahnwesen, Dampfschiffahrt und Maschinenkunde,* vol. 1 (1845), pp. 114–15. (the article reprinted from *Frankenstein's Allgemeines Industrie- und Gewerbeblatt*).
4. This process of the assimilation of initially disturbing new phenomena has been excellently described by Peter Wexler in the context of the development of French railroad vocabulary (*La formation du vocabulaire des chemins de fer en France, 1778–1842* [Geneva and Lille, 1955]). Wexler states that the initial phase is a "descriptive" one, characterized by cumbersome and pedantic circumlocutions for processes and parts of machinery that are still unknown; in the last phase, we get a new concretized conceptual vocabulary, which is an expression of the new "almost unconscious familiarity" with the formerly frightening technology.

5. Ernest Bloch, *Spuren* (Frankfurt and Berlin, 1962), p. 208.
6. Felix Tourneux, *Encyclopédie des chemins de fer et des machines à vapeur* (Paris, 1844), pp. 2–3.
7. *Capital,* vol. 11, p. 126. In this context, reference should be made to central concepts of Freudian psychoanalysis: psychic apparatus, economic principle, free and contained energy, etc. The balance between the Ego and the Id is assumed to be as unstable as the balance between the parts of a nineteenth-century machine. The psychic apparatus, according to Pontalis and Laplanche, "performs a particular kind of *labor,* described by Freud in various ways: it transforms free energy into contained energy, postpones frustration, psychically *reworks* stimuli, etc." (*Das Vokabular der Psychoanalyse* [Frankfurt, 1972], p. 358.) It might be profitable to consider, in terms of the history of these concepts, the connections between accident, crisis, and neurosis.

Chapter 9: Railroad Accident, "Railway Spine," Traumatic Neurosis

1. In England the corresponding law, the Campbell Act, is passed as early as 1846. However, only an amendment passed in 1864 makes this act applicable to victims of railroad accidents, as literature by medical experts only begins to appear after that date.

It is worthwhile to investigate how the industrialization process is reflected in accelerating accident rates and the new institutions such as liability laws and accident insurance policies which grow out of these. Thus the increase in railroad accidents is a part of the general increase in industrial accidents. The more sophisticated the mechanization of production becomes, the more vulnerable it also becomes, especially in the initial period of adjustment, as people are not yet accustomed to the new machines. The connection between industrialization and accident frequency can be seen in the Registrar's Office annual report of 1842, which notes the remarkably higher (i.e., double) rate of fatal accidents in England as compared to other countries, and demands a statistical analysis of its causes: "The violent deaths in England appear to be nearly twice as frequent as in other countries of Europe from which returns have been procured. . . . The coroners' informations, although not made at present on a uniform plan, furnish many valuable facts, and when compared with the occupations and other circumstances recorded in the registers, or ascertained at the census, become doubly interesting. . . . It is very desirable that in all cases in which inquests are held the coroners should instruct the juries to state in their verdicts with greater minuteness than at present the cause of death, recording more in detail the nature of the injury, and the circumstances in which the death happened." (Quoted in Cornelius Walford, *The Insurance Cyclopedia* [London, 1871], vol. 1, p. 4.) According to Walford, a French survey of the year 1865 shows "that accidental deaths nearly everywhere increase more rapidly than does the population." (Op. cit., p. 5.) In the Registrar's Office annual report of 1856 we read: "The progress of science has created new forces often fatal, and has produced new substances, of which our forefathers had no knowledge. Machinery is organized on a large scale, so that the lives of numbers of men are liable to be destroyed, *not by malicious intent, but by the negligence of other men who have their lives in charge.*" (Op. cit.; italics added.)

The notion of negligence is a modern one; it did not exist before the seventeenth century. With the increasing differentiation of bourgeois life it becomes ever more important. (Cf. William S. Holdsworth, *A History of the English Law* [Boston and London, 1922–52], vol. 8, pp. 449 ff.) In the nineteenth century, industrialization gives a powerful impetus to this development: Eldridge even states that "there is practically no law of negligence prior to the nineteenth century." (Laurence Eldridge, *Modern Tort Problems* [Philadelphia, 1941], p. 32.)

It is within the context of the increasing importance of the negligence problem, that the Campbell Act, "An Act for compensating the Families of Persons killed by Accidents," passed in 1846, has to be understood. It is the legislative response to the increase in accidents; as the commentary in *Halsbury's Statutes of England* points out, it elevates negligence, for the first time, to a clearly defined breach of the law: "No such liability existed at common law" (vol. 12, p. 335).

In addition to liability laws, industrial development creates the institution of accident insurance. This begins with the railroad (W. A. Dinsdale, *History of Accident Insurance in Great Britain* [London, 1954], p. 52). According to Walford, eleven out of the thirteen accident insurance firms founded between 1845 and 1850 include the word *railway* in their names. (Op. cit., vol. 1, p. 7.)

2. Esther Fischer-Homberger: "Railway Spine und traumatische Neurose: Seele und Rücken-mark," *Gesnerus* no. 27 (1970), pp. 96–111; "Die Büchse der Pandora: Der mythische Hinter-grund der Eisenbahnkrankheiten des 19. Jahrhunderts," *Sudhoffs Archiv* (1972), pp. 297–317; *Die traumatische Neurose: Vom somatischen zum sozialen Leiden* (Bern, 1975).

3. In an extended sense, these include shock reactions to bad news, to experienced catas-trophes, etc.

4. *Moniteur parisien,* May 10, 1842, quoted in Pinard, *Relation exacte de l'affreuse catastrophe du 8 mai* (Paris, 1842).

5. J. A. Delcasse, *De la commotion* (Paris, 1834), p. 5.

6. Op. cit.; similarly, in the *Dictionnaire des sciences médicales,* "commotion" is defined as a "gen-eral or local shock to the nervous system, following either a fall or a violent percussion" ([Paris, 1813], vol. 16, pt. 1, p. 152.)

7. In Jack Simmons, ed., *Journey in England* (New York, 1969), pp. 210–11.

8. Calvin Colton, *Four Years in Great Britain, 1831–35* (New York, 1835), vol. 1, p. 68.

9. William Camps, *Railway Accidents or Collisions: Their Effects, Immediate and Remote, upon the Brain and Spinal Cord . . .* (London, 1866), p. 12.

10. Erichsen (1866), pp. 95–96.

11. Op. cit., p. 99.

12. Buzzard, *Lancet* (1866), p. 454.

13. Erichsen (1866), p. 95.

14. Op. cit., p. 9.

15. Let us compare the previous quote on the violence and peculiarity of the railroad accident with another one that states the exact opposite, i.e., that railroad accidents are *not* essentially different from other accidents: "I cannot, indeed, too strongly impress on you the fact that there is in reality nothing special in railway injuries, except in the severity of the accident by which they are occasioned. They are peculiar in their severity, not different in their nature, from injuries received in the other accidents of life. There is no more real difference be-tween that concussion of the spine which results from a railway collision and that which is the consequence of a fall from a horse or a scaffold, than there is between a compound and comminuted fracture of the leg by the grinding of a railway carriage over the limb and that resulting from the wheel of a street cab across it." (Op. cit., pp. 46–47.)

16. Op. cit., p. 18.

17. John Eric Erichsen, *On Concussion of the Spine, Nervous Shock, and Other Obscure Injuries of the Nervous System, in Their Medical and Medico-Legal Aspects* (London, 1875).

18. Erichsen (1875), pp. 194–95.

19. Op. cit., p. 195.

20. See note 15 above.

21. In 1866, Erichsen strictly rejects the designation of the pathological symptoms as hysterical; however, in 1875 he says: "It is this condition that is so apt to lead to an emotional state, which, for want of a better term, may be called hysteria." (P. 195.)

22. Erichsen (1875), p. 196.

23. Thus Fischer-Homberger can still represent Erichsen as a proponent of the purely patholog-ical conception, while pointing out her unfamiliarity with the second version of his book.

24. In the early 1880s, the psychopathological explanation gains ground. After M. Bernhardt's initial attempts in this direction in 1876, Moeli publishes an article in 1881 (*Berliner Klinische Wochenschrift,* No. 18) which states that psychic causation is the most likely one. In 1883, Hodges publishes an article, "So-Called Concussion of the Spinal Cord" (*Boston Medical and Surgical Journal*), in which he criticizes Erichsen and stresses the psychic component. Sub-sequent literature can be found in Fischer-Homberger's listing.

    While psychic causation gains thoroughgoing acceptance, there remains, in the back-ground, the continued notion that even the psychic cause ultimately has a "molecular" effect.

25. Page (1883), p. 83.

26. Op. cit., p. 147.

27. Op. cit., p. 147.

28. Op. cit., p. 147.

29. Quoted in Fischer-Homberger, *Traumatische Neurose,* p. 33.

30. Cf. Fischer-Homberger, *Traumatische Neurose.*

31. Thomas Atkins Street, *The Foundations of Legal Liability* (Northport, L.I., 1906), vol. 1, p. 458.

207

32. John D. Mayne, *Mayne's Treatise on Damages* (London, 1899), p. 51.
33. *Winfield on Tort* (7th ed., London, 1963), p. 249. The latest accessible handbook from the year 1970 again reduces liability to the somatic pathological symptoms that may accompany the psychological shock: ". . . mere grief, anguish, unhappiness, humiliation, outrage and so on, however distressing they may be, are never compensable at all unless they follow on some physical injury. Only if the plaintiff suffers some actual illness, usually referred to by lawyers somewhat unscientifically, as 'nervous shock,' does any question of compensation arise." (P. S. Atiyah, *Accidents, Compensation and the Law* [London, 1970], p. 63.)
34. Fischer-Homberger, *Traumatische Neurose,* p. 79.
35. J. Laplanche and J. B. Pontalis, *Das Vokabular der Psychoanalyse* (Frankfurt, 1975), vol. 2, p. 523.
36. Op. cit., p. 517.
37. Walter Benjamin, "On Some Motifs in Baudelaire," in *Illuminations,* pp. 160–163.
38. Fischer-Homberger, *Traumatische Neurose,* pp. 86–87: "The shell explosion now became, as it were, the trauma *par excellence.* In that explosion . . . sense impressions and physical shock acted on the bystanders with the highest degree of intensity. According to the old doctrine of traumatic neurosis, the shell explosion had to be generative of neurosis to a greater degree than any other trauma. It proved, indeed, to be thus: as we know, World War I, particularly in its first years, was a time of enormous epidemics of neuroses, many of which were traced back to shellshock."
39. On Freud's preoccupation with the war neuroses, see Fischer-Homberger, *Traumatische Neurose,* pp. 151–59.

Excursion: The History of Shock

1. Hans Delbrück, *Geschichte der Kriegskunst im Rahmen der politischen Geschichte* (Berlin, 1908), vol. 4, p. 62.
2. *Trübners Deutsches Wörterbuch* (Berlin, 1955), vol. 6, p. 192.
3. Lynn White, Jr., *Medieval Technology and Social Change* (Oxford, 1962), p. 2.
4. Werner Sombart, *Krieg und Kapitalismus* (Munich and Leipzig, 1913), p. 28.
5. While Delbrück perceives the modern squadron formation as in many ways a kind of resurrection of the phalanx of antiquity, he believes that the impact of collision experienced in the warfare of modern times was not known in that of antiquity (vol. 4, p. 63), because the phalanx, although it was a closed formation, did not function as a unified body of troops, but rather as a sequence of individual warriors who were replaced by others as they fell or were wounded. (Delbrück, vol. 1, p. 32.)
6. Delbrück, vol. 4, p. 12.
7. *Krieg und Kapitalismus,* p. 28.
8. "Observation and anticipation of the intentions of the adversary are the objective. . . . For their own interest, adversaries in battle are in closer communication and are compelled to cooperate with each other far more intensively and deliberately than dancers. . . ." (Rudolf zur Lippe, *Naturbeherrschung am Menschen,* vol. 2, *Geometrisierung des Menschen und Repräsentation des Privaten im französischen Absolutismus* [Frankfurt, 1974], p. 152.)
9. *Krieg und Kapitalismus,* p. 28; see also Zur Lippe, vol. 2, *Köpererfahrung als Entfaltung von Sinnen und Beziehungen in der Ära des italienischen Kaufmannskapitals,* p. 102.
10. *Krieg und Kapitalismus,* pp. 28–29. In M. D. Feld's extremely interesting paper, "Middle Class Society and the Rise of Military Professionalism" (*Armed Forces and Society,* no. 4 [1975]), pointed out to me by Lutz Unterseher, the development of the modern Dutch army in the seventeenth century is described as a process of industrialization. According to Feld, this army was "the only industrialized system of the age" (p. 429), its creation "this earliest of industrial revolutions — the industrialization of military behavior" (p. 434).
11. Op. cit., p. 427.
12. Delbrück, vol. 4, pp. 307–8.
13. Summarized by Delbrück, op. cit., p. 308. Due to the use of the salvo as a tactic, there hardly ever was any hand-to-hand combat in the eighteenth century (Delbrück, op. cit., p. 309).

14. Quoted in H. A. Davis, *Shock, and Allied Forms of Failure of the Circulation* (New York, 1949), p. 1. In the original French edition of 1737 the word *choc* does not yet occur; the corresponding passage is as follows: ". . . le bale . . . poussé par la poudre à canon, l'est avec tant de vitesse et de force, que toute la machine animale se ressent plus ou moins de la *secousse* et de *l'ébranlement.*" (Pp. 1–2; italics added.)

15. G. H. Groeningen, *Uber den Shock* (Wiesbaden, 1885), pp. 3–4. Like most non-English authors of the period, Groeningen uses the English spelling of the word.

16. Quoted in Groeningen, op. cit., p. 101.

17. Groeningen, p. 101.

18. Quoted from Groeningen, p. 101. Ernest Jünger provides an example from first-hand experience: ". . . a blow on my left thigh felled me to the ground. I thought that I had been struck by a flying clod of earth, but the copiously flowing blood soon convinced me that I had been wounded." *Stahlgewittern* [Berlin, 1929], p. 25.

19. It would be of some interest to investigate the relation between shock and pain. As modern bullet wounds are generated unexpectedly, one might assume that the sensation of pain occurs after a longer interval than in former times. Copland, among others, notes that shock and absence of pain are closely connected: "In most of these severe injuries, and especially those produced by fire-arms, the amount of pain is very small compared with the intensity of the shock; and even where the shock is the greatest, the pain may be the least, or may even be entirely absent." (James Copland, *Dictionary of Practical Medicine* [London, 1858], vol. 3, p. 785.) Following wound shock, there is an absence of pain, due to the unexpectedness of the physical trauma. This may be parallel to what happens in cases of psychological trauma. In these, according to Freud, the traumatic neurosis will occur due to the absence of *fear* on the occasion of the traumatic experience.

Chapter 10: Stimulus Shield; or, The Industrialized Consciousness

1. G. Claudin, *Paris* (Paris, 1867; pp. 71–2).

1a. Mumford posits an inverse ratio between actual technical differentiation of machinery on the one hand, and its external surface presented to the consumer for use, on the other: ". . . a simplification of the externals of the mechanical world is almost a prerequisite for dealing with its internal complications. To reduce the constant succession of stimuli, the environment itself must be made as neutral as possible." (*Civilization and Technics*, p. 357.) Mumford also hints at an analogy between the development of technological and social forms: "The machine has thus, in its esthetic manifestations, something of the same effect that a conventional code of manners has in social intercourse: it removes the strain of contact and adjustment." (Op. cit.)

1b. H. J. Berger, G. Bliersbach, R. G. Dellen: *Zur Psychologie des Sicherheitgurtes* (Frankfurt, 1973, pp. 128–133).

2. In connection with the concept of reification developed by Lukács in *History and Class Consciousness* on the basis of Marx's concept of commodity fetishism, we would like to quote an aperçu by Adorno, conveyed in a letter to Benjamin in 1940, concerning the relationship between reification and forgetting: "All *reification* is a forgetting: objects become mere things at the moment they are fixed without being actually present in all their parts — the moment when some part of them has been forgotten." (Adornoto Benjamin, 29 February 1940, Benjamin, *Gesammelte Schriften* [Frankfurt, 1974] vol. 1, pt. 3, p. 1131.)

3. Freud, Sigmund; *The Standard Edition of the Complete Psychological Works,* London, Hogarth Press, Vol. 18, p. 12. (1) "Anxiety (angst) has an unmistakable relation to expectation: it is anxiety *about* something." (p. 165.) (2) "Anxiety is a reaction to a situation of danger." (p. 128). (3) "The ego subjects itself to anxiety as a sort of inoculation, submitting to a slight attack of the illness in order to escape its full strength." (p. 162)

4. Vol. 18, p. 32.

5. *Illuminations,* pp. 160–163.

6. *Grundrisse,* op. cit., p. 92.

7. Op. cit., 27.
8. Op. cit., pp. 28–29.
9. Op. cit., p. 31.
10. *The Sociology of Georg Simmel,* ed. Kurt Wolff (Glencoe, Ill., 1950), pp. 410–11.
11. The proposal to call this process of assimilation of the journey "interiorization" was made by Fritz Heubach, in a letter to the author: "By means of it [the concept of interiorization] we can understand the development of fearlessness, the taking for granted of structures formerly connected with fear and expectation, and finally the congruence of psychic matter with what the psyche has at some point experienced; the 'dulling' of a stimulus (qua stimulus) — i.e., the cancellation of a sensibility — can thus be seen as its recession into the interior, its interiorization. Thus we also find the repressive mechanism of 'identification with the aggressor'."
12. Norbert Elias, *Über den Prozess der Zivilisation,* 2nd ed. (Bern and Munich, 1969), vol. 2, p. 317.
13. Franz Reuleaux, *Theoretische Kinematik.* p. 234.
14. Reuleaux, op. cit., p. 37.

Chapter 11: The Railroad Station: Entrance to the City

1. Auguste Perdonnet, *Traité élémentaire des chemins de fer* (Paris, 1865), vol. 4, pp. 401–02.
2. Hermann Muthesius in his lecture "The Unity of Architecture," 1908: "In the commercial buildings, the railroad stations, the market halls, the convocation halls, modern conditions have been able to create modern types of buildings. . . . These edifices of novel form served commerce and traffic, which experienced rapid development in the nineteenth century. In the requirements of that traffic we see the shaping idea that the art of architecture now uses preferentially." (Quoted in Monica Hennig-Schefold and Helga Schmidt-Thomsen, *Transparent und Masse: Passagen und Hallen aus Eisen und Glas,* 1800–1880 [Cologne, 1972], p. 19.)
3. P. J. Wexler, *La formation du vocabulaire . . .,* p. 83.
4. A. G. Meyer, *Eisenbauten,* p. 146.
5. ". . . Ferrovitreous construction . . . certainly moved to a climax around 1850 and before 1845 had amounted to little." (Henry Russell Hitchcock, *Early Victorian Architecture in Britain,* 2 vols. [New Haven, 1954], vol. 1, p. 511.)
6. See Meeks' hitherto unsurpassed standard work on the architectural history of the railroad station (Carroll L. V. Meeks, *The Railroad Station: An Architectural History* [New Haven, 1956], pp. 37 ff.) The roof of Euston Station (1839) was only 40 feet wide, and the railroad station of Liverpool (1850) was the widest in the world at 153 feet (op. cit., pp. 38–39.)
7. Meyer, p. 146.
8. Richard Lucae, "Über die Macht des Raumes in der Baukunst," *Zeitschrift für Bauwesen,* vol. 19 (1869), p. 298.
9. It is interesting to consider, in this context, the idea of the railroad station as the modern successor to the town or city gate. The gate certainly exerted some influence on the form of the reception buildings; this is most clear in Philip Hardwick's Euston Station (1835–39), with its monumental Greek portico, which was deemed provocative even by contemporary architecture critics, as the ornamental aspect had become entirely emancipated from the practical function, leaving a facade without a building in back of it. (Meeks, pp. 40 ff.)
10. Here, too, American development proceeded quite differently. In the nineteenth century, Americans do not see the railroad as entirely different from other thoroughfares, as Europeans do. Frequently the railroads are referred to as simply "roads," and this familiarity gives rise to a situation that is unheard of in Europe: the train appears in the middle of the city, but with the locomotive disengaged and replaced by horse teams. "In several of the principal American cities, the railways are continued to the very centre of the town, following the windings of the streets and turning without difficulty the sharpest corners," observes Lardner, describing the American railroads of the 1840s (*Railway Economy* [London, 1850], p. 338). That situation continues until the turn of the century: "The railroads proceed for long distances at the same level as the highways, and railroad crossings within the city disrupt

traffic, but the public endures this disruption with incredible patience. Furthermore, while it travels through inhabited streets, the locomotive continuously rings a loud and nerve-wracking bell." (Alfred von der Leyen, *Die Nordamerikanischen Eisenbahnen in ihren wirtschaftlichen und politischen Beziehungen* [Leipzig, 1885], p. 221.)

11. The spacious railroad station hall disappears at the beginning of the twentieth century, and does so first in the U.S. It is replaced by the less expensive roofing of the individual platforms by means of "bush sheds": "Such a shed was cheaper to build and more economical to maintain, and gave nearly as much protection as the colossal ones." (Meeks, p. 122.) As the train hall disappears, the reception halls clearly adopt the form of the train halls of the nineteenth century, i.e., the form of their "adversary": this, too, is a kind of architectural variation of the "interiorization" principle discussed in chapter X, note 11.

12. Perdonnet, describing this regulation of access to the platforms, contrasts it with the freedom of such access in England and recognizes this freedom as the result of advanced industrialization: ". . . this is truly a grand and beautiful spectacle which gives a good idea of the power and liberalism of the companies that have given their country these magnificent instruments. The travelers, who can freely enter the station at all hours, familiarize themselves with the machines by studying them. By admiring them, they lose their fear of them, and thus the railroads become popular." (*Traité . . .*, 1st ed., [Paris, 1856], vol. 2, p. 30.)

13. Meeks, p. 79.
14. Op. cit.

Chapter 12: Tracks in the City

1. John R. Kellett, *The Impact of Railways on Victorian Cities* (London and Toronto, 1969), p. xv.
2. Op. cit., p. 2.
3. The stations of English industrial cities such as Birmingham, Liverpool, and Manchester are located in the center of town. (Kellett, pp. 9 ff.)
4. A. Perdonnet, *Traité élémentaire . . .* (Paris, 1865), vol. 4, p. 401.
5. In London, the railroads are built exclusively through proletarian residential districts, because the real estate prices (and those of the buildings that have to be demolished) are the lowest there, and the properties mostly belong to a few magnates — thus, negotiations are simple (Kellett, pp. 324 ff.) Kellett estimates that at least 120,000 inhabitants had to be resettled (p. 328). In a historical irony, the arches of the viaducts that enabled the trains to cross over former proletarian housing districts were turned into shelters for those who had been evicted from their homes (Kellett, pp. 344–46).
6. This *ex post facto* incorporation of the stations into the city has not been noted by the otherwise knowledgeable historian of urban development, Lewis Mumford, who writes that the railroad "was invited to plunge into the very heart of the town and to create in the most precious central portions of the city a waste of freight yards and marshalling yards." (*The City in History* [New York, 1961], p. 461.)
7. *Morgenblatt für gebildete Leser*, 1838, no. 294, p. 1176 (quoted in Manfred Riedel, "Vom Biedermeier zum Maschinenzeitalter," *Archiv für Kulturgeschichte*, vol. 43 [1961], no. 1, p. 121.)
8. Kellett, p. 313; and, on the stations as traffic nodes in the city: "No single business-district function attracted and focused more traffic than the railway stations. They were the originating points of a great part of the cab traffic, and their names figured on the destination boards of many of the new horse omnibuses which replaced the short stage coaches in London in the 1830s." (P. 312.)
9. Kellett, p. 287.
10. It would be worthwhile to investigate exactly which of Haussmann's thoroughfares are indeed motivated by exclusively strategic considerations, how the strategic and commercial interests were balanced out, and what conflicts, agreements, and compromises resulted therefrom.
    Basically, the process of Haussmann's constructions is only a variant of what happened to the railroads during the era of the July monarchy: the railroads were planned in as centralized a fashion as was Paris when it was remodelled under Napoleon III. (This is in contrast with the English practice of laissez-faire.)
11. Victor Fournel, *Paris nouveau et Paris futur* (Paris, 1865), p. 40.
12. J. M. and Brian Chapman, *The Life and Times of Baron Haussmann* (London, 1957), p. 77;

Françoise Choay; *The Modern City: Planning in the Nineteenth Century* (New York, 1969), p. 17.

13. Chapman, pp. 77–78.

14. Walter Benjamin, "Paris, die Hauptstadt des 19. Jahrhunderts," in *Illuminationen* (Frankfurt, 1961), p. 197.

15. Andre Morizet, *Du vieux Paris au Paris moderne* (Paris, 1932), p. 195. The only access to the Gare de l'est before the construction of the Boulevard de Strasbourg was "the narrow Rue de Chabrol [which could] ill accommodate the 12,000 vehicles that used it daily." (David Pinkney, *Napoleon III and the Rebuilding of Paris* [Princeton, 1958], p. 39.)

16. In every European city connected to the railroad, that street becomes the *Bahnhofstrasse* (railroad station street).

17. Chapman, p. 181.

18. Choay, pp. 17–18. Siegfried Giedion on Haussmann's streets: "The streets themselves, not squares or single buildings, dominate the scene." (*Space, Time and Architecture* [Cambridge, Mass., 1976], p. 770.)

19. If the avenue of the baroque era was straight, it was so for reasons of symmetry and perspective. "The straight road provides its triumphal, *dominating,* regulating note in the antique manner; it also expresses the need for order and classification that systematized Descartes and this desire for perspective." (Gaston Bardet, quoted in Michel Ragon, *Histoire mondiale de l'architecture et de l'urbanisme modernes*, vol. 1, *Idéologies et pionniers, 1800–1910*, p. 95.) Haussmann's avenues are rectilinear for the sole reason that, in terms of traffic technology, the straight line *is* the shortest connection between two given points. The baroque avenue had as its destination and vanishing point an edifice representing regal might: its essential function is to point and lead to that building in terms of perspective. Haussmann's avenue either totally rejects such vanishing points or creates artificial eye-catchers such as the Opera House. Haussmann, Pinkney says, "thought of the streets first as traffic arteries, then sought architectural embellishments that might be attached to them" (op. cit., p. 218). In addition to this, Haussmann's traffic arteries are so long that any building at the vanishing point would literally vanish "in the blue distance" (Giedion).

20. Op. cit., p. 32.

21. "That which one knows one will soon no longer have in front of one's eyes becomes an *image,*" says Walter Benjamin, discussing Meryon's etchings of the old Parisian quarters; "that is what seems to have happened to the streets of Paris of that time." (*Charles Baudelaire: Ein Lyriker im Zeitalter des Hochkapitalismus* [Frankfurt, 1969], p. 94.)

22. Fournel, p. 220.

23. Fournel, p. 22.

24. Giedion, pp. 758–59.

25. Thiers complains: "For the promenaders, what necessity was there to walk from the Madeleine to the Étoile by the shortest route? On the contrary, the promenaders like to prolong their walk, which is why they walk the same alley three or four times in succession." (Quoted in Giedion, op. cit., p. 771.) "The straight line has killed the picturesque and the unexpected. The rue de Rivoli is a symbol — a new, long, broad, cold street on which people travel as cold and formal as it. The Paris of yesterday still had its Cour des Miracles, whose multicolored inhabitants we knew; they have just expropriated it for the cause of public utility. . . . The street [in the old sense] existed only in Paris, and now the street is dying; it is the reign of the boulevards and their outcome, the great arteries." (Charles Yriarte, in *Paris guide: Par les principaux écrivains et artistes de la France* [Paris, 1867], part 2, p. 929.)

Even the overall street plan of Haussmann is misunderstood by those who do not recognize its traffic orientation: "One cannot grasp the intention and scope of the plan . . .," says one commentator in 1867, "one sees only long straight lines striking out at random, illustrating all possible variations of the triangle and quadrangle" (quoted in Chapman, pp. 183–84.)

26. Thus, for instance, Claudin remarks that Haussmann's work had "hardly changed anything in the beautiful quarters. War has been waged only on side streets of obscure thoroughfares and on those insanitary labyrinths in which the fractious, in times of trouble and mutiny, tended to entrench themselves. Their amputation has been complete: entire quarters have disappeared under the hammer. The boulevard Sebastopol on both banks, the prolongation of the rue de Rivoli, the isolation of the tower of Saint-Jacques and the Hotel de Ville, the new Louvre all exist on terrain previously occupied by smoky factories and insalubrious shops." (G. Claudin, *Paris* [Paris, 1867], p. 57.)

27. In Alexandre Dumas, Arsène Houssaye, Paul de Musset et. al., *Paris et les parisiens au XIXe siècle* (Paris, 1856), p. 40.

28. Émile Zola, *Die Beute* (Munich and Gütersloh, n.d.), p. 293. (German translation of *La Curée.*) The novel, written in 1869–72, around the time of the final phase of Haussmanization, can be seen as a contemporary description of the newly completed boulevards.

Chapter 13: Circulation

1. H. Pasdermadjian, *Le Grand Magasin: Son origine — son evolution — son avenir* (Paris, 1949), p. 2.
2. Pasdermadjian, p. 8.
3. Émile Zola, *Paradies der Damen* (Munich and Gütersloh, n.d.), p. 489. (German translation of *Au Bonheur des Dames*.)
4. Ibid., pp. 371–72.
5. Ibid., p. 371.
6. Ibid., p. 393.
7. The railroad "made personal travel a 'commodity' whereas previously it had usually been undertaken only under some compulsion. The main effects of the railways were not on production possibilities in other sectors, but in making available a much-improved consumer service." (G. R. Hawke, *Railways and Economic Growth in England and Wales, 1840–1970* [Oxford, 1970], p. 54.)
8. Naturally, even coach travel is a commodity that has to be paid for, but its commodity character is still undeveloped, preindustrial. The coach journey still has as much "use value" as the goods in the old-fashioned retail store.
9. Obviously, the concept of the panoramic is used here in a general, i.e., ahistorical sense, as a category, although it was initially discovered in connection with a specific historical subject. It would, naturally, be necessary to develop a corresponding concept for each and every historical reorganization of perception. The panoramic merely serves as a model here.
10. Utz Haltern: Die Londoner Weltausstellung von 1851, p. 182, (Münster, 1971).
11. Werner Hofmann, *Das Irdische Paradies* (Munich, 1960), p. 153.
12. Quoted in E. Littré, *Dictionnaire de la langue française* (Paris, 1956), vol. 2. One might object that Say's definition originated at a time before the railroad was known, but if we remind ourselves that in the decades immediately preceding the railroad, traffic capacity was increased while traffic was still based on the old technology (a great need for traffic already existed at the beginning of the nineteenth century), then we can see Say's definition as anticipatory of the modern traffic that was realized by means of the railroad.
13. The biologization of social and economic processes, and conversely, the influence of underlying social conditions on biophysiological notions, are of course older than the nineteenth century. Thus William Harvey's discovery of the circulation of the blood has been related to the bourgeois revolution in England: "Harvey dethroned the heart in the same year as the English Republic was proclaimed." (Christopher Hill, "William Harvey and the Idea of Monarchy," *Past and Present*, no. 27 April, 1964]; reprinted in *The Intellectual Revolution of the Seventeenth Century*, ed. Charles Webster [London and Boston, 1974], p. 163.)
    It would be worthwhile to trace the changes that have occurred in the last 300 years in this area of the interpenetration between biological and social concepts, and to investigate which biological metaphors are stressed in which historical periods. To cite only one example, Marx's notion of "metabolism" was obviously borrowed from the physiologists of his day.
14. Choay, p. 19.
15. Quoted in Ragon, p. 96.
16. Remarkable analogies can be demonstrated between the remodeling of Paris and the (slightly earlier) prison reform. The replacement of the medieval dungeon by a type of building based on Bentham's Panopticon was caused by the same intentions as the remodeling of the city and led to very similar results. The intention, to provide more light and air, is humanitarian and sanitary; the result, as Michel Foucault has noted, is the more effective control of the prisoners. Light is what makes such control possible. It enters through the cell windows and shows the prisoners to their guards as easily controllable silhouette figures. (M. Foucault, *Surveiller et punir: Naissance de la prison* [Paris, 1975], p. 197.) "In Short, the principle of the dungeon is inverted; or rather, of its three functions — to lock in, to deprive of light, and to conceal — only the first one is retained, the other two eliminated. The strong light and the stare of a guard are better captors than the dark, which, finally, was protective. The visibility is a trap." (Op. cit., p. 202.)
17. "On Some Motifs in Baudelaire," in *Illuminations* (New York, 1969), p. 172.
18. Ibid., p. 197.